CHILE, PINOCHET, AND
THE CARAVAN OF DEATH

CHILE, PINOCHET, AND THE CARAVAN OF DEATH

by
Patricia Verdugo

with an introduction by
Paul E. Sigmund

translated by
Marcelo Montecino

North·South Center Press
UNIVERSITY OF MIAMI

The publisher of this book is the North-South Center Press at the University of Miami.

The mission of The Dante B. Fascell North-South Center is to promote better relations and serve as a catalyst for change among the United States, Canada, and the nations of Latin America and the Caribbean by advancing knowledge and understanding of the major political, social, economic, and cultural issues affecting the nations and peoples of the Western Hemisphere.

Originally published as *Caso Arellano: Los Zarpazos del Puma* © 1989 Patricia Verdugo. Ediciones ChileAmérica CESOC.

All copyright inquiries should be addressed to the publisher: North-South Center Press, 1500 Monza Avenue, Coral Gables, Florida 33146-3027, U.S.A., phone 305-284-8912, fax 305-284-5089, or e-mail mmapes@miami.edu.

To order or to return books, contact Lynne Rienner Publishers, Inc., 1800 30th Street, Suite 314, Boulder, CO 80301-1026, 303-444-6684, fax 303-444-0824. Lynne Rienner Publishers is the distributor for books published by the North-South Center Press.

Cover: The cover is a composite of two photos: a background photo of two helicopters, © Crown Copyright, the UK Ministry of Defence and Foreign and Commonwealth Office; the foreground photo of General Augusto Pinochet is by Santiago Llanquin, © AP Wide World Photos.

Library of Congress Cataloging-in-Publication Data

Verdugo, Patricia.
  [Caso Arellano: Los zarpazos del puma. English]
  Chile, Pinochet, and the Caravan of Death/by Patricia Verdugo
    p. cm.
  ISBN 1-57454-084-X (hc:alk.paper) — ISBN 1-57454-085-8 (pb:alk.paper)
  1. Arellano Stark, Sergio. 2. Assassins—Chile 3. Political prisoners—Chile. 4. Political atrocities—Chile. 5. Miltary helicopters—Chile. 6. Chile—Political government—1973-1988.

  F3101.A74 V47 2001
  986.06'5—dc21   00-069571

Translated by Marcelo Montecino for the North-South Center Press at the University of Miami. This first English edition, entitled *Chile, Pinochet, and the Caravan of Death*, was updated by Patricia Verdugo in 2000-2001 and edited by the North-South Center Press.

Translation of *Caso Arellano: Los Zarpazos del Puma*
Ediciones ChileAmérica CESOC
José Miguel de la Barra 508, Dept. 6, Santiago
Inscripción No. 73.672, septiembre de 1989

Printed in the United States of America/TS
∞ The paper used in this publication meets the requirements of the American National Standards for Information Sciences — Permanence of Paper for Printed Library Materials, ANSI Z39.48.1984.

05 04 03 02 01   6 5 4 3 2 1

This book is dedicated to Sola Sierra, president, until her recent death, of the Association of Families of the Detained-Disappeared of Chile (Agrupación de Familiares de Detenidos-Desaparecidos de Chile), for her steadfast loyalty and valor in the defense of human rights.

Table of Contents

Foreword

*"I could have rested, relaxed, breathed, but the duty to the dead does not
give me pause: they died, you lived. Do your duty so that the world will
know everything."* —Alexander Solzhenitsyn

Alexander Solzhenitsyn's words address the main reason why the
investigative reporting for this book began. After General Augusto
Pinochet's military coup of September 11, 1973, which overthrew President
Salvador Allende, 75 Chileans trusted their uniformed compatriots and the
laws of our country. Some of them were arrested — without putting up a
fight — in their homes or places of work. Others, the majority, appeared
voluntarily before the new military authorities when they saw their names
in the official lists, either because they had held politically sensitive jobs
with the previous government or because they belonged to leftist political
parties. In October 1973, while these people were in jail, awaiting sentencing or serving their sentences, a "special commission" from the capital,
headed by General Sergio Arellano Stark, traveled by helicopter to four
locations in northern Chile and one in the south, took some of these prisoners
from the jails, and murdered them. This was an enormous crime, completely
without legal justification, which also violated the faith placed in the
military by Chilean "citizens who entrust us with weapons, so that we can
defend and not kill them," as one of the generals who speaks in these pages
acknowledges.

For more than two decades, the application of the "amnesty law,"[1]
decreed by General Augusto Pinochet in 1978, prevented the legal investigation of the facts connected to this special commission's actions, which
later came to be known as the "Caravan of Death." However, nothing could
stop a journalistic investigation. That was our duty. But that research,
undertaken by several journalists in Chile, including myself, led to an

---

1. The amnesty law of April 19, 1978, pardoned all individuals who committed crimes
between September 11, 1973, and March 10, 1978, also known as the "state of siege
period." This law included authors of crimes, their accomplices, and those who covered
up the crimes. It also benefited some political prisoners sentenced throughout that period
who were granted amnesty. The law specifically excluded those eventually found
responsible for the 1976 Letelier-Moffit murders. (See *The Truth About Pinochet:
Chile's Legacy of Torture, Murder, International Terrorism and 'The Disappeared'* at
<http://www.lakota.clara.net/derechos/chrono2.htm>.)

i

unknown labyrinth: the discovery of what happened to the soldiers in the provinces — as well as to the 75 victims — who were visited by the special commission.

A large dose of terror was required to paralyze the actions — and even the consciences — of millions of Chileans. Thus, from our investigation, two faces of fear began to appear. It was not enough simply to have uniforms and weapons to apply fear. The men who wore the uniforms and carried the weapons had to be willing to use them against their compatriots. The testimonies from members of the military and their families and from the families of the victims, gathered during the course of this investigation, showed that the special commission turned out to be an efficient and tragic instrument for achieving its goal. In most cases, these personal accounts reveal that the witnesses in the military were just as terrified as the victims of the operation.

Those two faces of fear also appeared in 1998, when Judge Juan Guzmán was able to begin investigating the Caravan of Death, the same year of General Pinochet's arrest in London. Judge Guzmán, in fact, considered the details of the journalistic investigation a well-ordered source of data and included this book as part of the judicial process. In the last chapter of this book, the reader will find a summary of the legal procedures that allowed the Supreme Court of Chile, in the year 2000, to revoke the immunity that protected General Pinochet.

Finally, I would like to clarify that I did not gather these testimonies in search of a useless and painful voyage to the past. These testimonies are a festering and present wound that can only be partially mitigated by the understanding of those who did not know or did not want to know what happened. Therefore, this book is intended to make a contribution to fraternal reconciliation.

Patricia Verdugo
Spring 2001

Introduction

Chile, Pinochet, and the Caravan of Death is a translation and updated edition of *Los Zarpazos del Puma* (*The Claws of the Puma*), by Patricia Verdugo, first published in Chile in 1989. It is an account of the executions without trial of 75 political prisoners in five provincial cities of Chile, carried out by a military team later dubbed "The Caravan of Death," sent out by General Augusto Pinochet to "harmonize judicial standards" following the September 11, 1973 coup that overthrew the elected President of Chile, Salvador Allende. This book, published after the October 1988 defeat of Pinochet's bid to extend his presidential term for eight more years but before the December 1989 victory of Patricio Aylwin, presidential candidate of the opposition coalition, contains revelations that have had an important influence on the development of Chilean politics down to the present.

When it was first published, this book revealed the extent and intensity of the repression that followed the 1973 coup to those Chileans who had been ignorant of or in denial of the facts because of media censorship. Widely available in paperback on newsstands, Verdugo's book contributed to Aylwin's substantial victory in the 1989 elections. The substantial evidence that it uncovered was reviewed and incorporated into the 1990 report of the Commission on Truth and Reconciliation (Rettig Commission), which documented with names and dates those killed or "disappeared" by agents of the military government. After the report was published, however, the relatives of the victims were not able to get satisfaction from the Chilean courts because the judges continued to recognize the validity of an amnesty covering the 1973-1978 period that had been decreed by Pinochet in April 1978. The case received further publicity when General Sergio Arellano Stark, the leader of the 1973 mission, who had traveled with full powers as Officer Delegate of General Pinochet, sued Patricia Verdugo for libel. After lengthy hearings, the Chilean courts found "no merit" in the suit. In 1998, Judge Juan Guzmán took up the cases of those who had disappeared before 1978, arguing that since the bodies had not been found, the 1978 amnesty did not apply to the continuing post-1978 crime of "aggravated kidnapping." Drawing on the extensive documentation in this book, Judge Guzmán gave special attention to the 19 (out of 75) victims of the Caravan of Death whose bodies had not been found.

In March 1998, Pinochet moved from his post of commander in chief of the army, which he had occupied since March 1990 when he gave up the presidency, to become senator-for-life, as provided for ex-presidents in the 1980 Constitution, which was written under his direction. In October 1998, during a visit to London, he was arrested by Scotland Yard on an extradition warrant by a Spanish judge for crimes of torture and genocide. In March 2000, after extended court hearings and appeals in which the Chilean government argued that the Chilean courts should have priority in the case, the British Home Minister allowed Pinochet to return to Chile on grounds of poor health. After his return, many law suits (as of this writing, 200) were filed against him, and in August 2000, the Chilean Court of Appeals lifted his parliamentary immunity, specifically citing the evidence in the Caravan of Death case (see below) to support a "well-founded presumption" of Pinochet's direct responsibility. Judge Guzmán continues to investigate the cases of the disappeared, visiting the sites of the executions and attempting to identify bodies. This book is a major source of evidence for Judge Guzmán's investigation.

Author Patricia Verdugo has published 10 books on human rights-related topics, beginning in 1979 with *Detenidos-desaparecidos: Una Herida Abierta* (*The Detained and Disappeared: An Open Wound*), which circulated clandestinely until the abolition of censorship in 1983. Her writing is motivated by personal as well as political factors. Her father, a union leader and Christian Democratic activist, was arrested in 1976, and his body was found in the River Mapocho. For her work, she has received many awards, including the Maria Moors Cabot Award from Columbia University (1993), Chile's National Journalism Award (1997), and the Media Award from the Latin American Studies Association (2000).

The book begins with an account of the military plotting before the 1973 coup, which focuses on the role of General Sergio Arellano Stark and, in contrast to claims made in his memoirs, documents General Pinochet's hesitancy to participate until forced to do so by the other commanders. It also examines several cases of post-coup persecution of officers suspected of insufficient enthusiasm for the coup. General Arellano reappears in the second chapter, arriving at the Talca Regiment on September 30 in a Puma helicopter as Officer Delegate of Augusto Pinochet, army commander in chief and head of the Junta, in order to remove the regimental commander for not moving quickly enough against the local government officials of the

Allende regime. Arellano later presided over a court-martial of the same officer, which sentenced him to three years in jail.

As described in chapter 3, a similar fate befell the officer of the Calama Regiment, who carried out the post-coup courts-martial of 16 persons, including David Silberman, the manager of the Chuquicamata copper mine, sentencing them to prison terms of 61 days to 20 years. Seen as too "soft" on the Allende officials, the officer was arrested, detained, and tortured in Santiago for a year and a half and then sentenced by General Arellano to 270 days in jail "for not performing his military duty." After his arrest, new trials imposed death sentences on three of the prisoners, and Silberman was transferred to a penitentiary in Santiago where he disappeared.

The next five chapters are an account of the Caravan of Death, the military team, headed by General Arellano, that traveled in a Puma helicopter (thus the original Spanish title of this book, *The Claws of the Puma*) to five provincial cities, ostensibly to "standardize sentences" but, in fact, to "toughen" the military in the provinces by executing political prisoners who were awaiting trial or had received "lenient" sentences. (The smoking gun, that is, the formal order investing Arellano with full powers as Officer Delegate of Pinochet, later disappeared from the government's files, but there was sufficient evidence, some of it detailed in the book, that the Chilean courts could later connect Pinochet directly to the case.) Upon his arrival in Cauquenes on September 30, and in La Serena, Copiapó, Antafogasta, and Calama from October 16-19, General Arellano would review the list of prisoners, place checkmarks against certain names, and those persons would be taken out of jail to another location and executed. Arellano made sure that he was not present at the executions, so that he could have an alibi in the future — which he has used to deny that he authorized the murders. Newspapers reported that prisoners had been shot while trying to escape or, in the case of La Serena, that they had been sentenced by a military court. In Calama, a court-martial was convened only after the prisoners had been executed. In a number of cases, the families could not obtain the bodies or were told to bury them in unmarked graves. Among those killed were Jorge Peña, the conductor of the Children's Symphony of La Serena, and Eugenio Ruiz-Tagle, a cousin of Eduardo Frei Ruiz-Tagle, the president of Chile from 1994-2000. A total of 75 persons were killed as a result of the Caravan of Death. The chapters include extensive verbatim interviews with family members, retired army officers, and witnesses of the executions. Patricia Verdugo's updated Epilogue summarizes new evidence that has emerged as a result of more recent court cases, effectively refuting the arguments of General Arellano's defenders, including those of a 1985 book by his son, Sergio Arellano Iturriaga.

The last three chapters deal with the aftermath of the executions. Chapter 9 includes an interview with General Joaquín Lagos, who was army commander of the First Division, which gave him power over three of the five cities. In his defense, Lagos argues that he only found out about the executions after they took place and that he protested to Pinochet, who was passing through Antafogasta, and offered his resignation. Later, when he submitted a report that specifically referred to the executions ordered by General Arellano, the "Delegate of the Commander in Chief," he was summoned to Santiago to sign a new document that described the executions in general terms, omitting all references to Arellano and Pinochet. (The original document, retained by Lagos, was part of the evidence considered by the Supreme Court when it lifted Pinochet's parliamentary immunity in August 2000.) In the same chapter and in the Epilogue, the principal members of Arellano's staff are discussed, including Pedro Espinoza Bravo, later sentenced to six years in jail for his involvement in the September 1976 assassination of Orlando Letelier in Washington, and Armando Fernández Larios, who surrendered to U.S. authorities in 1987 and was sentenced to 27 months in a U.S. jail for his part in the assassination (Fernández Larios was also involved in the September 1974 assassination in Buenos Aires of General Carlos Prats, Pinochet's predecessor as commander in chief — a case that, at the time of this writing, is being tried in Buenos Aires and has produced extradition requests for Fernández Larios and Pinochet.) Chapter 9 also records the unsuccessful efforts of families and relatives to get a hearing from the Chilean courts in the 1980s, because of their adherence to the 1978 self-amnesty decreed by Pinochet. Chapter 10 tells how the relatives of the victims struggled to obtain justice and how the amnesty law aborted those efforts.

The Epilogue reviews the legal developments in the 1990s, particularly since 1998, when under the continuing crime of "aggravated kidnapping," Judge Guzmán began to gather evidence on the disappearances of 19 of the 75 people executed.

The North-South Center Press's updated edition of Patricia Verdugo's book makes available — for the first time to the English-speaking world — a wealth of historical documents, interviews, and other materials needed to understand a period of Chilean history on which the world has continued to focus attention, during the prolonged detention of General Augusto Pinochet in England and most recently with Judge Guzmán's December 1, 2000, prosecution of General Pinochet for the crimes of "kidnapping and homi-cide" involving the victims of the Caravan of Death. It is published at a time when Chileans on all sides, through such efforts as a government-sponsored dialogue between the military and civilians, a church effort at reconciliation, and proposals for "justice with mercy," are attempting to turn the page on the last 30 years of Chilean history. To do this, however, requires knowledge and understanding of how and why what was one of the most civilized countries in the world descended into barbarism. This book is a major contribution to achieving that goal.

Paul E. Sigmund
Professor of Politics
Princeton University

Map of the Route of the Caravan of Death

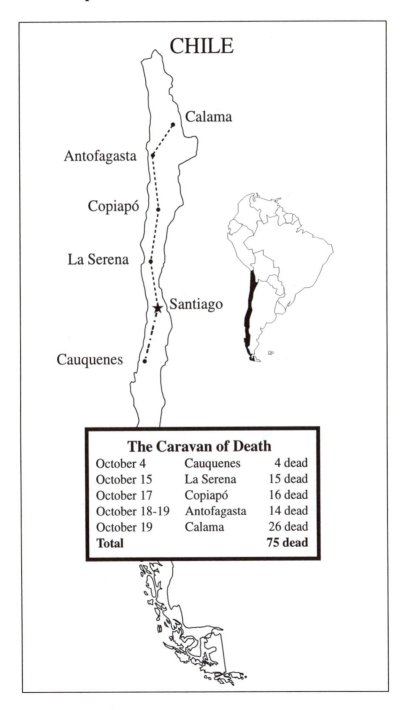

CHILE

Calama

Antofagasta

Copiapó

La Serena

Santiago

Cauquenes

The Caravan of Death

October 4	Cauquenes	4 dead
October 15	La Serena	15 dead
October 17	Copiapó	16 dead
October 18-19	Antofagasta	14 dead
October 19	Calama	26 dead
Total		**75 dead**

CHAPTER 1

The Man of the Coup

This is the tragic history of the Caravan of Death, a mission that, in 1973, took the lives of no fewer than 75 political prisoners in five Chilean cities. Most of these citizens had voluntarily given themselves up to the new authorities just days after the military coup. The citizens trusted the military authorities, given the Chilean culture's strong legal tradition. Some of the prisoners had already received their sentences from the military court-martial — from 61 days to several years in prison. But the majority were waiting in prison to be judged. Their crimes? For the majority, holding political views and participating in political organizations that could be characterized as liberal, leftist, socialist, or, in a few cases, communist. For others, simply being in the wrong place at the wrong time.

This is also a history that tells, in their own words, how many Chilean military officers — educated in the traditions of a humanistic and demo-cratic society — were forced into fratricidal violence.

We do not know where, when, or how the term "Caravan of Death" originated. We only know that these fearful words traveled from mouth to mouth for the 12 years that the truth lay hidden, silenced by the military regime's mandated censorship. Perhaps the words, "Caravan of Death," were first used by the members of the military community who were abused by the criminal actions of the Caravan. Or maybe the Caravan was named by its victims' families.

This is a painful history that began during the months prior to the military coup of September 1973. The person who led the Caravan of Death — under orders from General Augusto Pinochet — was General Sergio Arellano Stark. A renowned officer who, in fact, led the conspiracy for the military takeover, General Arellano was the man of the coup.

For those who plotted in the Chilean army, air force, and navy, General Arellano was known as "the man" of the coup against President Salvador Allende during the midwinter of 1973, even though General Arellano did not command many men. He was in charge of the troop command of Peñalolén in the eastern sector of Santiago, which included telecommunications and military aviation. General Arellano's innate gift for leadership, along with his knowledge of local politics, anticommunism, and contacts with the Christian Democratic Party (he had been President Eduardo Frei Montalva's aide-de-camp), led him to direct the coup initiative that moved silently in the barracks and military academies.[1]

After the failed coup attempt (called the *tanquetazo* because tanks were used)[2] on June 29, 1973, the plotters were given a perfect smokescreen to justify their subsequent meetings and behavior: the high command authorized a new Committee of 15, a working group composed of five high-ranking officers from each branch of the armed forces, to study the situation and propose solutions to the executive. Not all of the generals and admirals participated in this secret. But General Arellano carefully planned every detail of the design. He took over Plan Campana, with the stated objectives of assessing the amount of weaponry held by factory workers in the "industrial belts"[3] around Santiago and proposing a plan to overcome the danger of further coups. To accomplish these objectives, he had to contact officers stationed at the Army War Academy. Arellano did not have to worry about downtown Santiago. The ballistics investigation ordered by General Augusto Lutz, director of the Intelligence Service,[4] had indicated clearly what type of weaponry and from what positions the military had been fired upon during the coup attempt of June 29.

By the end of August 1973, Arellano and the other conspirators feared that they were in grave danger when General Carlos Prats resigned as commander in chief of the army. In the first meeting they attended with General Prats' successor, General Augusto Pinochet, the conspirators heard Pinochet say openly and angrily, "What has been done to General Prats will be washed with the blood of generals." Pinochet then asked for the generals' resignations.

However, Generals Arellano, Palacios, and Viveros did not hand in their written resignations. As the hours went by, they feared that everything would be lost if Pinochet fired them. General Arellano decided that the time had come. He entrusted his son, Sergio Arellano Iturriaga, a lawyer, to contact the son of Comptroller General Héctor Humeres and ask him to notify Arellano Iturriaga immediately if the dismissal decree arrived at the comptroller's office. Arellano's son would then try to stop the process of "public documentation of intent."

The next tense weekend should have culminated with the "go ahead" on Monday, August 27, for the military coup to be implemented on Wednesday, August 29. Generals Arellano, Palacios, Nuño, and Viveros fine-tuned the details: the professors at the Army War Academy would transfer the orders to unit commanders. It was hoped that a large part of the army and all of the navy and air force would participate. Representing the national police, General Yovane assured them that he could neutralize the pro-government forces.[5]

But it was Pinochet himself who broke up the movement. That same Monday, August 27, he met with the military high command and suddenly changed his tune. Instead of insisting on their resignations, he spoke of closing ranks within the army and within the other branches of the armed forces. Pinochet brought up the possibility of a "military intervention" if circumstances made it necessary.

What were the members of the high command to do? Was General Pinochet trustworthy? Until then, "We all believed that Pinochet was opposed to the coup," remembered General Nicanor Díaz Estrada, one of the principal architects of the plot on behalf of the air force.

Federico Willoughby MacDonald, a participant in the coup plotting on behalf of extreme right-wing civilians and spokesman for the military government after the coup, explained what happened:

"Allende trusted Pinochet a lot; after all, he had named him commander in chief! There is an aspect of the personality of General Pinochet that could make him appear to be a traitor, in the sense that he is a man who quickly changes from one position to the other. My explanation, given what I know, is that he is 100 percent a military man, a man who went into the army when he was 15. He's been in the institution almost 60 years, and he had to stay in the army to advance and be promoted. He must comply with the currents of the times, following prevailing opinions, because a person who doesn't operate that way is out, is expelled by the system. Therefore, if it's necessary to be a Catholic, he is a Catholic; if it's necessary to be a Mason, he is a Mason; if it's necessary to salute the politicians, he salutes the politicians — if it's Fidel Castro, he salutes Fidel Castro.

"But Pinochet wasn't [the only one like that]," Willoughby continued. "Everyone who has remained in military institutions has acted that way. He has always been the most loyal collaborator with his superiors. Of course, he was his predecessor General Prats' most trusted man. When his turn came up, he could also be betrayed. What happened is that Pinochet didn't confide in anyone. He was absolutely cautious and suspicious."[6]

Equally cautious and suspicious, General Arellano discussed the matter at length with the other conspirators. With the support of the entire navy, all of the air force, a large part of the army, and a good part of the national police, victory seemed assured. Obviously, costs could be minimized if the commander in chief of the army led the movement, given the Prussian education of the military, with their blind obedience to their superior officer. They decided that Pinochet would think along the same lines.

For General Arellano, Saturday, September 8, was the turning point. The coup already had its "D day": it could not occur after September 19, because they did not want to risk rendering military honors to President Salvador Allende during the traditional military parade scheduled for that day — to avoid the danger of being together where they could be arrested if the plot leaked. "D day" could not be on a Monday, because the slightest preparations on a Sunday would be cause for alert. Yes, it had to be on Tuesday, the conspirators agreed. Let it be on Tuesday, September 11!

Willoughby pointed out, "Indeed, the rumor circulated that General Sergio Arellano Stark visited General Pinochet on Saturday, September 8, to inform him that if he did not go along [with the coup], he would just be left behind. And that's the way it was. Arellano, it's true, for all practical purposes, was the man who best embodied these sentiments within the army. His was the voice of dissatisfaction."[7]

Chilean Air Force (Fuerzas Aéreas Chilenas — FACH) General Díaz Estrada recalled those days just before the coup almost 16 years later, in his apartment located in the Providencia neighborhood:

"We were almost ready, and nobody had spoken with Pinochet. I had been talking only with Arellano. On Saturday morning, the 8th, I insisted, 'So, when are you going to speak to Pinochet?' Arellano answered, 'I am going to his house this afternoon.'

"Since Admiral Carvajal was in Viña del Mar and was coming back that night with news, I told Arellano, 'Let's meet at Carvajal's house at 9:30 p.m.' But Arellano did not come to that meeting. I remember I said to Carvajal, 'They must have arrested him after he spoke with Pinochet.' Since we were playing with fire, we didn't know how Pinochet was going to react."

General Díaz Estrada continued:

"I said goodbye to Carvajal at 11:30 p.m. and left in my car. As I approached the exit of the Quinta Normal [a large enclosed park] by Santo Domingo Street [on the western edge of the capital], I was just making that turn when I saw General Arellano, who was walking along looking very elegant.

"'Where are you coming from, General?' I asked.

"'From a wedding,' Arellano answered very calmly.

"'Did you speak to General Pinochet?' I asked in an urgent tone.

"'No, I didn't speak to him,' Arellano said tersely.

"'So then, what are you doing here?' I asked loudly, feeling angry with myself that I'd feared Arellano had been arrested."

General Díaz Estrada went on to say that at that point, two navy captains who had been at the meeting at Carvajal's house came up to him and suggested that they go inside the nearby home of one of the captains and continue their dangerous conversation there instead of on the street.

"General Arellano," Díaz Estrada concluded, "had not dared to speak with Pinochet."

But General Arellano, speaking through his son, gave a different version of the events leading up to the military coup to overthrow Allende. That Saturday, September 8, after briefing the other army generals, Arellano said that he arrived at Pinochet's house around 8:30 p.m. "His [Pinochet's] reaction was a mixture of surprise and annoyance. When he became aware that the only thing required of him was his support of a decision that had already been made, he seemed overwhelmed."[8]

Arellano said that when he told Pinochet that the Commander in Chief of the Air Force, General Gustavo Leigh, was expecting his telephone call, Pinochet "asked for some time, assuring me that he would call soon but that he needed some time to think it over."

That moment became the key to General Arellano's later defense: the moment when he revealed to his commander in chief that the plans for the coup were in their final stage and offered Pinochet leadership.

General Leigh did not receive any telephone calls that day. After Leigh had written the proclamation for the coup, he decided to go to Pinochet's house, at around 5:00 p.m. on Sunday, September 9, interrupting Pinochet's young daughter Jacqueline's birthday party. General Leigh's recollection of the conversation[9] indicates that Pinochet had already spoken with Arellano:

"He was very relaxed. He listened to the proposal as if he saw no other solution.

Leigh remembered pressing Pinochet, saying, "'What are *you* going to do? As for us, *we* can't take it anymore. If we don't act, the whole country will sink into chaos.'

"Pinochet told me, 'Have you thought about the fact that this can cost us our lives and the lives of many others?'

"'I've thought about it,' I answered."[10]

The meeting between Leigh and Pinochet was interrupted by the arrival of emissaries on behalf of Admiral José Toribio Merino, Admirals Carvajal and Huidobro, and Commander González. They brought a brief handwritten text that sealed the coup. Leigh signed immediately. Pinochet hesitated.

"If this leaks, it could have serious consequences for us," Pinochet said, according to Leigh's recollections.

"Pinochet hesitated briefly, and General Leigh pushed him, saying, 'Decide, General, sign.' Pinochet went to his desk, opened the drawer, took out a pen and his stamp. And he finally signed," General Díaz Estrada recalled.

****

From that moment on, the invisible red alert began to signal unrelentingly. Only 36 hours before the military coup was to begin, General Augusto Pinochet became part of the plot. And Pinochet had decided that if something were to go wrong with him, General Oscar Bonilla was to replace him.

One of the first arrangements the coup leaders made was to put their own families out of harm's way in case something went wrong. Each man decided on the safest place. General Pinochet chose the Escuela de Alta Montaña del Ejército (Mountain Warfare School of the Army). At an undetermined time on Monday, September 10, Lucía Hiriart Pinochet and her young children reached the military compound commanded by Colonel Renato Cantuarias Grandón. What reason did Lucía Pinochet give to explain the presence of the family of the commander in chief? That they needed to rest from the tense situation in the capital? What is clear is that she could reveal nothing about the imminent coup because Colonel Cantuarias was considered "unreliable" by the conspirators.

Why, then, did Pinochet choose the Escuela de Alta Montaña, under the command of Colonel Cantuarias, as a "safe haven"? Colonel Cantuarias' cousin, former Minister of Mining Orlando Cantuarias, who had served in the Allende administration, gave one answer, "My cousin was a gentleman; he was very proper, loyal, and noble. And I have no doubt that, if the coup had failed, he would have done everything possible to get Pinochet's wife and children out of Chile. I have no doubt that he would have taken them to the other side of the border, only a few kilometers away."

Another explanation, given by military sources, was more severe: "Pinochet directed the coup from Peñalolén, where he had helicopters ready to fly to the Escuela de Alta Montaña quickly. If the coup failed, he could escape by that route and cross the mountains. Moreover, if he decided in time, he could use Colonel Cantuarias, known for his Unity sympathies

[Allende's party, Popular Unity — Unión Popular], to initiate an offensive against the insurgents from there and try to save the situation, keeping himself in military power."

The truth about what really happened in the Escuela de Alta Montaña was buried along with the bullet-ridden body of Colonel Cantuarias before the end of that September. Fifteen years later, conspirator Federico Willoughby responded to journalist Sergio Marras' questions:

"Was there resistance in the army?" Marras asked Willoughby.

"No, not that I know of. As far as I know, there were places where orders were not followed, and disciplinary measures were immediately adopted to deal with those people. In the place where the Pinochet family had gone, the Guardia Vieja Regiment in the Andes Mountains, Commander Cantuarias died. That's where Mrs. Lucía [Pinochet] and the children spent September 11th," Willoughby answered.

"Did the commander resist?" the journalist inquired.

"I don't know the details, but Cantuarias died."

Marras also interviewed General Díaz Estrada, who gave this account of Colonel Cantuarias' death:

"The colonel who was in charge of the Escuela de Alta Montaña, where Mrs. Pinochet sought refuge on the 11th, was arrested and brought the following day to the military school where they left a revolver on the table so that he could commit suicide."

"He wasn't put before a firing squad?"

"No, he committed suicide."[11]

What really happened? Orlando Cantuarias, Allende's minister of mining, visited briefly with his cousin, Colonel Renato Cantuarias, shortly before he died. In an interview with me, he emotionally recalled their encounter:

"After September 18, 1973, I was in hiding and in the process of dismantling the operations of the Radical Party. One day when I thought they wouldn't be looking for me any more, I returned to my house. That same day they came to get me. They went through everything. After the police officer directing the search found everything in order, he told me that, unfortunately, he had to follow orders and take me to the military school.

"At the school, they led me into an office, and suddenly my cousin Renato came down, dressed in combat uniform with the brightly colored bandanna they used. Renato asked me, 'What are you doing here?' I answered, 'I don't really know — they forced me to come here.' And he said, 'What's my aunt going to say? She'll kill me if she knows.'

"He seemed normal," Orlando said, describing Renato Cantuarias. "Perhaps I was the one who was upset. Was he armed? I don't remember. He called a lieutenant and ordered. . . ."

"He could give orders?" I asked.

"Yes, everything seemed normal. He was something like an aide to the General Staff. The more I thought about it, the more he seemed to be a subtly undeclared prisoner. They had him there, well protected, but without any troop command. The fact is that he called a lieutenant who was his aide, named Allende, and ordered him to take me home under escort. When he said goodbye, he told me, 'Don't tell my aunt anything. What is she going to say?' He loved my mother very much.

"A little after 2:00 a.m., they took me home. Then, a short time later, I sought asylum in the Swedish Embassy and went into exile. Three or four days after I saw Renato at the military school, I heard that my cousin had committed suicide. That's it. I never wanted to find out anything else."

"And does suicide seem possible to you?"

"No. He was a Catholic and full of life. Someone told me, as an official explanation, that he had been summoned by a military court, which found out that he did not follow the order to bomb the workers of the Andina Mines. The appropriate sentence was stripping him of rank or for him to commit suicide. But I'm convinced that, one way or another, they killed him," Orlando Cantuarias concluded.

Another version of Colonel Renato Cantuarias' death came from Lieutenant Colonel Olagier Benavente, who found out — in the Talca Regiment — that Colonel Cantuarias was punished for not arriving on time in Santiago with his troops.

As the result of an exhaustive investigation, journalist Ignacio González discovered that the movement of troops from the Andean mountain town of Los Andes on Monday, September 10, "had originated with an order sent from Santiago: A battalion from the Andino Regiment, part of the Escuela de Alta Montaña, and a regiment from San Felipe were to travel to the capital."[12] There is no more reliable data.

One cannot talk to Colonel Cantuarias' immediate family. The mere mention of the colonel's name by General Díaz Estrada during his testimony in 1988 resulted in an indignant visit from Cantuarias' widow and his daughter, who angrily demanded a retraction. The widow, María Antonieta

Bernal Cantuarias (her late husband's cousin), had remarried; her husband was a high-ranking officer in the army. The daughter had married an army officer, and the son was also an officer in the army.

Former Minister Orlando Cantuarias remembered his cousin Colonel Renato Cantuarias as "a very good man, cordial, cheerful. He loved life. He loved reading, which made him different from the rest of the military. My father, who was a history professor, had a large library, and I remember Renato reading a lot. He wasn't a man of the left, or anything of the kind," the former minister insisted. "He was aware of the need for change, for progress, for the conditions of the poor to improve but without affecting the framework of the society in which he was living as a member of the military. He had an unrestricted respect — in this he was as dogmatic as he was about his own Catholic faith — for the will of the people. That is why he felt close to Generals Schneider and Prats [former army commanders]. Both had given him their friendship, just as Pinochet had done until the military coup."

Former Minister Orlando Cantuarias continued, "I saw him many times during the Popular Unity administration. I used to go see him at the Guardia Vieja Regiment in the Andes, where he was executive officer, and he used to come to see me. Later, he was commander of the Escuela de Alta Montaña, near Portillo. I know that when President Allende visited there, Renato said to him, 'Mr. President, welcome. You are in charge, but from this moment on, the responsibility for your security is in my hands. I have prepared everything so that the members of your security detail will be comfortable outside. But they cannot come into my regiment.' I know that Renato was annoyed with the presidential personal guard, the GAP [Group of Personal Friends — Grupo de Amigos Personales], just as I know he was annoyed that we were not able to solve the problem of shortages of essential products."

Major Fernando Reveco Valenzuela, who had acted as chairman of the court-martial in the Calama Regiment, heard what happened to Colonel Cantuarias when he was first interrogated.

Major Reveco Valenzuela, interviewed more than 15 years after the events, recounted, "They said he [Cantuarias] was a traitor to the fatherland, just like Major Iván Lavanderos Lataste, who was my classmate and who they said committed suicide at the Army War Academy. In the first interrogation session he had with me, 'Polaco' Rodríguez, threatened me, saying, 'Two have already killed themselves, Cantuarias and Lavanderos.'"[13]

Did Lavanderos commit suicide?

"I don't believe in his suicide. He was unmarried, the only son of a widowed mother, without any tendency toward depression. They said that he had a group of prisoners and that he took pity on them and left them in front of an embassy. And later, something happened in the War Academy: they forced him to shoot himself, or they killed him," said Reveco Valenzuela.

Another version states that Major Lavanderos Lataste was shot in the National Stadium, along with 100 other prisoners. As to the action that cost him his life, it was said that Lavanderos "decided to spare the lives of 41 Uruguayans and that he gave them to the Swedish ambassador in Chile."[14]

Notes

1. Chapter 1 establishes historically that the plot of the military coup against President Salvador Allende was headed by General Sergio Arellano Stark on behalf of the Chilean military. Because the army is the oldest and most powerful weapon in Chile, whoever leads the army would also automatically be the leader of any conspiracy. General Augusto Pinochet was named commander in chief of the army by President Allende on August 23, 1973. Both Pinochet's reputation as a top military officer and the military intelligence report given to President Allende indicated that Pinochet was a constitutionalist, that is, an officer who would respect the Constitution and uphold the laws of the country, an officer who would not become involved in military coup-type adventures.

The research for this book revealed that General Pinochet first became part of the coup and accepted his leadership role in the conspiracy on the evening of Sunday, September 9, 1973, joining the conspirators only 36 hours before the event. If the coup were to fail, he knew that he would be court-martialed. That is why he took his family to a safe haven located very close to the Argentine border, the Mountain Warfare School of the Army (Escuela de Alta Montaña del Ejército). This School was located in the same region as the Guardia Vieja Regiment, under the direction of Colonel Renato Cantuarias Grandón, a commander who was known to be sympathetic toward Allende's government, so when the coup proved successful, Pinochet had Commander Cantuarias arrested with the understanding that he would "commit suicide" at the Military Academy in Santiago.

2. The *tanquetazo* was a failed military coup attempt to overthrow President Salvador Allende a few months before Pinochet's rise to power. On June 29, 1973, the Second Armored Battalion in Santiago, led by Lieutenant Colonel Roberto Souper, drove a column of 16 armored vehicles, including tanks, and encircled both the presidential palace, La Moneda, and the building housing the Ministry of Defense, in downtown Santiago. *Ed.*

3. "Industrial belts" were poor neighborhoods surrounding Santiago containing many factories.

4. The Intelligence Service of the Army (Servicio de Inteligencia Militar del Ejército — SIM). Its Director, General Augusto Lutz, died under strange circumstances in 1974.

5. Sergio Arellano Iturriaga, 1985, *Más allá del abismo: un testimonio y perspectiva* (Santiago: Editorial Proyección).

6. Sergio Marras, 1988, *Confesiones / Federico Willoughby . . . et al.; entrevistas de Sergio Marras* (Santiago: Ediciones Ornitorrinco).

7. See Marras 1988.

8. See Arellano Iturriaga 1985.

9. See Marras 1988.

10. Florencia Varas, 1979, *Gustavo Leigh: El general disidente* (Santiago: Ediciones Aconcagua).

11. See Marras 1988.

12. Ignacio González Camus, 1990, *El día en que murió Allende* (Santiago: Ediciones ChileAmérica CESOC).

13. Colonel Manuel Rodríguez (alias "Polaco" or "Polish" Rodríguez), was known as a riding champion. He was in charge of the inquiry into cases in the army and was later named Chile's ambassador to Austria.

14. Ascanio Cavallo Castro, Manuel Salazar Salvo, and Oscar Sepúlveda Pacheco, 1990, *Chile, 1973-1988: La historia oculta del régimen militar* (Santiago: Editorial Antártica).

CHAPTER 2

I Don't Know What War You Are Talking About, General

The news of the strange death of Colonel Cantuarias spread rapidly through the barracks. The news ran like a chill — from the north to the south — along the spine of Chile's Andean region, setting off a reign of terror within the ranks of the military. This chill turned into a maelstrom a few days later, with the arrival of the Caravan of Death.

Years later, I interviewed Commander Efraín Jaña Girón of the Talca Regiment. Regarding Colonel Cantuarias' death, Commander Jaña Girón said, "Someone told me that he committed suicide in the Escuela de Alta Montaña. Knowing Cantuarias, that seemed very strange because he was so full of life, so proper, an old-fashioned soldier. But I must admit that in those days I had so much work to do that I did nothing to find out more."

The executive officer of the Talca Regiment, Lieutenant Colonel Olagier Benavente, agreed and told me during a similar interview:

"We all knew that he [Cantuarias] had been killed. Because it is impossible that while under arrest at the Military Academy and in the middle of his testimony at his trial, he would ask for permission to go to the bathroom and commit suicide, shooting himself. We all knew that a soldier under arrest could not be armed. The charges? We knew that he was late when they ordered him to transfer troops from the Escuela de Alta Montaña. And people used to say that he was one of the colonels loyal to General Prats, and that's why he was put on trial."

Lieutenant Colonel Benavente, who was a military prosecutor[1] back then, had the Cantuarias case very much on his mind on September 30, 1973, when the Puma military helicopter landed in the Talca Regiment and General Sergio Arellano Stark and his entourage arrived, initiating a tragic journey that would ultimately claim the lives of 75 Chilean citizens.

This is how Lieutenant Colonel Benavente remembered that particular day during an interview with me in the late 1980s, while General Pinochet was still in power:

"General Arellano's caravan arrived on Sunday, without any prior notice. They called me on the phone at home, and I went in immediately. I lived very close. Everything seemed very strange to me from the very beginning, because General Arellano arrived with unusually heavy military protection: everyone wore helmets and had submachine guns. In fact, when I arrived at the commander's office, he was already there, and his guards did not allow me to go in. But, since the barracks had so many interconnected passageways, I went in through another room and just walked in."

Lieutenant Colonel Benavente recalled the scene clearly during the same interview:

"General Arellano was using the direct telephone, the one that doesn't go through the telephone company, speaking with someone in the town of Concepción. When he hung up, he asked me what problems I had in Talca. I replied that, fortunately, we didn't have any problems. He insisted on knowing which were the most difficult cases among the political prisoners. I told him that there were none at that time because the week before we had shot Governor Castro at the base."

"In what capacity was he acting?" I asked him.

"He told me that he came with broad powers — as the delegate of the commander in chief of the army."

"Did you know some of the members of his entourage?"

"Yes, I knew at least two who were with him, Marcelo Moren Brito, who had been one of my lieutenants in Cauquenes and who had a history of being impulsive because he was very high strung. There was also Antonio Palomo, who was the pilot of the helicopter and also one of my lieutenants in Cauquenes, a very good kid."

Meanwhile, the Commander of the Talca Regiment, Efraín Jaña Girón, was in the governor's office, and Lieutenant Colonel Benavente phoned to tell him that General Arellano wanted to see him immediately.

"I got in my Jeep," Jaña recalled, "and I arrived at the regiment in a couple of minutes. General Arellano received me in the officers' mess hall: he was standing, holding a glass in one hand and a submachine gun in the other. He skipped the required salute that is always exchanged between gentleman and soldiers. In an imperious way, he abruptly asked me about the number of casualties in my jurisdiction."

Commander Efraín Jaña, as host to the visiting general, said that he remembered feeling surprised and offended by General Arellano's manner.

"General, all is quiet in the Talca Regiment," Commander Jaña said.

"What do you mean, all is quiet? How many casualties?" Arellano inquired in an annoyed tone.

"There are no casualties or cases at this time, General. The only problem we had that could have been avoided with timely orders has already been resolved. The former governor was tried and shot," Commander Jaña answered.

"Don't you know that we're at war?" said General Arellano, raising his voice.

"I don't know what war you are talking about, General," Jaña answered, snapping his words.

Commander Jaña explained, "I could speak to Arellano like that because he had been my student. I was an intelligence professor of the military attachés on the General Staff. Palacios, Lagos, Álvarez, Benavides, and Arellano had been my students. Also, Arellano had written to me from Spain, calling me 'my dear friend.' So when I saw him in the mess hall of my regiment, cold and arrogant, I couldn't avoid answering him caustically.

"I told General Arellano that we were proud of the fact that in Talca everything was normal. I said that when regiment intelligence reported that it was possible that the harvest might be burned by unhappy farm laborers, I went in my Jeep without any weapons, just my driver and myself, and I met with more than 1,200 laborers. Everything was settled that day, and the workers wound up supporting my work as the local authority. And I did the same thing with the workers at a meeting in the Municipal Stadium. I told him that I understood that the military Junta needed the greatest number of people to actively support the new government. As I was saying this, General Arellano interrupted me and threw a piece of paper on the table.

"He said, 'And this order, what does this 'military proclamation' mean?'"

Commander Jaña remembered looking at the paper that Arellano had thrown onto the table, and he recounted how he had explained it to him:

"I told him, 'It is a military proclamation calling on the city of Talca to come together to reconcile differences. I asked everyone to put aside antagonistic positions and unite with their armed forces to ensure internal peace.'

"General Arellano rejected my explanation. He was very angry, and in retrospect I understood why – I was calling for civil-military friendship at a time when this sort of thing did not fit into plans at the top, when they were seeking to stir up the military's fury against the left for devising the so-called

'Plan Zeta.'[2] So Talca did not fit into that plan. Everything was quiet just at the time when the Junta needed many prisoners and cases so that they could accuse them of organizing Plan Zeta."

Commander Jaña said that he finally told General Arellano that Colonel Juan Von Chrismar had reviewed everything done in Talca and had submitted a report to General Washington Carrasco, division chief, who had been in total agreement with his [Jaña's] actions. "But Arellano didn't want to listen. He was very upset," said Jaña.

"General Arellano ordered me to wait in a room next to my office while he met with other officers of the regiment. While I waited, I was aware that I felt a sense of calm, that I was in an unusual frame of mind – calm because I knew that I had carried out my duties yet very concerned about General Arellano's attitude," Commander Jaña explained.

"An hour later he told me that, as delegate of the commander in chief of the army and of the government Junta, he ordered me to give up my command but to continue my service in the high command of the army.

"'Take all the time necessary,' Arellano told me.

"'I will hand over command first thing in the morning,' I said and immediately saluted him, turning about face."

General Arellano informed Lieutenant Colonel Benavente that he would have to assume temporary command of the regiment, and Arellano left after signing the following document and classifying it as secret.

TOP SECRET

Chilean Army

Troop Command of the Army

Delegate of the Military Government Junta

Talca, September 30, 1973

Order No. 1 of the Delegate of the Government of the Military Junta and the Commander-in-Chief of the Army

1. Whereas: The Governor of Talca and Commander of Talca Mountain Regiment No. 16 Lt. Col. EFRAÍN JAÑA GIRÓN has not duly complied with the orders of the Military Junta Government and the Commander in Chief of the Army.

2. Whereas: The searches starting on September 11, 1973, were carried out late and without the due intensity that the case demanded.

3. Whereas: The order of the Commander-Chief of the III Army Division sent on Tuesday, September 11, 1973, by the Chief of the General Staff, COLONEL LUCIANO DÍAZ MAIRA, naming CAPTAIN CARLOS VALVERDE VILDÓSOLA, Director of the Regional Hospital, to replace DR. ALBERTO CONTRERAS GARRIDO, affiliated with the Communist Party, who was kept on active duty until Thursday, September 11, 1973, on which date the HEALTH CAPTAIN OF POLICE CARLOS CAPONASSI was appointed.

4. Whereas: He kept the Directors of the Popular Unity Party government in their positions at their various public or state-run institutions until Thursday, September 13, 1973, with all the problems that this implied, giving said persons the opportunity to destroy compromising documents and perpetrate every type of irregularity. All this without considering the danger that could have been posed to the Regiment insofar as the civilian population could have had an unfavorable reaction if they had been so incited by the Popular Unity Service Directors who were kept in their positions on the 11th, 12th and 13th of September 1973.

5. Whereas: He did not follow the order to arrest the former Governor of the province, GERMÁN CASTRO, affiliated with the Socialist Party, the order given by telephone by the Commander in Chief of the III Division, General WASHINGTON CARRASCO FERNÁNDEZ, on Tuesday, September 11, 1973 at 8:30 a.m., but rather, instead of immediately sending a patrol led by an officer to arrest this person, he called the person on the telephone and told him to come to the Regiment to be arrested, which gave him the opportunity to run away, organize a guerrilla force and assault the police station in Paso Nevado that same day at 12:30 p.m., seriously wounding CORPORAL ORLANDO DEL C. ESPINOZA FAÚNDEZ, who later died.

Whereas the notice to come to the police station to comply with the arrest warrant arrived late, since GERMÁN CASTRO had been duly notified by the aforementioned telephone call and had escaped from the Governor's office.

ORDER:

1. LT. COL. EFRAÍN JAÑA GIRÓN is hereby dismissed from his positions as Governor of the Province of Talca and Commander of the Talca Mountain Regiment No. 16 on September 30, 1973.

2. LT. COL. OLAGIER BENAVENTE BUSTOS will assume the interim post of Governor of the Province of Talca and Commander of the Talca Mountain Regiment No. 16, effective on the above said date.

3. LT. COL. EFRAÍN JAÑA GIRÓN will report to the Chief of the General Staff of the Army, DIVISION GENERAL ORLANDO URBINA HERRERA, on Monday, October 1, 1973.

Sergio Arellano

Officer Delegate of the President of the Military Junta and
Commander in Chief of the Army

DISTRIBUTION

1 President of the Government Military Junta
1 Chief of the General Staff of the Army
1 Commander of the Army III Division

1   Lt. Col. Efraín Jaña Girón
1   Lt. Col. Olagier Benavente Bustos
1   Brigadier General Sergio Arellano Stark

****

Commander Jaña Girón said that he was never given his copy of the document (translated above). However, almost 16 years later, he and I reviewed the charges against him together, and I listened as he defended himself, remembering and reliving the events of those days between the military coup in 1973 and the inspection visit of General Arellano that put an abrupt end to his impeccable military career.

I asked former Commander Jaña, "Were those searches really carried out late and without the 'due intensity' demanded by the situation?"

"Look, until September 11th, my forces were deployed in a defensive position to guarantee constitutional stability and keep security in areas of strategic interest. Moreover, on the night of September 10th, I increased the number of soldiers on patrol because terrorist attacks had intensified."

"Who were the terrorists?"

"People from the extreme right. They burned tires to set up barricades, they put nails on the streets and highways, they detonated bombs, there was shooting. Therefore, from the night of the 10th to the 11th, I was up until 6:00 in the morning, inspecting different areas. I had barely slept a couple of hours in my office when four officers woke me up to tell me that something was happening in Santiago. It was the coup."

"How many officers did you have in your regiment?"

"Only 22."

"Was the political situation discussed before the coup took place?"

"When I received command of the regiment, General Prats told me, 'Look Jaña, the officers of 1973 have been specifically selected because we want first-rate professionals commanding troops. We want men who can handle the job; we want officers who are not removed from command by adventurers like what happened in the Tacna Regiment in 1969.'[3] The fact is, I was given a regiment with very low morale, because in Talca the situation had been very bad since the strike in October 1972. I did a study, and I proposed ways to counteract the situation. And my direct superior, General Carrasco, decided to extend these strategies to the whole division.

"I saw how the people of the Fatherland and Liberty group (Patria y Libertad)[4] sought to win over my officers. So I tried to stay with my men at all times to keep them from being infiltrated."

"But then came the military coup," I interjected.

"Yes, and from having my regiment deployed defensively to protect the legally constituted government, I had to withdraw my forces quickly and reorganize them. There was terrible confusion among my officers. Now, when I recall those days, I ask myself, what did General Arellano consider 'due intensity' during the searches? Did he mean to use physical violence against my compatriots, to use compromising material against public officials, to provoke unnecessary reactions on the part of those affected, to destroy property and documents?"

"And what is your answer?"

"This is an answer that history will demand from General Arellano himself. But no one could know the situation in my jurisdiction better than I did, and, therefore, I had the professional authority to determine what the priorities were. That's what I did, and the decisions were reported immediately to General Carrasco, my direct superior, who approved them.

"Besides, the actual events confirmed the accuracy of my position. Order was, in fact, maintained, and there were no unnecessary victims. In my double duty as commander and military intelligence specialist, I wanted to avoid creating imaginary situations — such as finding weapons in places where none existed before and stirring up confrontations with unarmed civilians, causing unjustified and serious injuries to innocent people.

"All of these considerations made me decide to give the searches secondary priority, a decision that now — after so many years have gone by — my companions in arms can understand in its strategic logic. I can't help but ask myself what would have happened in Talca if there had been people awaiting trial when General Arellano came around."

"And what do you think would have happened?"

"The relatives of the victims of Calama, La Serena, Copiapó, Cauquenes, and Santiago know the painful answer. As an army officer, doing my duty, I never disobeyed an order, but I always made due reflection my top priority, to avoid regrets later on the part of those who gave the orders and those who followed them."

"The first order you received on the day of the coup was to arrest the Socialist Governor, Germán Castro. What happened? Did you help him get away, as the charges state?"

"I received that order at around 8:00 a.m. on the day of the coup by telephone from Concepción. The connection was poor. I knew that it was General Washington Carrasco. His message was terse: proceed to arrest the governor. Then the line went dead. I was surprised and decided to confirm it. But I wasn't able to get a line. Then I chose two captains to arrest the governor. But after quick reflection, I decided that, for reasons of time and space, the police were better equipped to carry out that task — they were located across from the governor's office.

"I decided to call Governor Castro and tell him, diplomatically, to come immediately to the base for his own security and protection. He told me he would do so immediately. I hung up, and I called General Gallardo, provincial chief of police of Talca, and asked him to arrest the governor and transfer him to the barracks."

"And it seemed proper to call the governor, asking him to appear at the regiment?"

"It was the same request that many regimental commanders made, for example, the one in Curicó and in Linares. Even General Forestier, commander in chief of the Sixth Division, did it. He called Governor Burgos of Iquique on the telephone. Because normally there's a kind of friendship between the commander of the regiment and the local governor."

"That's the way it was in 1973?"

"That's the way it was, because it's a fact that our relations with the political leaders and chief representatives of the executive in the provinces were traditionally harmonious. There was a high degree of cooperation and mutual respect. That's why the majority of us provincial military chiefs acted in a similar fashion, within the parameters established by the consideration, respect, and awareness of the importance of the positions they held. Obviously, it was very difficult for us to use violence to comply with an order of that nature, which forced us to arrest officials with whom we had been exchanging information about the situation up to the day before."

"Was that true in your case?"

"Not as to friendship. Because Governor Castro was an intelligent guy, but he was very immature and lacked judgment. Look, for a ceremony honoring Bernardo O'Higgins on August 20, Castro arrived disheveled, unshaven, wearing boots. I was forced to tell him that his appearance did not fulfill the minimum standards of deference that representatives of the executive should have for the troops that would parade before him, and I said, 'The troops will be dressed in their best clothes, and you are not,' and I offered him my chauffeur so that he could go and wash up. He refused, saying that he was a revolutionary. Then I told him that he was not going to preside over the event, that I would. He agreed and stayed in the area designated for the public during the ceremony.

"I reported what happened, and then President Allende himself called me to apologize. He told me he was ordering a change of governors because Governor Castro had been causing problems for awhile."

"The fact is that the governor fled."

"I think he did so because he was terrified of Patria y Libertad and not because he was afraid of us. As a matter of fact, while he was speaking on the telephone with me, he had a Jeep with the motor running waiting for him at the door of the governor's office to escape with three other men. They had a confrontation with the police as they were escaping to the mountains, and Corporal Espinoza was badly wounded. Later, when the police captured the four men, they almost lynched them. A military patrol headed by Captain Meza intervened and brought them to the base," Jaña explained.

"And you brought them before a court-martial?" I asked.

"Of course. The prosecutor was Lieutenant Colonel Benavente. The military judge, General Carrasco, decided on the death penalty for all four. I intervened and stated that the death penalty was unjust for his companions because the head of the group was Governor Castro. Finally, the penalty was lessened, and the other men were spared at that time."

"Where was the former governor executed?"

"The execution was carried out on the base. I refused to order my people to shoot him, so I asked for volunteers. All who volunteered were policemen. Before that, I called the Bishop of Talca, Carlos González, to come spend some time with Castro. A few minutes before he was shot, the governor told me, 'Forgive me for all the troubles that I have caused you. I die for what I believe, for my cause. And I'm sure that I have acted correctly.'

"So, on September 30th, there were only two casualties in Talca, the policeman and the governor. And both could have been avoided if I had been told of the measures that I should have foreseen for September 11th. In Talca, troops controlled the city from the very beginning — without shedding blood."

"Finally, General Arellano accused you of having kept the director of the Talca Hospital, a member of the Communist Party, in his post, as well as other high-ranking public officials, for two days until September 13th."

"Yes, and I'll explain that to you. I had dealt with the director of the hospital, Doctor Alberto Contreras, three times before. The first time was when I inspected the hospital on June 29, 1973, as a result of the armored regiment uprising [*tanquetazo*] in the capital. The second time was when I formulated a plan for natural disasters for Talca and, finally, during the special ceremony of pledging allegiance to the unit's flag. During this last meeting, I witnessed an interesting dialogue between Dr. Contreras and Bishop González that impressed me favorably with regard to the personality of Dr. Contreras.

"Anyway, I did not consider the doctor someone capable of endangering the security of the hospital or anything along those lines. And I was right. When I proceeded to follow the order, I chose to replace Dr. Contreras with the police doctor because I had been told that the police doctor had previously worked as director of the hospital and was experienced. Logic told me that a military doctor would be needed for his logistical expertise in case of any problems in my jurisdiction.

"I contacted the division commander and reported my reasons for replacing Dr. Contreras. General Carrasco approved my decision," former Commander Jaña Girón concluded.

Talca's Deputy Commander, Lieutenant Colonel Olagier Benavente, shared with me his recollection of how that episode led to the personal intervention of General Pinochet:

"Two days after the coup, General Pinochet called, and, since Commander Jaña was not there, I had to answer. General Pinochet said, 'What is going on in Talca? Tell Commander Jaña to immediately change the director of the hospital because I don't take any shit, and this must be done right away.' I reported the general's orders to Commander Jaña immediately at the governor's office, and the change was made that same day. Instead of appointing the Talca army doctor, he appointed the police doctor of the town of Linares, a few kilometers away form Talca, because the one from the army, Dr. Valverde, was too hard-line. Commander Jaña thought that the people would be more protected with the doctor from the police, who was more humane.

"In any case, the 'hard-liners' in Talca were right-wing civilians and retired military who would come to the regiment, denouncing people from the left and pressuring us to act against them."

Benavente continued, "Once I was criticized in headquarters because I had not called in a man named Venegas, a prestigious accountant, to make a statement. We called people in to make statements through military proclamations that were published in the newspaper. Mr. Venegas came with his lawyer, and I remember that he was very afraid. He told me that he had been very good friends with President Allende and that the president had even stayed at his house when he came to Talca. I listened to him and told him that was all, that he was free to leave. What more could I do, since he had not committed any crimes?"

Commander Jaña also received a note signed by the National Party of Talca, he recollected, "instructing me as to how I should act as the new local authority. I considered it an insult, and I sent it to the Intelligence Director, General Lutz. Another time, the cousin of former President Jorge Alessandri[5] showed up with a list of people 'who should be arrested.' I asked him what crimes he was denouncing. He answered, 'This one is a communist, this one is a socialist, and this one is a radical. . . .' I told him that nothing in the penal code defines political affiliation as a crime. He was very upset when he left."

"And who gave the order to replace the service directors by militants from the National Party and the Christian Democrats?"

"That was ordered by the chief of the General Staff of the division. Finally, I decided to name only Christian Democrats."

However, on September 30, 1973 — after having served as Governor of Talca for only 19 days — Commander Jaña was punished by General Arellano. "On that date, a fog settled over my small military camp," Commander Jaña said, paraphrasing what General Carlos Prats had written in his memoirs.[6]

Lieutenant Colonel Benavente pointed out, "He [General Arellano] took away his [Commander Jaña's] command immediately, and that is not normal. You always transfer command, and a colonel comes from Santiago to see that everything is in order for the transfer."

That night, Commander Jaña ate with his officers without completely comprehending what had happened. Commander Jaña recalled the scene:

"We were very emotional. With their words or with their gestures, everyone there was telling me, 'Commander, this is unfair, an injustice.' That night, the officers decided to place a guard (two privates) in front of the door of my apartment to protect me against any attempt on my life. It was clear that I had fallen into disgrace and that anything could happen.

"The next day, I said goodbye to the assembled regiment. I asked them to continue to do their duty, and I told them that their regiment could be proud that no Chilean citizen had been unjustly treated. But I was as sad as I was confused. I had earned the best grades of my professional life while I was commander, I had the best job within the division, and I had obtained three sevens [seven is the highest mark] in my category. I could not understand what was going on. I left in my car with an officer who offered to accompany me, Lieutenant Gumucio," Jaña concluded.

At that point in the Talca Regiment, a combined regiment of about 1,200 men, "all hell broke loose," as then-interim Commander Benavente admitted.

"Yes, that's right, everything was upside down because they took away the commander overnight. The officers and noncommissioned officers refused to swallow any of the [official] versions we gave of the story. They asked me, 'What really happened to the commander — is he going to be shot?' And I answered, 'How can you believe such a thing?' But I also thought that they could kill him."

"How could you think that?"

"Because the Colonel Cantuarias affair had just happened, and all the army had found out about it."

"Were you afraid?"

"Yes, very afraid. And that fear that General Arellano aroused in Talca spread quickly throughout Chile. Everybody found out in a few hours, and from then on, we all knew that we had to bow if he [Arellano] showed up. You had to accept whatever he ordered without hesitation or causing any problems."

"And did your attitude change after that episode?" I asked Benavente.

"Yes, of course. I understood that procedures had changed, that you had to be tougher if you wanted to survive."

"And there were no hard-line officers in your regiment?"

"No, we were all similar. Some liked to play cowboys and Indians. I remember that on the same day of the military coup, September 11, I went home for lunch in my Jeep. But one particular captain, by 10:00 in the morning, had already taken his Jeep's top down and mounted a machine gun in the back. Different temperaments, that's all. In the beginning, the younger officers and the recruits wanted to be the good guys in the movie. But then that disappeared, and everything returned to normal — until General Arellano came."

Lieutenant Colonel Benavente recalled something else that paved the way for the Caravan of Death. While he was commander of the regiment, he received the order from the Intelligence Service in the capital to send a list of the 100 townspeople who were closest to the Popular Unity government. "The captain in charge of intelligence," Benavente said, "who had just arrived, asked me what names who to include. I didn't know either. So we took the lists that the people from the Right sent us, and we copied it. Years later, a cousin of mine who had gone to England asked me for help to return to Chile. I made some inquiries for him, and it came up: 'Communist Party sympathizer,' according to report number such and such of the Chillán Regiment. But I couldn't do anything about it. And then I remembered I had done the same thing to 100 people in Talca. They are probably still catalogued that way. Jesus!"

Meanwhile, Lieutenant Colonel Jaña told me how he was living his own nightmare in Santiago:

"I arrived at my house in the fashionable district of Las Condes and was ordered by phone to go to the General Staff. I knew my career had come to an end. Generals Lutz, Urbina, and Álvarez were waiting for me — the director of intelligence, chief of the General Staff, and personnel chief, respectively. They told me that the Officers' Board had decided to retire me. 'Do you have any complaints?' one of them asked. I knew that everything was absurd, so I answered that there was no point in complaining and left.

"That night my wife and I spent the night at the Sheraton Hotel, as a way of celebrating the beginning of a new phase in our lives. There was nothing to celebrate, of course. The next morning, I saw two pickup trucks from the Police Investigations Headquarters[7] outside the hotel. When we went home, the house had already been searched. I called General Baeza, with Investigations, who was my friend. But he wasn't there, and an officer told me that they needed to ask me some questions. He said, 'Why don't you go to the Armored Regiment, please?' I went, and I was immediately arrested . . . for three years."

"You arrived at the regiment, and you were arrested. Did you do something — did you complain?"

"What could I do? The situation was terrifying. I thought about various things I had heard, about a couple of captains who had disappeared and the matter of Colonel Cantuarias. I was paralyzed. Approximately two hours later, an officer appeared and asked me, 'What are you doing here, Commander?' He was a friend of my son's. Then other officers arrived, and they took me out to have tea."

"How did they react when they found out what had happened?"

"They were upset. They said that my case was an injustice. That same day they transferred me from the base, and they took me to the Telecommunications School. There they practically held me incommunicado. I could only see my wife and my lawyer. My son, who was in the military school, visited once," Jaña Girón stated.

"What did your son say?"

"He was very bitter; he suffered a lot. I told him not to be ashamed of his father, that time would prove me right."

"Were you interrogated?"

"Of course. And once they took me to the Air Force War Academy (Academia de Guerra Aérea—AGA) to be interrogated. 'Polish' Rodríguez, Manuel, who was a very good friend of mine, came to get me. He said, 'Why do these idiots want to take you to the AGA?' I told him to follow orders and not to worry. We arrived, and we were received by Commander Lavín of the Chilean Air Force, who was also a very good friend of mine. He greeted me effusively. I was very solemn. He apologized, saying that he didn't know why I had been taken there. A military attorney asked me a couple of questions, and that was it. When I returned, Rodríguez told me that what was happening made no sense at all. On the way back, we even got out of the car to have a drink.

"Several times" Jaña Girón continued, "my guards were changed because they were punished for talking with me. Many of them were upset by the change in the situation, and they were afraid. They knew that if they did not follow orders blindly, they could be shot in the back. Others were happy with what was happening. I never shut up. I always told them that the army was debasing its role, that we were being used as instruments of the economic right, and that this would weigh heavily upon the army.

"Officers, noncommissioned officers, and recruits talked about the attrocities that were being done in other places. But no one ever told me that he had directly participated in anything specific. They spoke about the ill treatment of prisoners and that people had been thrown out of helicopters into the sea or in the mountains."

"You were detained for three years in the Telecommunications School?"

"No, after that they took me to the Infantry School. They took me in a Jeep under armed escort. Afterward, the captain in charge of the operation confessed to me that he took me to Chena Hill to be shot. I also had an intuition that something very bad was going to happen, and I left a farewell note to my wife. I thought they could shoot me. My brother-in-law, Colonel Figueroa, had told my wife that I was accused of treason. And that means the death penalty.

"Once there, instead of a firing squad, I was greeted by a butler whom I had met before, and I was given the suite for high-ranking visitors. My wife came to see me twice a week. Then they took me to a room in the officers' mess, and they boarded up the windows. I took the boards down, and they never put them up again.

"June 7th is Infantry Day. During the preparations, I opened a window, and I looked at the troops. When they passed in front of me, they saluted. I remember I felt a chill, and I closed the window. General Pinochet was there at that same ceremony. A captain asked him why I was in prison. He answered, 'Look, Captain, you shouldn't have asked that. As far as I know, he's imprisoned for his socialist ideas. But I'd like to give you some advice, Captain, don't involve yourself in something that is none of your business.'

"At the end of 1974," Lieutenant Colonel Jaña Girón added, "I was taken to the General Staff to be confronted by two officers who questioned me about my political contacts. I was asked about my relationship with Carlos Lazo, who had been my classmate in military school. I saw Lazo there, in very bad shape.[8]

"And then the court-martial began. I was accused of not fulfilling my military duties. The military judge was none other than General Arellano himself. Judge and jury, he sentenced me to three years jail. I was taken to the public jail to sleep on the floor of a cell. The intelligence officer who took me was very affected by the situation. And then I was taken to the Capuchinos Annex.[9] There I spent another year and a half."

"And how did you feel when you got out?"

"I wasn't defeated in jail. I kept my moral high ground. I peeled potatoes, I swept cells, and I did everything I had to do just like the others. With pride. And then my sentence was commuted to the sentence of exile: Colombia, Holland, and Venezuela. One more injustice, which caused my family to scatter."

Notes

1. In Chile, the military prosecutor — *fiscal militar* — has a judicial as well as a legal function. The role of this attorney is to gather evidence to determine whether a person should be indicted in connection with some crime. Once the prosecutor decides to press charges, the case is passed to the military judge for trial.

2. Plan Zeta was a reported plot to kill the military commanders and their families at the September 19 military parade. A document outlining the plan, clearly a forgery, was published by the Junta in its *White Book* (*Libro Blanco*), defending the coup. *Paul E. Sigmund.*

3. In 1969, General Roberto Viaux and a group of officers rose up in the Tacna Regiment, located in the heart of Santiago. They demanded a raise in salaries. The uprising took place toward the end of President Eduardo Frei Montalva's administration, and it lasted only for a few hours. General Viaux and the officers were dismissed. Later, in October 1970, Viaux himself, although he was retired by then, took part in a conspiracy to prevent President Allende from taking office after his election. The conspiracy — supported by the U.S. Central Intelligence Agency and a Chilean extreme right group — culminated in the assassination of then Army Commander in Chief René Schneider.

4. Fatherland and Liberty (Patria y Libertad) was a right-wing paramilitary group that opposed Allende's Unidad Popular government by sabotage and occasional violence. *Ed. and Paul E. Sigmund.*

The group's leader was the lawyer Pablo Rodríguez, who in 1999 assumed the defense of General Augusto Pinochet.

5. Jorge Rodríguez, cousin of Chilean President Jorge Alessandri Rodríguez (1958-1964).

6. See Carlos Prats, 1985, *Memorias: Testimonio de un Soldado* (Buenos Aires: Editorial Pehuén). General Carlos Prats was assassinated in Argentina in September 1974. *Ed.*

General Prats preceded General Pinochet as commander in chief of the army. General Prats was forced to resign by his fellow generals three weeks prior to the coup. *Paul E. Sigmund.*

7. In Chile, each city's police department has two divisions: 1) the Police Office for Investigations, whose officers do not wear uniforms, called Policía de Investigaciones and 2) the National Military Police, whose officers wear uniforms, called Carabineros de Chile.

8. Carlos Lazo, a socialist, was president of the Banco del Estado until the military coup.

9. Capuchinos Annex, a former Capuchin monastery, is the VIP jail in Santiago. *Paul E. Sigmund.*

CHAPTER 3

Two Have Already
Committed Suicide, Major

On September 30, 1973, a powerful dose of fear had inoculated the Talca Regiment with the arrival of General Arellano's Puma helicopter and his entourage. On October 2, the Calama Regiment, located in the city of Calama in northern Chile, experienced its first tremors of fear.

On October 2, 1973, Major Fernando Reveco Valenzuela, who had presided over the trials of political prisoners in Calama, was arrested. His arrest set the stage for what happened two weeks later, when the Caravan of Death reached Calama and 26 prisoners were massacred.[1] For Major Reveco, October 2 was the beginning of a nightmare that lasted 458 days and led to his sentence, given by General Sergio Arellano Stark, of 270 days in jail for "not performing his military duty." Almost 16 years after the episode that forever marked his and his family's lives, he recalled what happened in an interview at his house in Rancagua, next to his small optician's shop.

"What happened in your regiment on the day of the coup?" I asked.

"Nobody knew that there was going be a coup that day. I'm sure of that; neither the colonel nor the intelligence officer, nobody knew. At 8:00 in the morning, a little while after we found out, Commander Eugenio Rivera phoned and asked me how I perceived the situation. I told him, 'Colonel, it is very simple. If there is an uprising headed by a division commander or regimental commander to go against the legally constituted government, I'll oppose it. Now, if the Chilean Army, with its legally constituted command, takes a position as an institution, I belong to the Chilean Army and I'll go along with it. I imagine, Colonel, that the generals have weighed the step they are going to take. The only thing for us to do is to be loyal to the institution.' He shook my hand, saying, 'Reveco, I'm very grateful for your words. Go take charge of your unit.'"

"And all the officers supported the coup?" I inquired.

"All except one. Captain Jaque."

"Was he against it?"

"Yes. That very same morning of the coup on September 11th, he came to the office of Colonel Rivera and said that he was not taking part. He had spoken to me before. I told him my opinion about not being a disruptive factor in the army and that those orders must be obeyed. But he told me he could not, that he had a father (or a brother) in La Moneda, and that the military coup was not to his liking. Therefore, he went to the colonel and told him he was going to be in the mess hall. He arrested himself."

"What happened to him?"

"I found out later that 'Polish' Rodríguez had gotten a hold of him, and it seems that they tortured him."

"Before the coup, had you ever said that you were opposed to it?"

"In the political evaluation meetings we had every Monday, some officers bared their fangs at the possibility of the coup. I was always trying to quiet things down, pointing out that we were serving a legal government and that the only proper attitude was our obedience to military authorities. I supported the legal continuity of the system. Perhaps that's why some of them could have had the idea that I was a supporter of Popular Unity."

"According to what you knew about the army and the officers in your regiment, did you think that the mood would turn violent and bloodthirsty starting on September 11th?"

"No, absolutely not. Look, our regiment was large and diverse. There were infantry, artillery, everything — it was a combined regiment. In my opinion, the army was divided, and 25 percent to 30 percent of the officers supported the previous regime. They were not socialists or Marxists. No. They were constitutionalists, following the line of Generals Schneider and Prats. Somewhere between 10 percent and 15 percent were openly in favor of breaking with the government, wanting to carry out a coup. And they said so."

"And the rest?"

"That was the majority of the men, those who remained quiet and tried to get by unnoticed, those who didn't express opinions and were afraid — the ones who finally support whoever wins."

"And how many would you say were hard-line anti-Marxists and were willing to kill in cold blood?"

"If you had asked me before the coup, I would have said nobody. Later, there were some who wanted to see blood flow: Ravest, Robles, Minoletti, and Santander. I remember Captain Ravest saying that in Santiago the Maipo Regiment was being attacked and that we should go out into the streets. And we told him that Calama was peaceful, that we could not search houses and arrest people because of what was happening in Santiago and

Valparaíso. We had an oasis of peace in Calama — to the extent that the Popular Unity people trusted us and gave themselves up on the first day."

"Did the General Manager of the Chuquicamata copper mine, David Silberman, the communist engineer, also give himself up?"

"Yes, he turned himself in to Colonel Rivera at the base. I was up in Chuquicamata at the time."

"What were you doing there?"

"Colonel Rivera ordered me to take over the mine. And may I tell you something ridiculous? When I was in jail, the bulletin that promoted me to lieutenant colonel[2] appeared, and I was awarded the presidential medal for having participated in combat and having occupied Chuquicamata. Obviously, I never received the medal."

"And did you fight in Chuquicamata?"

"Never. Look, the chief of police of Calama had shown us (he was very excited and nervous) a sketch with the location of all the automatic weapons. Based on that information, we arrived armed to the teeth. I ordered the vehicles to stop about a hundred meters away from the mine, and I ran in with an assault weapon. I left the column outside with the artillery group, and I began the assault of the general manager's office of Chuqui. And there was nothing there. Everything was calm, not a single weapon. I was even foolish enough to kick open the door to Silberman's office when I simply could have turned the doorknob. Of course, it was more heroic to enter that way! Later, I began to open drawers, all of them unlocked, and I went through the documents.

"There I was able to verify that he [Silberman] was an extremely honest person. You should have seen the propositions his comrades made to him and with what decency he rejected them! Everything was very clear."

"Did you preside over the court-martial against Silberman?"

"Yes."

"And what sentence did you suggest to the military judge?"

"Twenty-five years, and he was finally sentenced to 13 years."

"Why?"

"Because he made the mistake of not giving himself up immediately. He fled toward the interior. And we thought he had gone to organize the people and to try to stop copper production. Later, he gave himself up to Colonel Rivera at the base."

"When you found out that finally, in October 1974, Silberman had been taken away by The National Intelligence Directorate (Dirección de Inteligencia Nacional — DINA)[3] from the penitentiary in Santiago and that he had 'disappeared,' what reaction did you have?"[4]

"Indignation! I could hardly believe it. But DINA left its imprint on everything — as always."

"Who made up the court-martial?" I asked Reveco Valenzuela.

"Five officers besides the prosecutor who presented the case to the court," Reveco remembered, "a secretary without the right to vote, and the defense, an officer who had been given the case a couple of hours before."

"A regular procedure?"

"No, it was highly irregular. Only formalities were followed. In the last analysis, the sentence was going to be handed down with or without a defense."

"And were there very hard-line officers?" I asked.

"Yes. They demanded the death penalty for the most innocuous misdemeanors. There was one who had very good reasons. He had been an intelligence officer, and he had U.S. dollars when it was an unavailable currency. He surprised all of us. I remember the deputy commander and I were wondering where the officer had obtained those $100 bills. That's why he wanted to kill the prisoners immediately, because he wanted to keep it a secret that they had given him money."

"Who?"

"The people in the Chuqui mine's finance office, which had been under Haroldo Cabrera. It seems that he gave a lot of them a quota of dollars on a monthly basis. But the intelligence officer told them that nobody could find out because the money was to finance intelligence work to pay for Chilean agents who were in Bolivia. That's why he wanted them to die before they talked. On the very same night of the coup, September 11th, he began to promote the idea of killing them. We were puzzled, and we talked about it with the deputy commander.

"On the night of the coup, Haroldo Cabrera called me, and we met. He told me he was stuck, that he had given the intelligence office approximately $1,000 for intelligence work in order to show that he had never acted against the regiment.

"That same night I told this to Colonel Rivera, and he was furious. He told me he could not accept one of his officers being under suspicion. I proposed an investigation, a summary investigation to protect the honor of the officer and to protect everyone's peace of mind. But Commander Rivera, despite being honorable and just, did not want to do anything to investigate such a serious charge. He was a very good friend of the intelligence officer."

"Were there any death penalties in the courts-martial you presided over?"

"No, none. I handed down sentences for 16 prisoners, sentences that ranged from 61 days to 20 years in jail."

"Was it really a surprise when you were arrested on October 2, or did you already know that they were not happy with your actions?"

"No, not at all. Furthermore, I was commanding the most powerful unit that the regiment had. They would have taken it away before that if they had been unhappy or had any doubts about me. I was in charge of a reinforced artillery group with three infantry companies and one engineering company. It was the most powerful of the combat units, and we were up there, in Chuqui. Every time Colonel Rivera went up [to the mine], he told me he was happy and grateful for how well we were performing."

"Hadn't you previously received pressure or suggestions to be careful in the court-martial, to be harsher?"

"Yes, there was one very difficult situation. While we were in the court, the intelligence officer, Luis Ravest, complained to the colonel because I had been handling things too mildly. Then the colonel decided to relieve me and told me to go to Chuqui. I did not like presiding over the court-martial. It was a very hard job, but on the other hand, I saw that the measure could have serious consequences. I told him [the colonel], with all frankness, that I was his only guarantee, as an observant Christian, that irreparable crimes would not be committed. Because killing a man with those courts-martial, without a defense, with the enormous power we had with those weapons — it was murder. And in the future, it was all going to be seen as murder, and those who participated in it were going to be the murderers. I asked him to please reconsider the matter, that he knew that there were other officers anxious to wash their hands in blood."

"What did he [Colonel Rivera] answer?"

"He agreed, and I continued to preside. But the next day he relieved me once again. It was a tragicomic situation. He said he was very sorry but that he had to remove me from my position because if they knew that things were being handled too leniently, this could have consequences. However, I repeated my same argument and convinced him again. I thought that our conversation was confidential, that only the colonel and I knew about it. I have never mentioned all this publicly until now. I even told him that if worse came to worse, I could sentence all the prisoners to life in prison, because a prisoner can be taken out of jail, but to sentence someone to death is irreversible – there is no way to bring a person back to life once he's in the grave. That's how I was able to finish the trial on September 29. Until that date, I presided over all of the courts-martial in the zone."

"Did Colonel Rivera confirm all of your sentences?"

"Yes, he even reduced a couple of them."

"How were you arrested on October 2?"

"The order arrived from Santiago, via Antofagasta. I was in the general manager's office in Chuquicamata, commanding my unit, when Deputy Commander Oscar Figueroa Márquez arrived. He was very confused. He said, 'Fernando, forgive me. I've been asked to take you to Antofagasta, and from there you will go to Santiago because the Junta wants to speak with you.' I was baffled. I didn't know what this meant. I told him that I had the right, and was in a position, to refuse. He said that would be a very dangerous step. I answered that what was being done to me was also very serious and that I would not move because they had not given me a clear explanation.

"He [Commander Figueroa] did not speak in terms of an arrest. I asked him under what terms I would be going, and he answered that he could not say anything and that the Junta was calling me to Santiago. I told him that it was my understanding, therefore, that I was under arrest and that I was going to do something to defend myself. Crazy! I didn't know what to do, and, in fact, I called my men, and I ordered my vehicle prepared."

"Why?"

"To go to the border."

"You prepared the vehicle to do what?"

"I was afraid that something very serious could happen, that I could be arrested since I knew about the things that were done without trial."

"But in the end you gave up."

"Yes, but I demanded to keep my weapon. He told me that he did not have orders to take it away from me. I said that I was going to go with my escort, but he did not accept. Commander Figueroa said that I had to go with his escort. When we reached Antofagasta, they put me in the office of the division headquarters. An officer who was a friend of mine came in and told me, 'Fernando, please give me the pistol.' I refused and demanded to know why I had been called because taking away my pistol was the same as taking away my rank and insignia. Finally, the five commanders of the Antofagasta regiment came in with threatening looks to take away my pistol. Colonel Sergio Cartagena, who was my friend, told me not to make a scene. I was arguing that they were ignoring the dignity of my rank. Moreover, I never imagined that my comrades would do this to me. Finally, I threw the pistol on the floor and said, 'Take this piece of shit, if you are so worried about it.' They took me to a bedroom, and they put a guard at the door.

"The next day, the commander accompanied me on a commercial airline flight to Santiago. I met with General Brady, who told me he was very sorry that I was there but that I should be confident because 'many have come back' (he used those exact words). I asked what that meant — what happened to those who didn't come back? He answered that he couldn't say any more.

"Then they handed me over to Manuel 'Polish' Rodríguez from the Tacna Regiment. Manuel Rodríguez had been named prosecutor to investigate all the cases of alleged Marxist infiltration of the army. Then he was promoted to general, and they [eventually] sent him as ambassador to Austria.

"You know what? I cannot forgive Rodríguez — neither him nor Quinteros, who acted as secretary in that pseudo-trial. They acted in the most undignified manner."

"Were you interrogated at the Tacna Regiment?"

"No. The following day, they took me to the Air Force War Academy. I was interrogated there, and then they took me to the Armored Regiment, where I was held incommunicado for six months."

"Wasn't it strange for an army officer to be interrogated at the Air Force War Academy?"

"Absolutely. It was very rare."

"Were the interrogators from the army or from the air force?" I inquired.

"I had a hood on, but I knew that the person interrogating me was 'Polish' Rodríguez. He was the only one who interrogated me. In the first session, he threatened me by saying, 'Two have already committed suicide, Major — Cantuarias and Lavanderos.'"

"Were you tortured?"

"Yes." (His chin began to tremble.)

"Was Rodríguez himself present [when you were tortured]?"

"I think so. I was wearing a hood."

"What type of torture?"

"I would rather not speak about that."

"Electricity?"

"No."

"Were you hung?"

"Yes." (Tears began to run down his face, and his breathing became more agitated.)

"Were you put in water?"

"No." (At this point he became very agitated.) He continued, "I was kicked a lot, but I also talked back to them, and that's why I was kicked more. I couldn't see them. I yelled at them, calling them 'shits.'"

"While you were under arrest for 458 days, could you understand that your own people were capable of doing all this?"

"No, I could not understand. The truth is that, with stupid naïveté, I told myself until the last moment that the court was going to recognize my innocence and they were going to apologize."

"And with regard to the torture?"

"It seemed so incredible to me that officers could inflict torture that all the time I was thinking, 'These characters are going to get caught, and they'll be eliminated.'"

"Did you really think that?"

"Sure, because I thought that the military as an institution could not tolerate something so barbaric. Years later, I found out through an officer, Major Cruz Loyer, who was artillery commander at Tacna, that very important people went to witness the torture up above in the 'rakes.'"

"What are the 'rakes'?"

"Where pieces of artillery are stored. Up above they have walkways where the most delicate parts are stored, and the guns are kept downstairs."

"Did you think it was possible to have a military government without the need to kill and persecute leftist militants?"

"Yes. I thought it was going be serious, that a little 'sweeping' would be done[5] and, in the short run, elections would be called, and there would be a return to democracy," Lieutenant Colonel Reveco explained.

"When did you understand that it was not going that way?"

"When I was in prison in the Armored Regiment. Something happened there that left me numb. When the six months of being held incommunicado ended and I could see my wife, I was transferred to another room, and they put me with Colonel Nelson Fuenzalida, who was imprisoned for one year with me.

"He spent a lot of time in the mess halls and talked until late at night with the officers. I didn't do that because I was very bitter about what was happening to me. I was very preoccupied about my own problems and was closed to the possibility that excesses were being committed outside. That's why I didn't inquire more. I didn't even ask myself why some officers were crying after coming back from night operations or why they would scream in their sleep.

"But one night at the end of October or the beginning of November 1974, Colonel Fuenzalida arrived in the bedroom with a few extra drinks in him, and he woke me up. He was very upset, crying. He told me that he had been talking with his brother, who was an army major, and his brother had told him that they were burning them."

"Burning them?"

"Because the summer was beginning, and the dogs had begun digging holes in Peldehue, attracted by the smell of the bodies. He told me that some bodies had even been dug up. Then an order was given to build a furnace right there in Peldehue, and those bodies were being burned. He [Nelson Fuenzalida] was very upset, and he said, 'Just like the Jews, Fernando, they're burning them.'

"Then I understood what was really happening. I was unable to sleep for several nights."

"Do you recall any other events that happened in the Armored Regiment?"

"Yes, there was another episode that left me very troubled. I remember that General Pinochet often visited the Armored Regiment and stayed for dinner with the officers. The night after one of Pinochet's visits to the mess hall, I spoke with the regiment's commander, and he told me, without thinking, something along these lines: 'What do you think about this bastard Bernardo Leighton and the things he's doing outside?' I was shocked because most people thought of Leighton as someone who was as kind as a priest. When I heard those harsh remarks, I was puzzled, and I thought for sure that the commander had heard something from Pinochet's own lips. I thought that probably Pinochet had called Leighton a traitor to the country or something similar in front of the officers. And before 15 days had passed, we heard about the assassination attempt against Leighton and his wife in Rome."[6]

"Are you suggesting that the military was being prepared to accept this assassination attempt?"

"Of course! There is no other explanation. In addition, there was a herd reaction, and they said, 'There is the enemy; every means to eliminate him is valid — period!' Without reasoning."

Lieutenant Colonel Fernando Reveco was certain that his arrest, on October 2, 1973, was a step toward a harsher treatment of political prisoners in Calama, and he explained during our conversation, "Colonel Rivera was a very good commander, a very good Catholic. He wasn't about to get his hands dirty with innocent blood. However, after my arrest, I have no doubt about the pressure that Rivera was under, along with the pressure from the tougher, hard-line officers."

On October 6, 1973, four days after Major Reveco's arrest, three people were executed in the Calama regiment: Luis Busch, Francisco Valdivia, and Andrés Rojas were sentenced to death for allegedly participating in the sabotage of the National Explosives Company (Empresa Nacional de Explosivos — ENAEX). Busch, 36, was an agricultural engineer who was a Bolivian national married to a Chilean. Valdivia, 34, was the president of ENAEX's labor union. Rojas was an ambulance driver for the Calama Hospital.

"I knew nothing about them. I did not try them," concluded Lieutenant Colonel Reveco. Of course, he could not have known about them because the three men had been arrested on October 4, and Reveco had been arrested on October 2.

*****

During my investigative research into the events that paved the way for the Caravan of Death in 1973, I realized that I needed to hear the explanation for the executions of Busch, Valdivia, and Rojas from the Calama Regiment Commander at that time, Colonel Eugenio Rivera Desgroux. The former colonel and I had the following dialogue regarding these executions and Major Reveco's arrest.

"Colonel, what happened at the ENAEX plant that led to the arrest of several workers?"

"First, the labor leader, I think, Francisco Valdivia, along with the ambulance driver of the Calama Hospital, Andrés Rojas, and a Bolivian gentleman named Busch, a well-known international activist, were arrested.

All three were arrested by the police and then tried. The court-martial sentenced them to death. And they were shot."

"And that was on October 6, 1973?"

"I don't remember the date. It must have been then, because it happened after Major Reveco was in Santiago."

"You mean after the date of Reveco's arrest, to be exact."

"Yes, his arrest."

"Do you remember who presided over the court-martial that sentenced the men to death?"

"It must have been one of the majors at that time, Ravest, Robles, or Aracena Romo."

"Why were those three prisoners condemned to death precisely after Major Reveco stopped presiding over the court-martial, when you appointed a hard-line officer in his place?"

"Because this was a real sabotage attempt that was denounced by the authorities of the ENAEX plant, and it was verified that explosive charges had been placed around the plant's perimeter."

"You confirmed those death sentences. Today, are you completely certain that they were guilty?"

"No, I'm not. There was a rather difficult situation and, after the court-martial decided the death penalty, I spoke to the three men. I did so especially with Rojas, the ambulance driver, because I knew him well. He came to the regiment to get bread every day because we supplied the hospital. On my rounds, I would often run into him and address him using a very common expression of endearment in the Chilean countryside, *mi regalón*, my special one.[7]

"I went to the court to speak to the three men. I asked them if they were sorry. And all three told me that they held firm to their position, that they would always act against any unconstitutional action of the military government."

"Did they confess to placing explosive charges?"

"No. The truth is I did not ask them directly. I realize now, because after 15 years I've learned from experience, that I should not have acted that way for any reason."

"What have you learned during these years?"

"Look, now that I've worked at ENAEX for 11 years and been head of security for some time, I realize that it was impossible to blow up the plant.

But, in 1973, the assistant manager of the company convinced me of the tremendous dangers threatening Calama at that time and the cataclysmic consequences of a large explosion in the plant."

"Was it painful to ratify the death penalties?"

"Just imagine what it means to a practicing Catholic to sign a death sentence! My wife always told me, 'Why didn't you ask beforehand?' I couldn't ask the bishop, because I was the commander, so I had to make a decision of conscience. On the one hand, I had a personal problem because, as a Catholic, I felt I should reject the death penalty. But at that time, I was a soldier, and I had the responsibility for making a decision. I swear I looked for mitigating circumstances, hoping that they would tell me that they were sorry. But they did not, and I had to make a decision."

"Did they have the right to a defense?"

"A formal defense. Nothing more, because they didn't have the lawyer they had chosen. So I appointed one of the two consulting lawyers I used; I don't remember which one."

"Did you give their bodies to their families?"

"Of course. Procedures were followed according to regulations. Chaplain Luis Jorquera heard their confessions, he gave them the last rites, they were shot, and their bodies were handed over."

"The widow of Luis Busch, Grimilda Sánchez, says you did not do so, that the family had to find the body with the help of a gravedigger in the cemetery."

"I cannot give you details about the return of the bodies. I don't know; I didn't see them. I ordered the bodies to be returned, but I am not certain that they followed through. I don't know if it's an aversion to corpses or to death, but after this matter was resolved, I ordered that their bodies be handed over, but I didn't want to participate.

"Regarding Mrs. Grimilda Sánchez, she was included among those to be killed by the firing squad, and I lowered her sentence to life imprisonment. Later, a relative came to speak to me, and she told me that Mrs. Sánchez had cancer and that they were asking for my authorization to take her to France. I agreed immediately, and she left Chile."

"Perhaps your decision was influenced by the fact that in addition to being a widow, a few days after her husband's execution, her son was killed. Colonel, Mrs. Sánchez said that she was imprisoned with her husband and the other two men who were shot and has stated that she witnessed the brutal tortures perpetrated on Francisco Valdivia in the rooms specially designated for that purpose in the ENAEX plant."

"I know nothing about that, I swear."

"Let's look at the case of Major Reveco. Did you receive pressures of any kind to relieve him of his duty as president of the court-martial?"

"No. The truth is that the court-martial over which he presided was not important. The sentences were minor; almost all were internal exile, with the exception of the cases of Silberman and Miranda. The only people who had weapons were four or five personal guards in Chuquicamata. There were no weapons there because what I found after the 11th was insignificant."

"No one mentioned that the sentences given by Major Reveco were too lenient?"

"No, because he wasn't too easy. What happened was that in our [professional military] world, denouncing people, squealing on each other, and clandestine activities affected morale."

"Please explain yourself."

"I received the El Loa governorship and had no problems with the Popular Unity governor. I sent the governor home without characterizing it as house arrest, because how could I justify arresting him and throwing him in jail? He had been one of the legitimate authorities, and he and I had a very good working relationship.

"The truth is that none of the authorities put up any resistance, and the Chuquicamata mine continued to operate normally, just as all other public services. I was ordered to take over the governorship at approximately 9:15 in the morning, and Police Chief Abel Galleguillos (he later became a general) reported to me that the whole area was peaceful. I ordered a meeting of all local authorities and heads of public services. Prior to that meeting, the first person who wanted to see me was a friend who was the top leader of the local right and the head of the Masons in this zone. He gave me a list, the list of people who had to be arrested or removed from their positions."

"So the first pressures for hard-line action came from the local right?"

"That's right. I didn't say anything to them, but I didn't do anything either. I took the list and put it in my pocket. The truth is that there was a lot of pressure on the part of civilians. Scores of anonymous letters betraying people would show up. Actually, there was a tremendous problem because I didn't pay attention to that list at all. Instead, at 10:00 a.m., I confirmed everyone in their jobs, demanding — imagine the foolishness! — that if I didn't see smiles on their faces again, that if someone complained of not being served with a maximum of efficiency and respect, that I would have to use my tool. And as I said this, I ostentatiously patted my pistol. Because our tools are our weapons.

"At approximately 11:00 in the morning," Rivera Desgroux recalled, "I was told that there were problems in Chuquicamata despite the fact that there had been a representative of the general manager's office at the meeting. Then I changed my orders, and I named Major Reveco as military area chief. I hadn't even thought of the military occupation of Chuquicamata or anything of the kind because everything was peaceful.

"Major Reveco went to Chuquicamata rather late, and later he was accused of hindering procedures to occupy the mine. If only I could tell you the numerous problems we all had — because we didn't have vehicles, because there were a lack of appropriate decisions on the part of my soldiers, and so on. Suffice it to say that the trucks I had belonged to MOPARE[8] and were driven by truckers who supported the Popular Unity. The local MOPARE authorities showed up and put the trucks at my disposal. Major Reveco, who was looking into the problems at ENAEX at that point, found out later about my order to go up to Chuquicamata. Reveco's unit was delayed in organizing itself. After 1:00 p.m., when everyone was in the trucks, there were no drivers. What had happened? At lunchtime, the drivers had been authorized by one of my officers to go home for lunch instead of going to the regiment's mess hall. No wonder Reveco was late. Nevertheless, this episode was taken into account among the charges against him when General Arellano decided to sentence Reveco."

With respect to Silberman, the general manager of the Chuquicamata mine who later disappeared, Rivera told me, "I had a very good relationship with David Silberman. He was very young, and his wife was the daughter of Colonel Abarzúa. Therefore, when Silberman saw a military unit arrive to occupy the mine, carrying artillery, he thought that we had declared war, and he fled with several others toward the interior.

"I went up to the mine at approximately 4:00 p.m., and after speaking with Major Reveco, I issued a military proclamation that all general managers should meet at 10:00 p.m. Neither Silberman nor Haroldo Cabrera, the finance manager, showed up. That was when I named Orompeyo Zepeda as general manager and confirmed all managers who were present, and I replaced the missing ones by their seconds in command. Mr. Zepeda was one of Silberman's deputies.

"Thus, Chuquicamata began to work the first shift on September 12 without using a curfew, because you could not coordinate the movement of 14,000 workers in three shifts with a curfew.

"That's when the problem of the informers' lists began. The first protest came, as I later found out, from a group of retired navy personnel who worked in Chuquicamata as well as in the thermoelectric plant in Tocopilla. I did not take into account these anonymous informants at all. But they continued to send letters to Antofagasta and Santiago.

"The person most affected, because he appeared to be responsible, was Reveco. He was the local authority, but the truth is that he was following my instructions. An investigating group composed of two captains was sent from Antofagasta at the end of September. I never cleared up this fact with General Lagos, head of my division. The two captains said they had come on his [General Lagos'] behalf to investigate some things that I did not think were important. I knew them, as they had been my cadets."

"From whom did you receive the order to arrest Major Reveco?" I asked Rivera Desgroux.

"From General Lagos. I received a call from him at approximately 6:00 p.m. on October 2. He told me he had received orders from Santiago to place Reveco under arrest. I expressed my surprise because I saw no reason to do so. Lagos insisted on his order, saying, 'Place him under arrest.' I trusted Reveco, so I decided that he would go there but not be under arrest, and I let him keep his weapon."

"Did you find out what happened to him?"

"I was told that he had been taken to Santiago under arrest. Moreover, as is usually the case, when the king falls, problems arise. His own colleagues denounced him."

"Did you know that he was tortured?"

"I found out later."

"Did you believe it possible that he was being mistreated?"

"No, never. It was not possible that this could be happening in our army. I could not conceive of it. The fact is that Reveco disappeared from Calama, and I expected, as his superior, to be asked about his background for his trial. They had to ask me for his file, his grades, all of the information that is pertinent in a normal trial. But they never asked for anything. I never imagined that he would be subjected to an irregular trial. And the case of Major Reveco, besides what happened in Calama later, cost me my military career."

"Could you explain yourself please?"

"I was punished for all of this in 1974. Formally, because I was not made general. And substantively, because I was considered no longer 'trustworthy.' I had been appointed as military attaché to Peru, and I was to leave in mid-July. When I went to the General Staff on March 4, 1974, I told General Arellano that I was worried about Major Reveco because he was in very bad condition. I added, 'They said that he's even been condemned to death, and I am his commander, and I have not been asked for any information. Reveco must think that I am very disloyal.' General Arellano responded tersely, 'Very well, I'll call you to make a statement.' And I did not notice the difference. He was going call me to make a statement in the trial, when what I wanted was to be asked, as his superior officer, about his background.

"During Holy Week of 1974, on Thursday, military attorney Melo told me to go down to his office to make a statement. I, very naively, went down and told them about Reveco's performance, which apparently contradicted all the other statements that had been gathered against him for the trial. A few days later, in April, I received a letter signed by General Pinochet, delaying my trip to Peru until June. I was then working in army operations headquarters on the restructuring of the army.

"In June, I went to the Secretariat of the Commander in Chief to speak with Escaurazia, who had been one of my cadets, and I said, 'Here I am, ready to leave.' The situation was tense. 'Listen, Colonel,' he told me, taking out a document, 'the thing is that General Arellano has requested that you stay here at the court's disposition.' I felt very annoyed, and I went to speak with the Chief of the General Staff, General Bravo. I complained, and there was a tremendous ruckus and very difficult moments. For the first time in my career, I felt I had no superior officers (*jefes*). Finally, General Bravo told me to speak with General Arellano. I went down rapidly, and I told Arellano, 'You've gotten me into this mess.' He looked at me coldly and answered, 'No, you're the one who got yourself involved.' I insisted that I owed loyalty to Reveco since I was his commanding officer, saying, 'I'm not defending him, General, I only demand that I be considered as his superior because I cannot leave him hanging.' Arellano, after discussing the matter, said, 'Come and testify again.' I answered, 'No problem, General.' I was called to testify, and I decided to give a copy of my statement to all my superiors. Then came the Council of Generals and I, who had been second in line of the colonels to be promoted, was put in 11th place. Ten of my colleagues were promoted, which was abnormal because they always promoted four or five.

I was offered a 'complementary position' (*complemento*). In this special situation, one is actually taken out of the chain of command and set aside to accomplish secondary-level activities. I did not accept it, and so I retired."

Postscript

In Calama, after Major Reveco's arrest, repression measures tightened everywhere, not only in the court-martial that handed down the three death sentences on October 6, 1973. On the day before, October 5, 22-year-old mine worker Ricardo Pérez Cárdenas, married and the father of a recently born son, died "in an escape attempt when national police took him to a reenactment of the crime that occurred on Montesuma Hill." This is what the military proclamation stated, but the family attests that he was already dying when he was taken from the police station en route to the Calama Hospital. They opened the coffin, and they saw that his body had sustained 25 bullet wounds, among them a gaping chest wound, plus evidence of torture. The death certificate gives the following cause of death: "multiple wounds to vital organs, numerous projectile wounds from firearms."

On October 16, 1973, Juan Matulic Infante also died in the police station in Calama. The report published by *El Mercurio* stated, "He was being held in one of the cells when he said he felt ill and requested to be taken out. The guards complied with his request, but when he was outside the building, he tried to escape, disregarding service personnel who shouted for him to stop, and, therefore, said personnel used their weapons. He died at the scene." Arica's newspaper, *La Defensa*, gave another version of the story, saying, "A dangerous MIR extremist, Juan Matulic, was killed when he tried to escape as be was being transferred from the police station to the court."

More deaths are known to have occurred in Calama, but the families have never made formal complaints.

Notes

1. See Chapter 8 for the details of the Caravan of Death's operations in Calama. *Ed.*

2. Throughout this chapter, as Lieutenant Colonel Fernando Reveco Valenzuela tells his story to Patricia Verdugo in 1989, he is called Major Reveco because that was his rank in 1973. As he said, he only found out about his promotion to lieutenant colonel while he was incarcerated. *Ed.*

3. The National Intelligence Directorate (Dirección de Inteligencia Nacional — DINA), was officially created in June 1974 by Law Decree No. 521 for the purpose of continuing the work of the "DINA Commission," which had been in existence since November 1973. During its years of operation, the DINA was directed by army Colonel Manuel Contreras, who was authorized to obtain any information he wanted from all state offices throughout the country. DINA was defined as "a military office with technical and professional characteristics, dependent on the military Junta and designed to gather data on a national level." DINA employees either belonged to one of the four branches of the military (army, navy, air force, or national police), or they were civil agents. Three of the articles — numbers 9, 10, and 11 — contained in the law decree that founded the organization were kept secret, and it was later discovered that, according to said articles, the intelligence services of all four branches of the Chilean defense worked for DINA and, as such, could make arrests and conduct searches of private homes. DINA created secret prisons all over the country, where inmates were tortured. Eventually, other members of the government Junta acknowledged that DINA responded solely to the orders of General Pinochet, and the organization's terrorist activities also were shown to have government support, some of its crimes extending outside of Chile, for example, in Washington, Rome, and Buenos Aires. DINA was dissolved at the end of 1977, after the U.S. administration pressured the Chilean government to explain the terrorist act that claimed the lives of former Chilean Chancellor Orlando Letelier and U.S. citizen Ronnie Moffit.

4. David Silberman Gurovich, age 35, a civil engineer, was married. DINA took him from the penitentiary on October 4, 1974. There are witnesses who have stated that they were imprisoned with him in the barracks in José Domingo Cañas and Tres Álamos. He has been among the "disappeared" ever since. The Silberman case was widely publicized by the international media.

5. In Spanish, the phrase, *que se iba a barrer un poco*, is close to the English euphemism, "that a little house cleaning would be done."

6. On October 6, 1975, Chilean Christian Democratic leader Bernardo Leighton and his wife, who were living in exile in Rome, were both seriously injured by bullets in an assassination attempt. The assassination was ordered by DINA, and final details were taken care of in Rome by Michael Townley, the same person who participated in the assassination of former Foreign Minister Orlando Letelier in Washington, D.C., one year later.

7. My "favorite one." *Ed.*

8. The Patriotic Transport Movement (Movimiento Patriótico del Transporte — MOPARE).

CHAPTER 4

Only the Colonel's Jeep Returned

A ccording to Lieutenant Colonel Olagier Benavente, General Arellano's caravan traveled from Talca on to Cauquenes on September 30, 1973. It is possible that fear and confusion in the face of an unprecedented situation — suddenly being left without a commander and having to assume interim command — caused Colonel Benavente to mix up the dates.

"I have the impression that not too many hours had gone by when we found out what had happened in Cauquenes. We supplied the base there, which was new and small. I was in daily communication with them, as our garrison served them logistically, even though to command, they depended on the Third Division," Benavente stated during an interview.

What is certain is the fact that it was October 4 when the Puma military helicopter arrived at the Andalién Regiment, carrying General Sergio Arellano Stark and his entourage. The exact time is not known, but it was mid-morning because witnesses recognized two of the people who accompanied the general. Major Marcelo Moren Brito was seen entering the Banco del Estado of Cauquenes at 11:00 a.m. (He was easily recognized because he had served in the city as a lieutenant and had earned a reputation as a hothead.) Captain Antonio Palomo Contreras, the helicopter pilot, was also recognized, not only from his days there as a lieutenant but because he had married a young local woman, América Domínguez. And General Arellano was seen lunching in the Social Club of Cauquenes with Lieutenant Colonel Rubén Castillo Whyte, commander of the Andalién Regiment and the local governor.

At approximately 4:30 p.m., a retinue of vehicles left the Investigations barracks: Commander Castillo Whyte's military Jeep, a bus full of soldiers, a truck, and another Jeep owned by the Banco del Estado that carried four young political prisoners. The next morning, the local radio, in a broadcast heard through loudspeakers in Cauquenes' main square, announced that the four prisoners had been shot for attempting to escape and for attacking soldiers.

The text of the radio announcement must have been nearly identical to the information published later by the newspaper *El Maulino*,[1] as in those days of the Junta all information was written by the military and passed through military censorship:

EXECUTED ON EL ORIENTE FARM
FOR ASSAULTING THE ARMED FORCES

On Thursday the 4th of the current month at 17:45 hours, in the place called El Oriente farm in Maule province, as the prisoners Claudio A. Manuel Lavín Loyola, Pablo Renán Vera Torres, Miguel Enrique Muñoz Flores, and Manuel Benito Plaza Arellano were being transferred by military personnel for questioning and to reconstruct the scene where they organized guerrillas on September 11 to oppose the armed forces and police, two of the prisoners proceeded to attack one of the sentries, attempting to take his weapons and wounding him in the arm, and, as the rest of the prisoners fled through the fields surrounding the place, the military patrol, in compliance with Military Proclamation #24 of the Government Military Junta, proceeded to stop and execute the aforementioned persons at the scene of the crime.

What really happened? Who were the people "executed?"

According to Luisa Vera, sister of Pablo Renán Vera Torres, one of the men executed, the four young socialists were friends "who had been lured in mid-1973 by a police major named Montt, who said he was a leftist. He suggested they should learn to shoot, and he took them to El Oriente farm to practice. A short time before the coup, Major Montt suddenly disappeared from Cauquenes, and my father died convinced that he [Montt] was an infiltrator who had informed on them."

Pablo Renán Vera Torres was the son of the regional secretary of the Socialist Party. Pablo was arrested on the street on September 11, 1973, the day of the military coup, and when he was freed, he was "a total mess" from the abuse he endured, his sister Luisa Vera said. "On September 15, Commander Castillo Whyte called a meeting of all political leaders to notify them that all political activity was forbidden. My father, Guillermo Vera, went up to him at the end of the meeting to complain about the mistreatment of Pablo. The commander asked him to put his complaint in writing. That same night, our house was searched for the first time. [Four days later,] during the second search on September 19, they arrested my father and Pablo," said Luisa Vera. Her brother, Pablo Vera, was killed on October 4, 1973, and their father, Guillermo, was held in jail until December 1976, when his sentence was commuted to exile. Guillermo Vera left Chile forever, taking his entire family with him to the German Democratic Republic. Guillermo's wife, Cira Troncoso, had also been held in prison in Chile for eight months. Guillermo died in exile, and as he lay dying, he continuously called his son Pablo's name.

Another one of the four executed men was Claudio A. Manuel Lavín Loyola, Jr., 29 years old, an agricultural technician, married, the father of two very young children. Claudio was the son of a well-known doctor and councilman from Maule. Because of his long friendship with President Allende, he was recognized as the socialist patriarch of the region. The younger Lavín worked in the Banco del Estado, and his colleague Juan León[2] recalled seeing Colonel Castillo Whyte arrive the day after the miltary coup [September 12, 1973]. Juan León described Colonel Whyte's visit to the bank: "He gathered us all together and harangued us. He said some things would be eliminated, that the military was giving the orders now." A week later, the young men were summoned, along with Lavín, to appear at the regiment's Investigations barracks. León told reporter Patricia Collyer, "They let us go after a little while, but a few days later, on September 25, they arrested me again. I was held in the barracks prison without knowing why. In the cell next to mine were Plaza, Muñoz, and Vera. I was interrogated about 'weapons' and 'Plan Z.'[3] I didn't know what they were talking about."

On October 3, Claudio Lavín was brought in to share León's cell. Lavín had been arrested the day before. León recalled, "Surprisingly, they agreed to his request to be with me, despite the fact that they had implicated us in Plan Z and those things. He was a dedicated Christian and asked them to let him keep a medal and a cross he wore around his neck. They allowed him to keep the medal. Claudio prayed a lot, he was very nervous, but we never spoke about the possibility that they would kill us."[4]

Lavín's widow, Gloria Benavente Franzani, remembered, "My father-in-law, Dr. Claudio Lavín, was summoned to the governor's office one week after the coup. He couldn't go for health reasons, so my husband went. There, the Chief of the Zone Under State of Siege, Rubén Castillo Whyte, told Claudio he had to go there and sign in every day with Investigations. He did so. I went with him every day. On October 2, we went to the barracks, and the detective on duty told Claudio that the police inspector, Exequiel Jara, wanted to talk to him about 'a problem with the bank's pick-up truck.' Since the pick-up truck had been assigned to Claudio, it didn't sound strange to us. We waited, and when Jara arrived, he asked Claudio to come to his office. Claudio came out five minutes later and told me, 'They've arrested me, so I have to make a statement.' They didn't give him any justification. I went to my father-in-law's house, got a sleeping bag and a thermos, and went back to deliver them to him."

On the next day, October 3, Gloria took her husband some lunch and [once again, later in the afternoon] tea. But on October 4, she could only deliver lunch because at 4:30 p.m., when she arrived with tea, the grounds were closed, and the duty officer told her, "Lady, you can't go in because there are soldiers in there. But hang around; maybe they'll leave soon." [5]

What was happening inside the Investigations barracks? Claudio Lavín's colleague, Juan León, remembered October 4 this way:

"That day, the atmosphere in the station was tense. At around 4:00 p.m., you could hear doors slamming, rapid footsteps, a lot of movement, and then absolute silence. Then the cell door opened, and they called Claudio. He told me, 'I'm probably being taken for questioning.'"

Half an hour later, León heard doors slamming again and, through the peephole, he was able to see Claudio being taken to the station's courtyard.

What happened in that half-hour was learned indirectly. León overheard it from a young Chilean Revolutionary Left Movement (Movimiento de Izquierda Revolucionario — MIR) prisoner, Ricardo Ugarte, who was the son of retired police Colonel Elías Ugarte, a cousin of General Augusto Pinochet Ugarte. In 1986, the magazine *Análisis* (in the same previously cited, well-documented piece by the journalist Patricia Collyer) published Juan León's testimony, which has never been disputed:

> Ricardo Ugarte was also held in Investigations and had been taken to a farcical 'court-martial,' which was held on the afternoon of October 4 in the station. And he told me the details. He was with Vera, Plaza, Lavín, and Muñoz when the five were taken from the jail cell to a room where there was a person wearing civilian clothes who gave orders, surrounded by soldiers with black berets and *corvos*[6] and hand grenades dangling from their uniforms. There was also a high-ranking officer. Ugarte told me that the soldiers — who were completely berserk — shouted and insulted them and that at a given moment, Pablo Vera shouted at them, 'You don't believe anything!' Suddenly, one of the black berets went up to Ugarte and struck him so hard that it made him and the person who was holding him fall down. At that moment, the prisoner felt himself being dragged on the ground, handcuffed, and thrown into a small bathroom. Ugarte did not know if he had fallen asleep or was knocked out, but suddenly he felt the doors slamming and he heard the group leave. And then a detective took him out of the bathroom and returned him to his cell. Some time later, he saw a newspaper with Arellano Stark's photograph and recognized him as one of the people present at the 'court-martial.' And he believes that his miraculous salvation was due to a telegram sent by Pinochet asking if Ricardo Ugarte was among the prisoners. From that moment on, he received special treatment.[7]

And while this court-martial was underway, Gloria Benavente, Claudio Lavín's young wife, was waiting outside Investigations, along with other prisoners' relatives, holding the food she had brought for her husband in her hands. Suddenly she saw a Jeep from Banco del Estado come out and she recalled, "There were Claudio and the other prisoners. I recognized him from a distance because he was wearing a red sweater I had knitted for him. He saw me and his sister Lily. He was sitting in the last seat, and he made a gesture as if to say, 'I don't know what's going on.' Then Colonel Castillo Whyte's Jeep came out, [followed by] a closed bus, and a truck owned by a well-known farmer of the area, Francisco Arellano." Other relatives recognized police Lieutenant Enrique Rebolledo, who was acting as secretary of the governorship, in the same Jeep with the prisoners.

Gloria and the others remained outside, waiting for the convoy to come back. Only the colonel's Jeep returned. The truck passed by but kept going. At that time, none of the waiting relatives could possibly have imagined that the four bodies of their loved ones were lying in the truck, en route to the local morgue. As time wore on, Gloria and Lily Lavín decided to go see Gonzalo Hurtado, a notary, to ask him to find out what was going on.

On the night of that same day, October 4, Gloria Benavente de Lavín returned to Investigations:

"I was received by Detective Mauricio Cerda, whose expression turned to surprise and desperation when he saw me. He already knew what had happened. I asked if I could leave some food for Claudio, and he replied that I should go to the governor's office because 'he was a prisoner of war' and they [Investigations] were no longer involved."

At the governor's office, a corporal referred her to the Andalién Regiment. There, after a lot of red tape, she was told, "You have to ask in the governor's office." She went back to the governor's office, a fruitless trip. It was already 11:00 p.m., and Gloria decided to go home to feed her one-month-old baby. "Claudio, Claudio, where are you?" she kept asking until she fell asleep.

Meanwhile, at the morgue of the Cauquenes Hospital, Dr. Mario Muñoz Angulo, head forensic doctor and acting director of the hospital, was experiencing another drama. When interviewed by Patricia Collyer, he recalled:

That October 4, a member of the army came in and ordered everybody to get out of the way — from the entrance all the way to the morgue. He gave no explanation. Then they brought in four bodies lying on sacks and dragged them down the corridor. They left a trail of blood as they went. I was ordered to perform the autopsies. This was extremely unpleasant, and it upset me tremendously, because I knew two of the boys, Pablo and Claudio. I was a friend and colleague of Claudio's father and I'd known him [young Claudio] since he was a child. All of them had sustained gunshot wounds to the head, some with their brains blown out. As soon as I looked at the bodies, I knew they had been murdered. It was a terrible shock. I felt literally sick, and I tried to forget everything quickly. Soon after I handed over the autopsy report to the commander, an army truck took away the bodies.[8]

The four death certificates, all identical, established the time of execution as "17:30 hours" and the cause of death as "gunshot wounds to the cranium." The four young men were buried in a common grave in the cemetery that same night. Only one civilian participated in that dramatic military task, the gravedigger. The helicopter carrying General Arellano and his entourage was already far from Cauquenes.

On Friday, October 5, Chief Baeza arrived very early at the Investigations headquarters. Juan León remembered the scene clearly:

"He [Baeza] called me and a communist prisoner aside. I will never forget his face. His face was contorted, and he was very pale. He told us, 'Guys, ask me for anything you want; if you want one, I'll bring you a priest.' We didn't understand what was going on, and we asked about Claudio. He said, 'Four are already resting.' We asked, 'They were taken home?' He said, 'No,' and gestured, pointing to the sky. We insisted, 'Did they go by helicopter?' And Baeza said, 'No!' and he made a gesture indicating someone's throat being slit."

At that same time on the morning of October 5, Gloria Benavente de Lavín was outside the Andalién Regiment. Nothing, no news of Claudio. Once again, they sent her to the governor's office building. She said to journalist Collyer years later, "I was standing in the street until around 9:30 a.m., when Castillo Whyte arrived with around 15 soldiers. He looked at me disdainfully and kept going, and the last of the soldiers asked me what I was looking for. 'I want to know about my husband,' I told him. He showed me in, and, after a long wait, a lieutenant appeared. I repeated my request to him. He replied that he would ask Castillo. He came back with a brief message: 'He says you should come back at 11:00 a.m.'"

While Gloria was searching for her husband, the radio — connected to the loudspeakers in the plaza — had already broadcast the military communiqué announcing the execution of the four young socialists. Gloria had not heard it. A little while later, she returned home, and her parents arrived. Gloria recounted the scene:

"My mother shouted, 'They shot Claudio!' From that moment on, my memory is a complete blank. It's a day of my life that doesn't exist. I don't know what happened. I only remember that I woke up the next day to the image of Claudio's sister kneeling by my bed, dressed in black."

Meanwhile, Dr. Claudio Lavín, the victim's father, was placed under house arrest with a military guard. Three days later, Claudio's other sister, Laura, arrived from Santiago. She was married to Colonel Carlos Alberto Lemus, of the Second Armored Division in Santiago. Gloria Benavente de Lavín described her sister-in-law's actions: "She met with Colonel Castillo and afterward only told me that visits to the cemetery were forbidden; that it was dangerous to go. I decided to go on All Saints Day, November 1. I went to look for the common grave where, according to the gravedigger, Alamiro Fuentes, they were buried. He told me he had been the only civilian present at the burial. I found two mounds of dirt with some tin cans full of flowers."

One month later, thanks to the work of Claudio's sister, Laura Lavín, and her husband, Colonel Carlos Alberto Lemus, the family was allowed to move the body to a private mausoleum, on the condition that no gravestone with Claudio's name be added for one year. The reason? It might attract pilgrims.

The medical examiner who had performed the autopsies, Dr. Muñoz Angulo, recalled his participation in the exhumation: "I received the order from the commander's headquarters. I was told that it would be carried out at a very strange time, 3:00 a.m. We worked by the light of a lantern. Everything was very terrible — nothing was normal. Everything had changed after the military coup."

Gloria Benavente de Lavín's account added important information:

"The exhumation took place at approximately 3:00 a.m., and the only person in the family allowed to attend was Colonel Carlos Alberto Lemus. Also in attendance were the soldiers who had participated in the firing squad and the forensic doctor, according to what Carlos Alberto later told me. The gravedigger was also present. I had asked to go, but Carlos Alberto said that no civilians could participate. I then asked him to bring me the medal and the cross Claudio wore around his neck. When he returned, he was all broken up. He gave me the medal and cross and said, 'Gloria, right now you can ask me anything, whatever you want to. But, for the rest of my life, never mention this subject again. You have suffered a lot, but what I saw, no one has ever seen before.' I asked him how many wounds Claudio had. He answered three or four — I don't remember — and that they were all in his face. I always knew that rifle or submachine gun bullets make a big hole in the place they exit. Carlos Alberto pointed out that the heads were destroyed and that all the bullets had entered from the front, through the face. In other words, the military communiqué about how the execution occurred was a gross lie."

Gloria continued, "My brother-in-law also saw the other bodies because at first they could not find Claudio. They had to dig them up one by one, and the last one was my husband." She also said that they had to take off plastic bags that had been tied around their heads and that the men were still wearing the same clothes they were wearing when they left Investigations. When Gloria Benavente de Lavín gave her testimony in 1986, she had just spoken with her children, telling them for the first time that their father had been murdered by the military: "My family is full of army people, and that's why it was so hard for me. It was so difficult. My oldest child, who was then 14, asked, 'Is there anything I can do for my father, Mommy?' And I answered yes, that we would all do it together."[9]

On April 30, 1986, the families of the four victims filed a criminal lawsuit for the homicides of Pablo Vera, 22; Manuel Plaza, 25; Miguel Muñoz, 23; and Claudio Lavín, 29. The plaintiffs' lawyer was Héctor Salazar, of the Vicarate of Solidarity,[10] who stated that the crime was aggravated homicide, with two aggravating circumstances: premeditation and malice. "Premeditation because the perpetrators chose the means to perpetrate the crime and decided the moment. Malice because they acted unopposed, knowing that the victims could not defend themselves."

The complaint identified four members of the military retinue of General Sergio Arellano Stark: Colonel Sergio Arredondo González, Major Marcelo Moren Brito, Captain Antonio Palomo Contreras, and Lieutenant Armando Fernández Larios.

In Cauquenes, the "October 4th Committee" commemorates the date every year with a vigil at the cemetery for the four murdered youths. However, they and their grieving families were not the only victims of this episode. One of those who did the shooting was a sergeant named Cárdenas, from the Andalién Regiment. Speaking about Cárdenas, Lieutenant Colonel Olagier Benavente told me, "He had to retire from the army because he could not stand it; his nerves were shot. He had to obey the order to shoot these young men he knew, with whom he had played soccer since they were all children. And he had to obey because he feared that, otherwise, he would be killed."

Luisa Vera, sister of Pablo Vera, one of the victims, stated that Lieutenant Jorge Acuña, another solider who participated in the executions, "is now crazy." Lieutenant Colonel Benavente added that Captain Palomo had to sell his house in Cauquenes "because things became very difficult for him there. He did not participate in the massacre, but he witnessed it. He knew Claudio Lavín well. The truth is that he was very shocked, and he became very introverted."

*****

I was only able to speak with General Sergio Arellano about what happened in Cauquenes through his son, attorney Sergio Arellano Iturriaga, the general's authorized spokesman. For more than one year, General Arellano rejected my repeated requests for a direct interview. He acknowledged that Colonel Sergio Arredondo, who belonged to his same garrison, had been in his retinue during a trip that took them to Concepción. He did not remember any other member of that entourage.

Attorney Arellano Iturriaga stated that in 1986, after being notified that the "Cauquenes case" would be made public, "We asked for his [General Arellano's] 1973 log, because my father thought he had gone to Cauquenes at the end of September. He asked General Humberto Gordon to release it to him, but Gordon refused. Arellano Stark remembered that, on the trip to Concepción, he decided to stop in Cauquenes because he had received a complaint: Bread was being distributed by military trucks during the curfew, and the trucks were being stoned. He went to speak with the commander of the regiment, had lunch at the Social Club with the commander, and left immediately after lunch."

General Arellano's spokesman added, "We have not been able to verify the dates, and, when we try to do so, all doors close in our faces. The point is, why Cauquenes? Does it seem logical that my father, a respected general, would personally decide to go to there, give the order, and witness massacres outside any legal procedure?"

The answer to this question is still pending.

Notes

1. The report was published in the local paper, *El Maulino*, on Saturday, October 6, 1973.

2. Testimonies gathered by journalist Patricia Collyer and published in *Análisis* May 6-12, 1986.

3. See Chapter 2, endnote 2, which explains Plan Z, also called Plan Zeta. *Ed.*

4. Collyer, 1986, *Análisis*.

5. Collyer, 1986, *Análisis*.

6. A *corvo* is a crescent-shaped knife still widely used by the Chilean army that dates back to Chile's war against Bolivia and Peru in 1879. A double-edged weapon that makes an open slash as it penetrates the skin, the *corvo* was allegedly utilized by some of the soldiers during Pinochet's military Junta to disembowel political prisoners before casting their bodies into the sea. *Ed.*

7. Collyer, 1986, *Análisis*.

8. Collyer, 1986, *Análisis*.

9. Collyer, 1986, *Análisis*.

10. The Vicarate of Solidarity is an office that was established by Cardinal Raúl Silva Henríquez, archbishop of Santiago, to give legal and humanitarian support to the victims of government repression and their families. *Paul E. Sigmund.*

CHAPTER 5

What Is This All About, General?

The Puma helicopter landed at the La Serena airport on Tuesday, October 16, 1973, at approximately 11:00 a.m. The Commander of the Arica Motorized Regiment (Regimiento Motorizado Arica),[1] Lieutenant Colonel Ariosto Lapostol Orrego, welcomed General Sergio Arellano Stark at the local airport and was notified of Arellano's extraordinary authority: Delegate of the Commander in Chief of the Army and the Government Military Junta.

There were hundreds of political prisoners in La Serena's jail. A local lawyer, Gustavo Rojas, testified before the United Nations Human Rights Commission: "The everyday routine there was to go at certain times to observe the police paddy wagons parked in front of the large wooden door, awaiting the load of prisoners that were going to the Arica Regiment to be interrogated, where the judge advocate and court-martial functioned."[2]

On October 16, two military Jeeps carrying soldiers wearing black berets parked in front of the jail at approximately 1:00 p.m., and the military guard at the door of the jail increased. Fifteen prisoners were taken in the direction of the regiment a little before 2:00 p.m. Their departure was recorded on page 35 of the *Book of Prisoners 1973* of La Serena's jail.[3] At approximately 4:00 p.m., loud, repeated bursts of submachine gunfire could be heard, coming from inside the regiment.

Around 7:00 p.m., Lieutenant Emilio Cheyre Espinosa telephoned the newsroom of the newspaper *El Día*, ordering the publication of a military proclamation on the front page of the next day's edition. This is the text sent by Commander Ariosto Lapostol Orrego; the newspaper added a large banner headline:

OFFICIAL COMMUNIQUÉ OF THE DEPARTMENTAL COMMANDER

SENTENCES OF THE MILITARY COURT CARRIED OUT

FIFTEEN PERSONS EXECUTED FOR DIFFERENT REASONS MADE KNOWN BY THE MILITARY TRIBUNAL

The Departmental Commander last night issued the following official communiqué:

Citizens are informed that today, October 16, 1973, at 1600 hours, the following persons were executed according to the decision of the Military Tribunals in Time of War:

a) José Eduardo Araya González
Víctor Fernando Escobar Astudillo
Jorge Abel Contreras Godoy
Oscar Aedo Herrera

These individuals were part of a terrorist group that planned to take over the police station in Salamanca on September 17 and kill all personnel and their children older than eight years of age.

As well as physically eliminating a group of almost 30 people from that city, whose names will not be made public for obvious reasons.

Once they finished this action, they were planning to attack the police station in Coirón, proceeding in the same way described previously.

The individuals' documents and explosives were seized, and all of them confessed their participation in the events just summarized.

b) Jorge Mario Jordán Domic
Gabriel Gonzalo Vergara Muñoz
Hipólito Cortés Álvarez
Oscar Armando Cortés Cortés

The reasons given for [their execution] were:

Burying and hiding a total of 15 weapons, abundant ammunition, and explosives, with the intention of attacking the police in Ovalle on last September 17.

Having participated as guerrilla instructors in the area, under the supervision of Hipólito Cortés Álvarez, who attended a course in guerrilla warfare in Santiago. In his absence Jaime Vergara Muñoz replaced him.

c) Carlos Alcayaga Varela

For stealing explosives with the use of force from the explosives magazine in the Contador mine in Vicuña on September 11, 1973; the explosives were found buried in his home and ready to be used. He was explosives instructor of the guerrilla school that operated in Vicuña, which was linked to Jorge Vásquez Matamala.

d) Roberto Guzmán Santa Cruz

For inciting the miners of the Desvío Norte camps and the surrounding area to take over the powder magazines and to put up armed resistance to the Government Junta.

e) Marcos Enrique Barrantes Alcayaga
Mario Alberto Ramírez Sepúlveda
Jorge Washington Peña Hen
Jorge Osorio Zamora

For participating in the acquisition and distribution of firearms and paramilitary instruction and organizational activities with the aim of attacking the armed forces and police and people in the area. Moreover, Ramírez tried to escape.

f) Manuel Jachadur Marcarian Jamett

For being in possession of buried explosives to attack the police station in Los Vilos, and for not having obeyed the military decree and personal warnings from the police.

ARIOSTO LAPOSTOL ORREGO
Lieutenant-Colonel
Commander of Fort Coquimbo
and the Departments of Freirina and Huasco,
Province of Atacama

At the same time that this official communiqué began to be printed on the presses of *El Día* newspaper, the helicopter that carried General Arellano and his entourage was flying north to Copiapó. Meanwhile, in La Serena's cemetery, a military truck had gone in with its macabre load covered by an olive-green tarp. A common grave at the end of the cemetery was the final destination of the 15 bodies. The officer in charge of the operation gave the names of the victims one by one to the administrator, who recorded them on pages 160 and 161 of the registry book. Also stamped in the registry book were the numbers of the burial authorizations given by the *Civil Registry* and the age of each of the victims after his name.

Pages 160 and 161 of the *Civil Registry* state verbatim:

235.	Araya González, José Eduardo	23
236.	Escobar Astudillo, Víctor Fernando	21
237.	Contreras Godoy, Jorge Abel	31
238.	Aedo Herrera, Oscar Gastón	23
239.	Cortés Álvarez, Hipólito Pedro	43
240.	Vergara Muñoz, Gabriel Gonzalo	22
241.	Jordán Domic, Jorge Mario	29
242.	Cortés Cortés, Oscar Armando	48

243. Alcayaga Varela ,Carlos Enrique   38
244. Guzmán Santa Cruz, Roberto   25
245. Barrantes Alcayaga, Marcos Enrique   26
246. Ramírez Sepúlveda, Mario Alberto   44
247. Peña Hen, Jorge Washington   45
248. Osorio Zamora, Jorge Ovidio   35
249. Marcarian Jamett, Manuel Jachadur   35[4]

The day after the execution and burial of the 15 men, the military decree printed on the front page of *El Día* shocked the city to its core: " . . . Jorge Washington Peña Hen executed — He was a favorite son of La Serena as well as Philharmonic Orchestra Director and creator of the Children's Symphony Orchestra, loved and esteemed even by his political adversaries. . . ! Also executed, Mario Alberto Ramírez Sepúlveda, respected university professor."

The pain from these executions penetrated many very different, very distant doors, from upper middle class homes in La Serena to modest peasant homes in the mountain village of Salamanca and the fishing enclave of Los Vilos, both about 250 kilometers from La Serena.

The horror spread through the streets, hills, highways, and university campuses. You could breathe the trauma in the spring air of the old city to such a degree that Commander Ariosto Lapostol decided, that same Wednesday, October 17, to try to calm the populace with a public response. He chose to do so by giving an interview to the local newspaper, *El Día,* published on October 18. A banner headline on the front page announced the story.

THE DEPARTMENTAL COMMANDER COMMENTS ON THE EXECUTIONS CARRIED OUT:

"THEY CONFESSED THEIR PARTICIPATION IN VARIOUS ACTIONS"

The sentences were imposed after profound study. The verdict of the Military Tribunal seems very sudden and drastic, but "so was what they were going do on September 17. We must respect other people's grief. We must respect the families that are suffering at this sad moment," stated Commander Ariosto Lapostol.

The events that occurred as a consequence of the sentence handed down by the Military Tribunal that tried and sentenced 15 people from the area, among whom were very well-known citizens, left the entire province and the whole country astounded, as this was the main event of the day.

In order to obtain details to inform the citizens, reporters from this newspaper yesterday requested official information from the Departmental Commander, Lieutenant Colonel Ariosto Lapostol Orrego.

All Confessed

"There was some very serious study before reaching that decision. The court-martial acted on the basis of concrete facts. They had all confessed to actions related to different events that had occurred or that were going to occur in different parts of the province, as could be observed. You must understand that a decision such as this was not to be adopted simply because someone has some kind of defect or because the court-martial didn't like the way they looked," expressed the Departmental Commander. "Here we're dealing with [a decision that comes from] very profound and serious reflection," he added.

He made it clear that "a tribunal that had come especially from the capital was the one that dictated this sentence."

Terrorist Friends

When asked about the impact produced when the news appeared that prominent citizens of the area had been executed, he said:

"It is very possible that many [of us] were acquainted with these individuals or knew them as friends and visited them in their homes, at a cocktail party, or other everyday situations. Nevertheless, this external facade had nothing to do with the other terrorist aspects of their characters, which was the other side of the coin. As the public knows, they had certain plans that, had they materialized, would have meant that neither you nor I would be sitting here face to face at this moment."

The Decision

Insofar as the decision to carry out the sentence of the Military Tribunal and how it appeared sudden to most people, especially since the vast majority of people in the province were not expecting a measure of this sort, because they had no knowledge of the terrorist plans of extremist elements who favored the old regime, Commander Ariosto Lapostol had few words to say, "What they were going to do on September 17 was also sudden."

Shocking

The carrying out of the sentence, which resulted in the execution of 15 people, was recognized as shocking. The Departmental Commander also agreed and said:

"Obviously this is something shocking. And more so because a terrorist doesn't go around telling everyone that he is a terrorist or that he is thinking about carrying out such and such a plan. That is why it has been shocking to learn that several of these people have been carrying out terrorist plans and were arrested and confessed."

Rumors

We asked the Departmental Commander about the fact that despite the military decrees issued regarding rumors, such rumors continue to circulate, even after the executions on Tuesday. Mr. Lapostol responded, "Rumors will exist as long as the sun shines. That is why we cannot deal with all these rumors."

Nothing New

When asked about similar new sentences, he stated clearly that he knew nothing. "The court-martial has not made any new decisions," he said.

He ended by pointing out the need to stop questioning what happened. "We must respect the grief of others. We must respect the families that are suffering in this sad moment."[5]

*****

The above newspaper story is very revealing. Commander Lapostol had to give explanations when faced with the people's outrage. He had to try to convince the people that the men who were killed were "terrorists" and "murderers" and that the court-martial had seriously analyzed the evidence before decreeing these dramatic sentences. He even had to appear compassionate and asked for respect "for the families that are suffering in this sad moment." And, above everything else, he had to attempt to wash his hands of the blood spilled, with the clarification: "a tribunal that had come especially from the capital was the one that dictated this sentence."

What Commander Lapostol did not explain was why he violated standard operating procedures. A military court in time of war can issue the death penalty and order the firing squad to carry out a sentence immediately. This is in the regulations. A military judge must, just as for the sentence itself, duly write his signature on the summary investigation. Lapostol knew that neither the families nor the few defense lawyers would dare to request copies of the trials. Moreover, he could not have given them anything because *nothing was put in writing*. But Lapostol did know that the families were going to claim the bodies, so that they could give their loved ones proper burials. Lapostol's obligation was to hand over the bodies of the people executed, bodies that were marked by one or more chest-high bullet holes.

However, Commander Lapostol ordered that the bodies be buried the same day of the execution. Did he do this to avoid funeral ceremonies that would alter the "order" of La Serena, Salamanca, or Los Vilos? What reason did he have?

*****

No clues have been discovered in all these years since October 16, 1973, to explain why these 15 prisoners were selected to be murdered. Were these the most difficult cases, the ones General Arellano had asked about in Talca, according to the testimonies of the commander and executive officer of that regiment?

On the one hand, we have three young countrymen in the registry from Salamanca, José Araya, Víctor Escobar, and Jorge Contreras, plus the subdelegate of Los Vilos, Oscar Aedo, sentenced for an alleged plan to kill policemen in Salamanca and Coirón, "their children older than eight years of age," and 30 unidentified people. No more information about these men can be found in the files of human rights defense organizations.

Then, in the second group, we find a physician, Jorge Jordán Domic, and three workers. Gabriel Vergara was president of the Ranquil Peasants' Union. Hipólito Cortés was a union leader of construction workers, and Oscar Cortés was a peasant. Young Dr. Jordán, who worked in the hospital in Ovalle, was the son of the director of the Psychiatric Hospital in Santiago, Dr. Jorge Jordán Subat. Dr. Jorge Jordán Domic was 29 years old, married, and had two very young children. He gave himself up voluntarily after being called by a military decree, and from the local jail he was transferred to La Serena. The archives of the Medical Association point out that Dr. Jordán Domic was scheduled to face a court-martial on October 18, two days after he was "executed." And in the case of the four prisoners from Ovalle, there is unquestionable proof of a mass crime because two months later, on December 20, 1973, the court-martial in La Serena issued a verdict in this case, list 45-73. In the "whereas" clause "j," the four cases were dismissed because the individuals were already dead.[6]

For Carlos Alcayaga, age 38, regional secretary of the Central Union of Workers (Central Única de Trabajadores), there is no data that can clarify this case. The military proclamation holds that he stole explosives from a mine in Vicuña, explosives he did not use because they were found in his house, and that he was a guerrilla instructor, along with Jorge Vásquez — Vásquez is a new name. Vásquez did not die with the others. A reliable source in the area assured me that Vásquez had been "persecuted and murdered" earlier. There is also no clear data with regard to Manuel Macaria, age 35, other than the fact that he was a farmer from Los Vilos.

Among the group of university victims, Marcos Barrantes was a student leader in the local technical university and was 26 years old. Jorge Osorio was an accounting official in the regional headquarters of the University of Chile. Mario Ramírez, age 44, was a professor of education at the University of Chile and regional secretary of the Socialist Party. Jorge Peña, age 45, was director of the Music Department of the University of Chile.

And, finally, there is a case that contributed undeniable proof of the mass murder, the execution of Roberto Guzmán Santa Cruz. He was a 25-year-old lawyer from Santiago who arrived in La Serena on the eve of the military coup, carrying out his duties as legal advisor to the workers of Minera Santa Fe. He was a member of MIR. His family stated that on September 14, he went to the home of Lorenzo Aguilera, who was the driver for the mining company in Los Choros. When they arrived at Aguilera's house, they could see that the house had been searched, so Guzmán Santa Cruz advised Aguilera to give himself up to the police voluntarily. They arrested Aguilera, and when Guzmán Santa Cruz went to the police to inquire about Aguilera's legal situation, he was also arrested. Both arrived at the La Serena jail on September 16, and, nine days later, the military judge, police Major Carlos Cazanga, asked for a sentence of 200 days for Guzmán Santa Cruz. The court-martial stiffened the sentences to five years for the attorney, Guzmán Santa Cruz, and three for the driver, Aguilera. These sentences were published later, along with 20 others, in *El Día* newspaper on Tuesday, November 6, 1973. No death sentences were listed.

*****

Josefina Santa Cruz saw her only son, Roberto Guzmán Santa Cruz, before he was killed. She located him after many long and fruitless trips to the Ministry of Defense and to the prison camp operating in the National Stadium in Santiago. Finally, the management of Minera Santa Fe told her that he was being held at the military base in La Serena. During an interview with me, Josefina Santa Cruz told her story:

"I went immediately. I arrived at the base, and there I was told that he was in the jail. A man who was leaving, when he saw my desperation, told me to go first to see lawyer Otto Cid, of La Serena, who could give me some information and take the case. He was the president of La Serena's Bar Association. I spoke with him, and he said, 'You want me to defend Roberto Guzmán Santa Cruz?'

"'Yes, sir,' I replied."

"'But don't you know that these people wanted to kill all of us?'

"'My son is not a murderer, sir!' I answered indignantly."

"'Is he your son?' he said, surprised."

"'Yes sir, he is my son.'"

"'I cannot defend him. I'm going to give you the names of some people who can do it in Santiago,' he said. At the same time, he wrote on a piece of paper: Alfredo Etcheberry, Manuel Guzmán Vial, Enrique Ortúzar Escobar, Enrique Eguiguren, Miguel Otero Lathrop, Pablo Rodríguez Grez.

"Finally, he told me not to worry, that Roberto, from what he knew of the case, was going to be sent to Santiago, and he wasn't going to get much jail time. I went to the jail, and I was able to see him. He was thin, pale, with traces of blows to his face. We embraced for long time, a very long time, and in silence."

Josefina Santa Cruz could not help herself. When she reached this point during the interview, she tried to continue talking, but the trembling of her hands and chin revealed a profound open wound. Her only son, Roberto had been her friend and companion since early widowhood.

"You know, we hardly spoke — only embracing was important. At the end, he whispered that I shouldn't worry, that he was going to be sentenced to five years and that he would be released even sooner. Desperate, I went back to Santiago to seek help. I spoke with several attorneys, but they didn't want to take the case. That's what I was doing when October 16 arrived," Josefina explained, weeping.

Roberto Guzmán Santa Cruz was already serving his sentence when, on that Tuesday, October 16, military Jeeps arrived at the jail. The driver, Lorenzo Aguilera Rojas, remembered, "We were painting our cell in the jail when a guard went to get Mr. Guzmán and another political prisoner, Manuel Marcarian. The guard said that the prosecutor had summoned them. They never returned. The next day we found out that 'they had been shot as a warning.'"[7]

Guzmán Santa Cruz' wife, Magdalena Hemard, arrived in La Serena on the night of October 16. When she found out about Roberto's death from the publication of the military proclamation, the next morning, she asked for the return of the body. When she was told that he had already been buried, she went to the cemetery and found the common grave.

In 1987, *Análisis* magazine published an interview with Magdalena Hemard. "They told me," she stated, "to follow the truck tracks. I found a hole covered by two slabs; everything was covered by a kind of wet talcum powder. I moved one of the slabs a little, and I knelt. There was a strange smell and large green flies that were fluttering, looking for the light. When I was able to see in the dim light, I was paralyzed with a strange mixture of repulsion and attraction. There they were, many bodies stacked together, all the heads toward the wall and all the feet toward the entrance. The same wet talcum was all over the bodies. There was no blood. Only bloodstains at the level of the heart, the stomach, thighs." She said that she stayed there, paralyzed by the macabre urgency of seeing her husband's body. But the manager of the cemetery interrupted her and forced her to leave.

Magdalena Hemard told her mother-in-law, Josefina, that Roberto's body was with the others in the mass grave. In her interview with me, Josefina recalled, "I became desperate; I couldn't believe it was true. And when I was able to accept that it was true, that they had already killed him, I felt I wanted to go out and look for the perpetrators and kill them. I locked myself up in my house. I felt that everyone, everyone who walked the streets, anyone who laughed, that they all were my enemies. What helplessness not to be able to do anything! I took over my three grandchildren, and I raised them. I locked myself up with the children and isolated myself. The truth is that no one came over, and I didn't want anyone to come over. Roberto's political friends didn't come to see me because all of them were also having problems. And the few members of my family also turned their backs on me. We had become dangerous."

"Did the children know about what happened to their father?" I asked her.

"No, it was my secret for many years. I thought that if they knew, they would be in danger. I thought that they could also be killed."

"When were you able to communicate with others?"

"I would break out of my isolation and fear only for anniversaries. I would go to La Serena and speak with people there to see if they could tell me anything. And when I went in 1976, I met Dr. Peña, Jorge Peña's father. Together, we began to look in the cemetery. When I was in La Serena, I would lose the fear that I had at home. I would arrive at the cemetery office, and I would ask, even with arrogance, 'Where are the graves of those killed in 1973?' I concentrated all my courage into that question."

"'No, I don't know,' they would tell me.

"'But you must know, where is the director?' I would scream.

"I spent hours there. We began to meet more people, more relatives. We visited the graves, and there was a lot of repression. We handed out pamphlets. The truth is that in La Serena and [every year] in October, I would get all my strength back. Here in Santiago, I was immersed in pain and loneliness."

"Before the military coup, what was your political position?" I asked Josefina.

"I was against the Popular Unity. That's the truth. I worked against Allende. I was an active militant of Fatherland and Liberty,[8] and I wanted the military to intervene to restore order. I'm so ashamed to say it!"

"What happened to you on that day of the military coup?"

"My apartment faces the street, in the middle of downtown Santiago. I asked the janitor for the Chilean flag to put it on the building, to celebrate. I even scolded his wife because the flag was wrinkled. And when the soldiers went by, I applauded them, and suddenly I thought — my son! He had always respected my position because we had the perfect right to think differently and still love each other. And I knew about all his activities, and I admired him for his idealism."

"When you found out he was a prisoner, did you believe that he was free from danger because he was in the hands of those you admired?"

"It never would have occurred to me that something bad would happen to him. Never! I was sure that he was going be released soon and that nothing would happen."

"Did you ask for help from the people from Fatherland and Liberty?"

"No, because I perceived them as enemies as soon as Roberto was in jail, because the mere fact that he was in prison was already an injustice. In 1974, one of the few times that I went out to do some legal errand, I ran into Pablo Rodríguez,[9] one of the lawyers recommended to me by the president of La Serena's Bar Association, and I told him, taking him by the arm, 'You are a murderer, because my son was murdered, and you work for this government of murderers.'

"He looked at me and he said, 'You're wrong, I don't work for the government.'

"A short time later they left a legal citation for me with the building's concierge. I went to see what it was all about. They made me go into an office, and a secretary told me that the government Junta had ordered that I be given a pension for the death of my son. I made a horrible fuss. Obviously, I rejected the offer — who do they think they are!"

"Who is guilty?" I asked Josefina to explain.

"First, General Pinochet. Because he was in charge of everything. Then, General Arellano, because he went with the mission to kill to the north. And after them, I am, . . . yes, I am also guilty, because I sided with those who supported intervention by the military, and that is how we opened the door to let this atrocity happen."

Josefina Santa Cruz ended her story in tears, apologizing to me for not being able to control herself. Her fine, trembling hands searched among some papers she had brought, and she pointed out a paragraph in one of them. When this lawsuit was brought for homicide in 1985, the judge sent a judicial order to the army's deputy commander in chief's office. And in April of 1986, Josefina received a report from the Santiago military judge and Commander in Chief of the Second Division, General Samuel Rojas Pérez, which was the chronological summary of case number 5A-73, containing the details of Roberto's trial. There you could see the tragic proof: on June 26, 1975, Roberto's five-year sentence was decreased to 541 days in jail. Roberto Guzmán Santa Cruz' premonition had turned out to be tragically correct, when he said, "And don't worry, mother, I'm going to get out earlier." If he had not been among those executed, he certainly would have been freed that very same day.[10]

*****

All of the men in the university group, executed along with the others in La Serena on October 16, 1973, were socialists. The Director of the School of Music, Jorge Washington Peña Hen, was arrested on September 19, after he had visited a female university colleague who was in jail. Peña was held incommunicado, but his father, the respected Dr. Tomás Peña Fernández, was able to visit him in jail on October 14 and 15. Dr. Peña was even able to visit his son Jorge on the morning of Tuesday, October 16, and said that it was a relatively calm meeting:

"I had spoken with the military judge, Major Cazanga, who told me he still did not know when my son would be brought to trial. And Jorge did not show any concern [on October 16]. He even asked me to do certain things for him, pay some bills and deliver some letters," Tomás Peña told me.

Meanwhile, in Santiago, the old Peña family home in Ñuñoa was searched. Jorge's sister, Silvia Peña, said, "The inside of our house was searched, and then it was surrounded by armored cars outside while Jorge was kept under arrest and held incommunicado in La Serena. They came to get my oldest son, who was 16 then, and my brother Rubén, who had just gone to La Serena to visit Jorge. In the end, they didn't take either of them.

"On October 16, my father found out about Jorge's death through a friend who went to the hotel [in La Serena] to show him the newspaper. My father called us on the telephone. I remember I had to call him back because we could not believe it. 'Papá, it's not possible; there must be some mistake; it's impossible,' we said to him. But it was true. Then he told us that they were not releasing the bodies and that he, as a physician, was doing everything possible so that Jorge's body would be released. We decided to go to La Serena immediately. I remember that the whole trip I was thinking that it was an error, that it couldn't be true because Jorge was very well-known in La Serena. He was a very prominent musician."

"You thought your brother's fame would protect him?" I asked Silvia Peña.

"Yes. I thought he was more protected than others were. I even felt safe because he was in jail, that nothing bad could happen, that the worst thing that could happen to him was that he would be tried, but he would have a defense. It was inconceivable to me that they could murder people from one moment to the next."

"And what happened when you arrived in La Serena?"

"We found out that our father, who was a very solid person, had already done all the paperwork that could be done. The hospital's Medical Director, Hugo Badiola, had talked to the regiment's doctor, and they finally told father that they would not surrender the bodies because they were already buried. They did not tell us where they had buried them.

"Suddenly, I was in despair. I wanted to go speak to Commander Lapostol the next day. My father and my brother did not let me go. Rubén and I went to get Jorge's belongings from the jail: a music notebook, where he wrote his musical ideas, and his clothes.

"Even the army major who was acting as warden was moved, profoundly moved, when he gave us Jorge's things. His eyes were tearing. I asked what happened. He answered in a thin voice that he did not know. And he referred to my brother as 'Don Jorge,' with respect.

"My brother Rubén and I went to the cemetery. Toward the back there was something — under a slab, some large tiles, there was something. I looked through a slit, and there were bodies, but they could not be recognized. I saw newly interred bodies, but I didn't know who they were."

"What reaction was there in La Serena?"

"Many people approached us. We were in the hotel, and many friends of Jorge's came to express their solidarity and their pain. Forgive me for crying, but I still haven't been able to get over it. I never have. Despite other tragedies that I've had in my life, I cannot overcome this. Why did they kill him? Why? He only communicated his love through music."

"One of Jorge's sons was a cadet in the air force. What happened to him?"

"Yes, Juan Cristián was a cadet in the FACH. His superior gave him the news at the School of Aviation, and they took him away for a few days. They gave him permission to take his exams [early and go], but, obviously, he didn't stay. Now he's a graphic designer, and he has begun a lawsuit against those responsible for Jorge's homicide. He needs to know everything that happened to his father," Silvia Peña told me.

"And in Santiago, what type of reaction was there around you?" I asked.

"Friends of ours and people from the music world quickly found out what had happened. The Symphonic Orchestra, directed by Agustín Cullel, interrupted its rehearsal. The director asked for a minute of silence. I know that many people were deeply grieved, but only a few came over to the house. Inevitably, people withdraw because of fear. They don't want to get involved, and they ask themselves what he had done to deserve that punishment. I found out that some believed what the military proclamations said, that Jorge had distributed weapons. They needed to believe that to justify what happened: 'There must be a reason; he must have done something.'

"In La Serena, Jorge's name was erased from the School of Music. His name was not mentioned until very recently. And when the children's orchestra came to Santiago in 1986, they played all the arrangements that Jorge prepared, yet they did not name him as the author. I went to Radio Cooperativa, and I asked to speak. I was desperate again, and I even went to the gala concert in the Municipal Theater. Before that, I spoke with the orchestra's director, a gentleman by the name of Domínguez, and I complained. He told me that he had not made the programs that had omitted Jorge's name as the composer of the arrangements. Later, at the gala performance, the vice-chancellor of the University of La Serena named him and recognized that the School of Music had been Jorge's work. And the applause brought down the roof. I don't know how people knew."

"After Jorge's death, were you able to carry out any legal proceedings?"

"Nothing. We were paralyzed, frightened to realize that it was worthless, that no one would listen. I don't know. And in 1975, when my son Roberto was 18, DINA[11] arrested him along with a group of young men in the street. He disappeared for two weeks. It was a horrible nightmare. I thought that they were also going to kill him. And at that time, you couldn't even say anything, except to those closest to you, about what was going on. I worked in the Music Department of the University of Chile, at the West campus. I couldn't speak, because I didn't know if I was next to some DINA agent.

"I asked for help from the head of the International Red Cross, and he told me that he [Roberto] was not in any detention camp. What desperation! I went to the National Prisoners Service (Secretaría Nacional de Detenidos — SENDET),[12] which was located in the old Congress building, and I would wait in line. They didn't tell me anything. But at that time we still didn't know about the 'disappeared.' I heard how the soldiers would tell the women, 'Your husband is really a good-for-nothing. We let him go a long time ago, and he must have run off somewhere. He left you; don't worry about him anymore.'

"I went to Tres Álamos several times, until he appeared on the list one day. I couldn't believe I would see my son again. I thought they had killed him. He wasn't in good shape, but he was alive. He had been in DINA's Villa Grimaldi detention center, located in the eastern end of Santiago.[13] He was there for about two weeks. He was tortured."

"And while he was there, your son was in the hands of the people who participated in the death of his uncle, your brother Jorge Peña Hen — the commander of that detention center was Marcelo Moren Brito, one of the members of the Caravan of Death."

"I had never thought about that; I had not made that connection before. The fact is that when Roberto was freed, we sent him to study in the United States. We didn't want to risk it again. And for the same reason, I didn't do anything about Jorge's case. I withdrew; I didn't want to know anything," Silvia Peña concluded.

*****

Hilda Rosas Santana, the widow of Mario Ramírez Sepúlveda, another of the prisoners killed in La Serena, was also unable to do anything for many years. Pain and fear paralyzed her. But during our conversation in the late 1980s, free from these restraints, she recalled each detail accurately. As she spoke, she evoked her husband's memory with a voice that seemed to revive and caress him.

Mario Ramírez had been regional secretary of the Socialist Party and professor of education at the regional headquarters of the University of Chile in La Serena. At the time of the military coup, he worked as general manager of the state tire company, MANESA.

"Mario participated actively in the Popular Unity government. He was a conscientious militant, committed to his cause. When the government asked for his cooperation, he requested permission for leave from the university and dedicated himself to creating MANESA. He worked very hard to get the company moving and, in 1973, he participated in a competition to recover his professorship at the University. He was able to teach some classes before the coup, and he kept his job in MANESA while they searched for a replacement.

"He loved teaching, loved being in contact with young people, with people in general. He was the author of several education books: *Didáctica de la Educación*, *Panorama de la Educación*, and others. He was a brilliant man. Right before September 11, the atmosphere was odious in La Serena. The people from Fatherland and Liberty harassed people from the left a lot. But Mario was so sweet, so affable, and so communicative that he made the atmosphere around him pleasant. He was charismatic; he was a beautiful person.

"On that September 11, at 8:00 a.m., he took me, just like any other day, to the school where I taught. We didn't know there had been a coup. When they told me, I couldn't believe it, and the first thing I decided to do was to go see Governor Rosendo Rojas. I had only exchanged a few words with the governor when Commander Ariosto Lapostol walked in to arrest Rojas," Hilda Rosas Santana recalled.

"I was able to get past the soldiers with helmets, and I left the building. I was heading for the apartment, and I ran into Mario, who was looking for me. He asked me to stay in the house, saying that he had to return to the company because he could not leave the workers alone. I refused, and I went with him. The truth is that I always wanted to go with him, and in the party, they said that I was more a '*ramirista*'[14] than a socialist. It's because he was a wonderful man who taught me so many beautiful things. He gave me two beautiful girls. What else could I do?

"In the large dining room of the company, Mario gathered everyone and, since the curfew was going to begin at 2:00 or 3:00 in the afternoon, he asked them to go home. He announced that he was staying, along with the person in charge of security, *compañero*[15] Crovaris. I saw that Mario was in pain and suffering. We didn't know what was happening in Santiago, and we saw that people were very afraid, so afraid that they all went to their homes without putting up any resistance. Mario asked me to go with our two girls to the house of the lawyer, Gustavo Rojas, whose wife was the minister of the court. Mario slept at the company that night.

"For the next several days, Mario continued to go to the company. On September 17, Commander Lapostol called all service chiefs and public companies to ask them to hand over their positions. Mario did so and continued to go to the university. I remember that Mario slept with his clothes on. He could not understand why all his friends and colleagues were imprisoned and he was not. He felt bad; he did not understand why he was free; he thought his duty was to be with them. It didn't even cross our minds to come to Santiago, much less to seek asylum. No!

"On September 27, they rang the doorbell at about 8:00 in the morning. An officer from Investigations named León came, accompanied by another individual." Hilda Rosas Santana gave this account:

"'Don Mario, good morning. We want you to go to Investigations,' León said.

"'Very well. Should I go with you, or can I go by myself a little later?' Mario answered.

"'No problem. Please go as soon as possible,' León said, and then he said goodbye.

"For Mario, it was a relief. Finally, the same thing that had happened to his colleagues was happening to him. He asked me not to go along, and he didn't even take clothes with him. He left for Investigations, which was very near our house, as if it was just another formality. Later, attorney

Gustavo Rojas called me to tell me that Mario had been arrested and to take him some blankets and clothes. I was able to see him twice. There were long lines of people to see the prisoners. The first time I saw him he was in a small room full of people. His beard and hair had been badly cut; he was pale, with black and blue marks on his face. He was emaciated, thin, and could hardly move. In such painful moments, one does not know what to say. I held his hands, and I stroked his face. Nothing else.

"I sent him pajamas, shirts, and underwear every day. Until, one day, he told me in a letter that I probably believed he was in a hotel. Imagine how silly: sending clean clothes every day when they were all crowded in a cell that was even used as a toilet. The second time I was able to see him was on October 8, in an inner yard of the jail. He had just come back from the base where they had taken him to make a statement. He was very emaciated. Then he was moved to a very small cell with a peephole, incommunicado. He was there from October 8 to 16, until they took him to the base — with his hands on the nape of his neck — to kill him."

Hilda handed me a piece of paper that Mario had written a few lines on during those days when he was held in solitary confinement. He hid it in a mattress that was later returned to the family. The note read as follows:

Mamita mía:[16]

I'm writing you, taking advantage of a little bit of light that comes in through the window of the door (10cm x15cm). You don't know how much I think about you and miss you. I hope that on Wednesday the 19th I'll be able to hold you and kiss you. I'm well, a little thin, and very tired. I hope you're calm and resigned, just like my dear Anitamaría. I send lots of big kisses to both of you.

Papito Mario[17]

Hilda put away this piece of paper, her treasure, and continued the story: "On that October 16, I came home at approximately 3:00 in the afternoon, and a young university student arrived to tell me that they had seen Mario being taken from the jail in the direction of the base. I jumped with happiness, thinking that his incommunicado status had been lifted, that he would be able to go back outside [to the prison yard] with his friends. I decided to go out and buy raisins and chocolates and wait until they brought him back so that I could throw him the package.

"I stood outside the penitentiary, waiting. And hours and hours went by. At around 8:30 p.m., a paddy wagon appeared. I ran and waited for them to let out the prisoners. They began to come out, and my Mario wasn't there. I became desperate. I screamed, asking for him. The driver told me to ask in the guard's office. I begged for an answer, and the guard told me to ask at the base, saying that he knew nothing. I became desperate because I had heard that the treatment on the base was horrible, that they hung them by the legs, that they sank them in buckets of excrement.

"I walked down the street; people greeted me, but I walked like a robot. That night, Ana María's boyfriend went back to his house a little before curfew. There he found out about the executions, and he ran back to our house. He said nothing to me, only that he came to be with us. But he told my daughter, and she decided to hide it from me. She told me she wanted to sleep with me that night. I felt she was restless, as if she was trembling all night. But I didn't guess what had happened.

"Very early the next day, some friends came over, and they told me that Mario was dead. I remember my first reaction was to run downstairs like a lunatic and to scream, to scream out in the street. I don't remember anything else about myself after that point. My whole family came from Santiago for the funeral, and since then we have not been able to hold funerals.

"I was paralyzed. I was in very bad shape. I could not believe it, and I would not accept condolences. I hadn't seen his body. They gave me a lot of pills, and I think I slept and I slept. The girls, who were very close to their father, were in very bad shape. I found one of them lying in our apartment building's park — she was crying because she thought she saw her father in an invisible airplane in the sky. I had to send her to get special therapy.

"My brothers, one of them a lawyer and the other a police officer, made some arrangements. They spoke with prosecutor Cazanga, who explained that it was a group that had arrived from Santiago — and that they [the officials in La Serena] were not the ones responsible. But my question is, who gave them the names of these men, who were shot, and not others?

"Later, my family begged me to come to Santiago to remake our lives. But I was not in good enough condition to work. I consulted the only psychiatrist in La Serena to get treatment and a medical dispensation. I remember the psychiatrist telling me that Mario was responsible for what had happened. He told me that I was young and should stop worrying and that I would be able to rebuild my life very soon and marry again. Every one of his words hurt, but I was in such bad shape that I listened to him, and I even began to accept what had happened. Today I think of that psychiatrist as a criminal. He was part of a scheme devised to convince people to accept everything that had happened.

"I was finally able to get to the cemetery on December 24. I went to a grave where they told me the men had been buried. I remember I took a

Christmas card and buried it next to that grave. On the other hand, I continued to think that everything was a mistake and that he was being held incommunicado in jail. Some time later, the Department of Education offered to transfer me wherever I wanted to go. Clearly, I had become a problem for La Serena. At the end of January 1974, I came to Santiago and worked until 1986."

Three years went by before Hilda could overcome her paralyzing fear that they could also kill her daughters. "I was so afraid that, after I had come to Santiago to live, one night my sister found me reading in the bathroom. In La Serena, I would turn off all the lights in the house and lock myself in the bathroom, the only place where I felt safe."

It wasn't until 1977 that Hilda began to find out about the other families. "In 1978, along with Dr. Peña, Josefina Santa Cruz, and eight other families, we founded the Association of Families of Persons Executed for Political Reasons. We opened a registry in the Vicarate of Solidarity,[18] and we discussed our cases among ourselves. That's all we did until 1985, when, thanks to attorney Carmen Hertz's tenacious initiatives, everything came out publicly."

Two years later, in 1987, Hilda Rosas Santana was told that it was the last year she could present a lawsuit for homicide, since the statute of limitations (15 years) would run out. "I decided to present a lawsuit in La Serena on the same day, on October 16. I wanted to see the newspaper *El Día* publish the presentation of the lawsuit on October 17, just as it had printed the news of the executions on that day in 1973. I felt so relieved when I did it. I said to myself, 'Hilda, now you can be at peace because you did it. I know that you must continue to struggle, but now you have performed an important part of your duty.'"

The various versions of the executions from these three women, a mother, a wife, and a sister — Josefina Santa Cruz, Hilda Rosas Santana, and Silvia Peña — leave one question resonating in our consciences: Why? Why was it necessary for those who had all of the power back then to kill those 15 prisoners outside every legal process? Was it a "warning" for the political left in the area? Was it necessary to harden the military's hand in the region even more?

The answers to these questions about the La Serena case can only come from Commander Lapostol and General Arellano.

*****

General Sergio Arellano Stark made the following statement, through his son, who served as his authorized spokesman, Sergio Arellano Iturriaga:[19] "In La Serena, three death sentences had been decreed for the prisoners Roberto Guzmán Santa Cruz, Manuel Marcarian, and Carlos Alcayaga. I remember that my father, before setting out on that trip to the north, said that such death sentences were the most thankless part of his mission. The fact is that he recognizes that he did not oppose those death sentences because court advocates from Santiago had participated in the drafting of the sentences, and they were technically well-constructed sentences, with 14 to 15 legal justifications for each one."

Insofar as what happened in La Serena, Arellano Iturriaga explained, "General Arellano, my father, found out only after he returned to Santiago. Moreover, he left La Serena without doubting that only three prisoners would be shot. He did not even think about whether this sentence would be carried out with or without his presence in the city. A minimum of political and practical sense should have told him to order the executions after he left. He did not do that."

Therefore, General Arellano's authorized spokesman stated categorically, "The execution of the other 12 prisoners was not his responsibility. Commander Lapostol should explain that, since he was the authority in the area at the time of the events — although we think that he is not responsible for what happened."

When the events were made public 12 years later, attorney Sergio Arellano Iturriaga looked for the text of those sentences in the Military Justice files. "I found out," he explained, "that something was added at the end of the death sentences [in the case] of those three persons, something along the lines of 'also condemned to death are . . . ,' and 12 more names were added. However, my father only saw the first text, and I saw the addendum that had been inserted to amend the injustice of the massacre. Also, there is handwritten proof that another person died 'when he resisted' a guard. That addendum has a scribble (a tiny, illegible signature) next to it, which kept that sentence, with several more addenda, from being signed by the military judge of La Serena, Commander Lapostol. So that sentence was never signed, and it remained a simple draft, without ever being transcribed or signed again. This could be due to a sense of self-respect on the part of Commander Lapostol, who had no involvement in the events."

General Arellano's defense flies in the face of two incongruities: First, how could attorney Roberto Guzmán have been condemned to death if his sentence to only five years had been publicly ratified? Moreover, as explained in his mother's testimony earlier in this chapter, Guzmán's case (number 5A-73) had an amendment almost two years later, and, on June 26, 1975, his term was reduced to 541 days in jail "through the sentence of the commander in chief who amended the sentence of the court-martial," according to a report to the court by General Samuel Rojas, military judge of Santiago.[20]

Second, if General Arellano had no responsibility in the events, and he states that Commander Lapostol was not involved, who had more power that day in La Serena than the delegate of the commander in chief of the army and the area commander under state of siege?

*****

I heard Commander Ariosto Lapostol Orrego's version of these events on a bright sunny day in 1989, after rain had cleared the smog from Santiago's air. From his window, one could see the green Santa Lucía hill, and there his glance took refuge during this difficult interview: to reveal the secret he had guarded for so many years, to speak the truth, continuously asking himself, "Do you really think the truth will be useful?"

"Let me start on September 10, 1973, when I received my combat orders for the next day. I had an isolated unit under my command, and, therefore, I had to resolve difficult situations by myself. One is told what to do but not how to do it. That same afternoon of the 10th, I decided to solve the problems in the best way possible. I had a good, harmonious relationship with most of the authorities in La Serena. So I never felt, after the coup, that it was the time to take revenge on anyone. Moreover, when I called all the service chiefs, more than 100 people, to the base, I did not request their resignations. No, I told them that the Popular Unity government had made an error and — I remember the phrase literally — that it was brave to admit when one was wrong, that when someone said, 'Sorry, I was wrong,' this was very valuable to me."

"But you arrested Governor Rosendo Rojas the same day of the coup?"

"That is right. He was a communist, and I decided to arrest him. He was not my personal enemy, but I saw him as an enemy of the new order. I knew that, during the strike in October 1972, he had ordered the locked food stores to be forcibly opened. And that, for me, was against legal principles. I remember I once spoke with him, bringing up the problem of lack of food for the soldiers on the base. He told me that to get the food I should sign the JAP[21] card. Obviously, I thought this was an inappropriate answer. Then he sent me an order so that I would be given, upon payment, 40 chickens in Ovalle. Forty chickens for 1,000 people? You must understand that I had no sympathy for him, but I did not hate him."

"General Arellano's defense states that there were three death sentences in La Serena, decreed by you."

"None. There were no death sentences. I was the president of the court-martial, and I can say that with certainty."

"At what time did General Arellano arrive?"

"At approximately 11:00 in the morning on October 16, 1973. I went to wait for him at the airport, and we headed toward the base."

"Who came with him?"

"Colonel Sergio Arredondo González, Lieutenant Colonel Pedro Espinoza Bravo, Major Marcelo Moren Brito, and Lieutenant Armando Fernández Larios. Regarding Moren Brito, he was the deputy commander of my regiment, and he had been assigned to Santiago. There was also the crew of the helicopter."

"What was General Arellano's first activity?"

"He asked me for a meeting with all the people in the regiment, that is, the officers and permanent staff. Accompanied by his entire entourage, he gave a presentation on the general situation of the country. Then, as we were leaving, he told me he had the mission of reviewing all the cases, that they had to be streamlined because it was not a question of keeping prisoners for minor crimes. He added that it was necessary to have the participation of a lawyer in the military prosecutor's office, that he would send me a legal officer as soon as possible to replace the military prosecutor, who was a police major and not a lawyer."

"And then?"

"We went to the commander's office, where he asked me to show him the registry of the prisoners. I called for the registry that was being kept by the military prosecutor, Major Cazanga. It was a huge book, with the names of 20 prisoners registered on each page. First you had the number, then the name, then the identity card, the crime the person was charged with, the decision of the court-martial (if there was one), and other personal data."

"What happened there?"

"General Arellano began to read the registry, surrounded by the people in his entourage. He had a pencil in his hand and began to make a mark, a check, in the column 'crime charged.' He went through the pages and made some check marks in that column. I was looking over his shoulder, and I began to sense something obscure. At that moment, Major Moren Brito turned around and asked me, 'Is the governor imprisoned in the jail?' For a thousandth of a second, I had an inspiration that I'm grateful for to this day. I answered immediately, 'No.' I did not lie because he was not being held in the jail. But I hid the truth, with regard to the substance of the question, because I was actually holding the governor a few meters away from there, under arrest while he was being investigated — he was staying in the doctor's room next to the clinic."

"Why did you say that you are grateful to this day?"

"Because my answer saved his life."

"Would he have died?"

"I have no doubts in that regard."

"What happened next in your office?"

"Suddenly, I saw that General Arellano made a check mark in Roberto Guzmán Santa Cruz's column. That was the case for which I had just rendered a sentence. I asked in a loud voice, 'What is this all about, General? That case was already tried.' Everyone, he and the four members of his entourage, turned around to look at me. No one answered, and they returned to concentrate on the prisoners' registry. They looked at me with contempt, as if to say, 'Who does this asshole think he is?' I left the office immediately, and I also left the base. I went to the garden outside."

"Why?"

"I did not want to participate; I did not want my presence to authorize anything improper, because obviously cases that had already been sentenced were going to be reviewed. And that was going over my head, an abuse."

"What happened then?"

"After I had been in the garden for about 20 minutes, General Arellano appeared. He told me he wanted to hold a court-martial. I answered that I agreed for those cases that still did not have sentences, but I disagreed for those that had already received sentences. I told him that that was neither appropriate nor legal."

"What arguments did he use?"

"Don't you think that the truth can sometimes be counterproductive? I choose not to answer."

"Colonel Lapostol, did General Arellano tell you that it was necessary to toughen the military's hand, that without being tough you would not be able to impose the order necessary to govern?"

"No, he didn't tell me that. Maybe he considered my actions in the zone lenient, but he didn't tell me that. He insisted that the cases of serious crimes were going to be reviewed. And I argued again that it was one thing to press a charge and another to prove the crime, that our obligation was to act in a legal and just manner."

"How long was General Arellano with you outside the base?"

"More than two hours, until approximately 5:00 in the afternoon."

"All that time with you?"

"Yes, all that time."

"In the meantime, was there a court-martial being held inside the base?"

"I don't know. I cannot prove it. I only know that none of my officers participated."

"Did something happen while you were with General Arellano in the garden?"

"Yes, I heard the shots inside the base. I asked General Arellano what was happening, and he answered calmly that it must be the result of the court-martial."

"Couldn't you have protested more?"

"I couldn't, and I can't tell you why."

"How did you feel at that moment?"

"Very bad, very bad."

"What did you do?"

"When I was able to speak, I told General Arellano to leave me a document in which everything that happened was written down. He didn't answer. I wanted a document signed by him. I asked him several times, the last time when I went to drop him off at the airport at about 6:00 p.m. on that same day, the 16th."

"You dropped him off despite everything that had happened?"

"It was my duty because he was a general and because it was my last opportunity to get that document. He did not give it to me. I asked him, Moren Brito, and Chiminelli for it. As I had been so insistent, they finally told me they would send it later. It never arrived."

"You returned to your regiment, and then what?"

"I had 15 dead prisoners."

"Did you see them?"

"Yes."

"How did they die?"

"They all had bullet wounds in the chest."

"Who executed them?"

"No one from my regiment. Except in the case of Mr. Ramírez."

"Are you referring to Professor Mario Ramírez?"

"Yes. His case was different. The soldier who participated in the episode told me that Mr. Ramírez realized that he was going to be shot when the column of prisoners crossed the courtyard. He became desperate, and he attacked the closest soldier, apparently with the intention of taking his weapon. In the struggle, the soldier fired a shot, and Mr. Ramírez died instantly."

"Regarding the other 14 prisoners, did the general's entourage shoot them?"

"Yes."

"Did General Arellano order you to issue the military proclamation in which you appear, explaining the executions decided by the 'military courts in time of war'?"

"No, I decided [to issue the proclamation] as soon as I returned to the base."

"You lied."

"Yes, I lied," Colonel Lapostol admitted. "But what was I to do? I had to explain to the country and the city that 15 prisoners had been shot. How was I to explain the next day to the mother or to the wife that her son or her husband was not in the jail any longer and that he was dead? I had to say something."

"And who ordered the bodies to be buried, violating the custom to return them to their families?"

"I did. I asked the regimental doctor to look at them and to issue a death certificate. Then I ordered the captain to take them immediately to the cemetery."

"Why did you do that, Colonel?"

"It was a mistake, and I'm sorry."

"The proper and legal thing was to return them to their families."

"Yes, I know. The only explanation I have is that I was psychologically stunned. I felt like a bum. I apologize to the families."

"You issued a military proclamation and ordered the burial of the bodies. Did you try to fix what happened from a legal standpoint?"

"No, I don't do things that way. I left everything as it was."

"So, as far as military justice is concerned, all the prisoners remained alive?"

"Apparently, that's the way it was."

"The next day, you said publicly that what happened was the responsibility of 'a tribunal that had come especially from the capital.'"

"Yes, I wanted to make that perfectly clear. And that phrase that cost me a great deal."

"Please explain."

"No, it's private."

"How were you emotionally after this episode?"

"I felt very empty and knew something totally irreversible had happened. Because nobody can be brought back from the dead."

"What was the condition of the officers in your regiment?"

"Stunned."

"Did you understand that, in the future, you had to act more harshly?"

"No. If that was the intention, I did not apply it. I knew that I had to continue to be just. Neither lenient nor harsh. And that is why I can return to La Serena and walk through the streets with my head held high. I know that the relatives must be distressed with me, and again, I ask for their forgiveness. But they must know that I did everything possible so that this would not happen."

"Did you hand out any death sentences afterward?"

"No, none."

"Reviewing the check marks made by General Arellano, what factor did they all have in common?"

"They were the cases with the most serious charges," the colonel concluded. "Nothing else. I'll tell you again, one thing is to press a charge, and the other is to prove that the crime has been committed."

Colonel Ariosto Lapostol Orrego refused to explain why his public phrase about the "tribunal that had especially come from the capital" cost him so dearly. However, a quick investigation into his military career provides an explanation: One year after the events in La Serena, he was transferred to Santiago — promoted to colonel by that time — and he stayed in the Recruitment Directorate until 1982, when he was asked to retire. A regimental commander with brilliant grades, certainly someone who should have become a general, was sent to a military corner to do clerical work.

Notes

1. This type of military unit is in charge of tanks and other such vehicles used to transfer troops across the desert. *Ed.*

2. Testimony before the United Nations Human Rights Commission.

3. Report from the Gendarmería de Chile (prison authorities) to the Crime Court of La Serena, signed by Assistant-Inspector Javier Galleguillos, Unit Director, dated February 17, 1986, from the *Book of Prisoners 1973*, 35.

4. The judge verified this list from pages 160-161 of the *Civil Registry* after conducting an investigation in the La Serena cemetery on February 25, 1986.

5. Published in *El Día*, on October 18, 1973. The author is only identified as J.S.

6. The court-martial was presided over by Lieutenant Colonel Mario Arriagada and was made up of Major Manríquez Núñez, Captain Daniel Verdugo Gómez, and Lieutenants Emilio Cheyre and Raúl Alvarado. The military attorney was Francisco Álvarez Mery.

7. *Análisis,* September 28, 1987.

8. See Chapter 2, endnote 4. *Ed.*

9. Pablo Rodríguez was the leader of the Fatherland and Liberty right-wing group. *Paul E. Sigmund.*

In 1999, Rodríguez assumed the defense of General Augusto Pinochet.

10. In other words, the undeniable proof of the mass murder on October 16, 1973, is particularly brought out in Roberto Guzmán Santa Cruz' case because, by the time his five-year jail sentence was officially published on November 6, 1973, he had already been executed.

11. See Chapter 3, endnote 3. *Ed.*

12. The National Prisoners Service (Servicio Nacional de Detenidos — SENDET) was formed at the end of 1973 in order to bring to one location all data pertaining to those arrested in mass detention centers (especially sports stadiums) and in the numerous concentration camps that sprang up all over the country. SENDET headquarters were located in the building that once housed the Chilean Congress, which was dissolved at the time of the military coup. In Chile, prisoners could be transferred from "public" detention centers to "secret" precincts belonging to DINA, and from these secret locations they would be categorized as "disappeared" (a euphemism for "killed").

13. Villa Grimaldi was a secret prison that was part of DINA, located southeast of Santiago. Today, the Park for Peace (el Parque por la Paz) marks the spot where the jail facilities stood. Tres Álamos was a concentration camp, also run by DINA, including a maximum security, inner compound where prisoners were allegedly tortured, just as in Villa Grimaldi.

14. Hilda Rosas Santana, the widow of Mario Ramírez Sepúlveda, is playing on her husband's last name. As she explains in her testimony, the townspeople in La Serena jokingly said she was more of a "Ramirist," a follower of her husband, than a socialist.

15. In Spanish, *compañero* literally means "companion" or "colleague," but it can also mean "comrade." *Ed.*

16. In the Spanish text of the letter, Mario addressed his wife as *Mamita mía.* Although this Spanish term of endearment literally translates as "my mommy," among many Spanish-speakers, the word has a more general affectionate or romantic meaning, like "Sweetheart" or "Honey" *Ed.*

17. See previous endnote. The same is true with *Papito,* a word often used for the male lover in Spanish. However, in the context of the letter, which was written to both the mother and the daughter, the English-language sense of "Daddy" seems appropriate as a translation. Mario also used the affectionate diminutive "ita" for his daughter, Ana María, calling her Anitamaría. *Ed.*

18. The Vicaría de la Solidaridad is a Catholic organization that investigates and reports on human rights violations affecting Chileans in Chile and abroad. See also Chapter 4, endnote 10. *Ed.*

19. In the late 1980s, his son, Sergio Arellano Iturriaga, was General Arellano Stark's only authorized spokesman. In the 1990s, his nephew, Claudio Arellano Parker, and other attorneys also spoke on behalf of the general.

20. Under the headline "22 Sentences are Awaiting the Decision of the Military Prosecutor," in La Serena's newspaper *El Día*, on November 6, 1973, the following text appears next to item number 7: "Roberto Guzmán Santa Cruz, 5 years imprisonment in La Serena." And on page 40 of Roberto's case for homicide, begun in 1985, there is the report of General Rojas, military judge of Santiago, stating that the prisoner's sentence was lowered to 541 days of imprisonment "by sentence of the commander in chief" on June 26, 1975. This date was one year and eight months after Santa Cruz was illegally executed.

21. As this organization's full name indicates, the Junta de Abastecimiento y Control de Precios (JAP) was responsible for the distribution of food and for price controls in Chile. It was established during the last part of the Allende administration. *Ed. and Paul E. Sigmund.*

CHAPTER 6

Copiapó and the "Special Commission"

E verything indicates that the Puma helicopter that carried General Sergio Arellano and his entourage landed in Copiapó at approximately 7:00 p.m. on October 16, 1973. Commander Lapostol bid goodbye to the general in the La Serena airport at around 6:00 p.m., and he was certain about the next destination: Copiapó. "I witnessed the arrangements made with the control tower for the flight plan. He went straight to Copiapó," Colonel Lapostol told me.

General Arellano was received by the Commander of the Number 1 Motorized Engineers Regiment of Copiapó, Lieutenant Colonel Oscar Haag Blaschke, who was responsible for holding dozens of political prisoners at the military base. One of the former political prisoners, Lincoyán Zepeda, recalled that all were "members or leaders of parties [branches] of Popular Unity, with the exception of four imprisoned priests. Our relationships with the soldiers and noncommissioned officers were good. However, that was not the case with the officers. They treated us very harshly."

There were also many prisoners in the Copiapó jail. Both the ones from the base and from the jail went through interrogations in the main office, where the court-martial, from what has been found out, was made up of Major Carlos Enriotti Bley (military prosecutor), Major Carlos Brito Gutiérrez, and Police Major René Peri. There is no further information on the operations of this court-martial.

Former prisoner Zepeda stated that on the morning of October 16th, the prisoners were told that a general from Santiago was coming. "We were made to get up very early, leave everything neatly arranged, and clean up. I remember that we were even told that this general could have some good news for us. The noncommissioned officers thought that he was coming to review the cases of the political prisoners and give them a quick solution.

"At approximately 2:00 in the afternoon, we had the first indications that nothing good could come from this visit. In a break from routine, we were forced to go back into our cells at approximately 2:30 p.m. The soldiers' treatment was harsh, and the atmosphere was very tense. At approximately 9:00 in the evening, the door suddenly opened, and a group of soldiers that we had never seen before on the base entered the area where we were. They looked us over, and they made the following comment, 'Here are the little pigeons,' and they left. My impression is that they were officers. Two hours later, the group returned, a list was read, and they made the people on that list leave. It was the last time we saw them alive."[1]

Another former prisoner, Juan Lafferte, age 66, said, "I still don't understand why they didn't take me that day. I remember that the soldiers came that night, asking if anyone knew Mansilla or Palleras. The political prisoners were held in tents and in one of the barracks. I was in the tents with a French priest. There was an atmosphere of great anxiety. The soldiers, who were not from the base, began to call the prisoners. Guardia was in the tent next to mine, and they took him away. They looked at me but didn't say anything. They left later, and we heard noises that sounded like people were being hit with gun butts and groaning. It seemed that one of the prisoners got cocky. After that, I heard screaming. Just imagine, I was about 10 meters away, and I heard it. Afterward, there was a noise that sounded like heavy bales being thrown into a truck. Then the sound of an engine and silence."[2]

What had happened that night was communicated to the people of Copiapó on Thursday, October 18, 1973, through a military proclamation, published on the front page of the town's local daily newspaper, *Atacama*. The following is a verbatim translation of the proclamation:

Diario Atacama Copiapó
Thursday, October 18, 1973
Province of Atacama
Chief of the Zone Under State of Siege
Copiapó, October 17, 1973

ESCAPE OF PRISONERS REPRESSED

Two days ago in the Copiapó Jail Penitentiary, a plan for the mass escape of prisoners arrested by the military justice system was detected. The plan was denounced by one of the prisoners implicated in this case.

Given the lack of security and the overpopulation of the Copiapó jail, the military prosecutor's office, after due communication yesterday, proceeded to transfer the most dangerous prisoners of the military justice system to La Serena's Jail Penitentiary .

The transfer was carried out yesterday, Wednesday, beginning at 0100 hours, by military personnel using a truck belonging to the regiment. According to the information supplied by the Chief of the Commission and after conducting a proper investigation, it was verified that the vehicle had an electrical malfunction when it had almost reached the summit of

'Cuesta de Cardones,' which forced it to stop on the shoulder of the road. Taking advantage of the fact that the driver and helper were busy trying to fix the electrical problem, the prisoners suddenly took advantage of the inattention of one of the guards, jumped from the truck, and escaped toward the fields. Despite the fact that the guards shouted "Stop!" several times and even fired warning shots into the air to frighten the prisoners, they did not stop. In view of this situation, the guards proceeded to shoot at the prisoners, wounding 13 of them who died immediately.

The affected persons were Fernando Carvajal González, Manuel Cortázar Hernández, Winston Cabello Bravo, Agapito Carvajal González, Alfonso Gamboa Farías, Raúl del C. Guardia Olivares, Raúl Leopoldo Larravide López, Ricardo Mansilla Hess, Adolfo Palleras Norambuena, Pedro Pérez Flores, Jaime Iván Sierra Castilla, Atilio Ugarte Gutiérrez, and Leonello Vincentti Cartagena. Their remains were buried in the local cemetery.

> Commander of the Zone Under State of Siege
> Province of Atacama
> October 17, 1973[3]

Based on the above military proclamation, the following information appeared in *El Día* newspaper, in La Serena, on October 18, 1973:

POLITICAL PRISONERS DIE IN ESCAPE ATTEMPT 23 KILOMETERS FROM COPIAPÓ

Thirteen fell in this suicide action.

They were being transferred to the jail in La Serena.

COPIAPÓ (Correspondent). On the morning of the October 16, a bus belonging to the commander of the zone of this province was transferring a group of political prisoners to the jail in La Serena, on the orders of military authorities. An electrical malfunction in the vehicle forced its personnel to stop to fix the breakdown. The incident happened 23 kilometers south of Copiapó. The prisoners decided to take advantage of the situation, rebelled against the military personnel, and tried to escape. Therefore, the fugitives were fired upon and paid dearly for their boldness.

The victims of this escape attempt were Alfonso Gamboa Farías, Director of Radio Atacama; Winston Cabello Bravo, former head of ORPLAN of Atacama; Leonello Vincentti, Professor at the UTE [State Technical University — Universidad Técnica del Estado, *Ed.*] of Atacama; Fernando Carvajal; Manuel Cortázar; Agapito Carvajal; Raúl del Carmen Guardia; Raúl Leopoldo Larravide; Ricardo Mansilla; Pedro Pérez Flores; Jaime Iván Sierra; Atilio Ugarte Gutiérrez; and Adolfo Palleras. The incident was made known by the Chief of the Zone of Copiapó through a military proclamation.

The families of the 13 victims received identical death certificates:

Place: Copiapó, Pan-American Highway south
Date: 0100 hours October 17, 1973
Cause: Gunshot wounds

Aside from the false official version of the facts — a report that will be proved to be a lie later on in this chapter — we note the first contradiction in the dates. Commander Lapostol saw General Arellano's helicopter take off at approximately 6:00 p.m. on October 16, en route to Copiapó. It should have arrived at 7:00 p.m. Prisoner Lincoyán Zepeda is certain of having seen the officers of the special commission at approximately 9:00 p.m. of that same day, when "a group of soldiers that we had never seen before on the base" arrived. The death certificates state that they died at 1:00 a.m. on October 17. So far the times fit. Why, then, did the military proclamation say that what happened occurred at dawn on October 16? A careful examination of the drafting of the military proclamation provides the first clue needed to clear up this confusion: Commander Haag Blaschke said, on October 17, that events occurred "yesterday, Wednesday, beginning at 0100 hours." Wednesday was October 17, not October 16.

*****

Who were the 13 prisoners who fell in Copiapó? I have gathered the following details from my investigation and other sources. For example, there is no information on Fernando and Agapito Carvajal González in the files of human rights organizations. They were probably two workers and, given their surnames, two brothers. Manuel Cortázar was 19, an only child, and student council president of the public high school for men. He was called by a military proclamation, and his father advised him to turn himself in at the base. His classmates remember him as "one of the most cheerful [persons], someone who always lifted everyone's spirits."[4]

A fourth victim, Raúl Larravide López, was a student at the local Technical University and was arrested when he went to class. Alfonso Gamboa Farías, a journalist, was director of Radio Atacama and gave himself up when called by military proclamation. He was transferred to the base, where he was interrogated. His wife and two children were able to see him, under heavily-armed guard, for only five minutes each day. Something similar happened with the young radio announcer, Jaime Sierra Castillo, who (other prisoners recall) was one of those who received the most torture. Raúl Guardia Olivares, who was arrested in Caldera, was tortured so much that he could hardly walk and had a broken arm.

The eighth person from Copiapó who was executed on October 17, 1973, was Pedro Pérez Flores, a mining engineer and professor at the local campus of the technical university, UTE; he was married with two children. His sister-in-law Doris said, "Pedro was taken from the university while he was teaching a class. He did not want to hide or run away. He had nothing to hide. And then we were never able to see him again. He was always kept in solitary confinement at the base. They say that it was because he refused to talk." Pérez' wife, Nuri, a secretary at Radio Atacama, was arrested a short time after he was. She was sentenced to five years in prison by the court-martial, but in 1976 her sentence was changed to exile.

Prisoner Leonello Vincentti Cartagena was a physics professor at the local UTE campus. The key to his imprisonment was, of course, his political post, regional secretary of the Socialist Party.

There is no data on Edwin Ricardo Mancilla Hess. The report from the intelligence officer of the regiment, Major Carlos Brito Gutiérrez, dated October 13, 1973, states that he was the local head of the Chilean Revolution Left Movement (MIR), along with Atilio Ugarte Gutiérrez. There is no further information on this other prisoner.

Victim number 12 in Copiapó was Winston Cabello Bravo, an independent leftist, economist, and the director of the Regional Planning Office (Oficina Regional de Planificación — ORPLAN) for Atacama-Copiapó. He was arrested the day after the military coup, on September 12, after going to a meeting of public service chiefs with Commander Oscar Haag Blaschke. Haag arrested Cabello while everyone was leaving the room, telling him that his Jeep had been seen in "suspicious maneuvers." Then Haag called for a military vehicle and sent Cabello, under arrest, to the Copiapó jail, where he was the first political prisoner from this region. From there, he was transferred to the base, where his family could see him three times each week.

On September 27, Winston Cabello Bravo's brother-in-law, a commercial engineer named Patricio Barrueto Céspedes who had replaced Cabello Bravo as the head of ORPLAN, was arrested. On the night of October 16, the two men saw each other at the base. According to a statement by Winston Cabello's sister, Zita Cabello, "My husband [Patricio Barrueto

Céspedes] was given the opportunity that night to call Malloco on the telephone, where our mother, Elsa Bravo lived. He told her that both [Barrueto Céspedes himself and Cabello Bravo] would be freed the following Saturday and that she should not worry because everything was all right."

Zita Cabello continued her dramatic narrative: "After 1:00 in the morning of October 17, Adolfo González (the secretary of the Judge Advocate[5] of Copiapó) came to my house to tell me that Winston had been taken from the base and had been killed. Adolfo was drunk, so we didn't believe him. He stayed at our house and slept on the sofa. The next morning Adolfo and I went to the base, but it was still cordoned off. I asked a lieutenant if they had shot political prisoners. 'No one was shot here,' he told me. We went to the house of Adolfo González' brother-in-law, who was in the military, and he confirmed that the men had been taken out and shot. On October 18, the newspaper said that they had been executed because they had tried to escape. Then Adolfo said that he had spent all of the 17th identifying bodies with the medical examiner. This was up on the hill as you leave Copiapó."

But there is more. According to Zita Cabello, Adolfo González told them that, "From the time he arrived on October 16, General Sergio Arellano Stark conferred privately with lieutenants from Copiapó, including González himself, looking at how to implement the order to kill 13 people. General Arellano had brought from Santiago five names out of those 13 people. Two of those names were those of my brother Winston and Professor Vincentti. 'Get eight more,' said Arellano. And the secretary began reviewing all the files. One of the lieutenants who participated in this review was named Ojeda. Adolfo said that Vincentti was killed on the base with a *corvo*. First, the lieutenants and Adolfo got drunk at the regiment. At approximately 11:00 that night, the lieutenants and the entourage from Santiago visited the prisoners' dormitories. Then another lieutenant appeared with a list. They read the list, and they took the men to the jail. They placed hoods on the prisoners' heads and put them in a truck. Then, on the outskirts of Copiapó, they told them to get off the truck and run. My brother refused to get off, so they killed him with a *corvo*. Lieutenant Ojeda participated in the execution." Zita Cabello heard all of these macabre details from a doctor who attended a soldier who had become disturbed and had to receive psychiatric care after participating in these events.[6]

The last of the 13 young men executed by the Caravan of Death in Copiapó was Adolfo Palleras Norabuena, 27, a shantytown leader and merchant in the Copiapó market, who was put in jail on October 15. His sister, photographer María Angélica Palleras, recalled that she and other family members visited him on October 16: "He was calm, but we knew he had been tortured because he had wounds on his wrist." Adolfo asked that they bring him breakfast the next day, the 17th, because he thought he would be facing the court-martial. As they were getting ready to take him his food the next morning, they found out that he was dead. Angélica remembered that, in her desperation, she crossed the city, and went to the base and grabbed the fence, cried and screamed, "Murderers, murderers!"

Angélica Palleras continued, "We were never able to see his body. They were all buried secretly, under heavy military guard. Some relatives received a death certificate signed by a civilian official from Copiapó, Mr. Víctor Bravo Monroy, who was dragged out of his house early on the morning of the 17th to do this paperwork. He was the only person they were able to find who could verify the state of the bodies. He later resigned. The certificates stated as cause of death: 'gunshot wounds.' Everything we did was futile. They even prohibited us from asking for more information. They only said that this had not been a decision made by local authorities, that a general had come from Santiago with superior orders and that they could not be held responsible for anything that had happened."[7]

While the families were learning about these tragic events, the commotion on the base was evident to the other prisoners. According to prisoner Lincoyán Zepeda, "The first information we received was given to us by a soldier. He told me that he had had a very bad night because of the horrible screams he had heard." At approximately 9:00 in the morning, some noncommissioned officers spoke with Zepeda and confirmed his suspicions, as he recounted, "Our comrades had been murdered. Some of the soldiers who gave us the news looked upset and sad. That day and the following we heard more details and were able to fill in the gaps. They told us that the men had not been shot but had been butchered while still alive. Some noncommissioned officers told us about the knife and *corvo* wounds on the dead bodies. They even told us that one of the prisoners was murdered at the base in the presence of the commander, who was so shocked by what he saw that he was unable to react to the brutality of the group accompanying General Arellano."

Here Zepeda's narrative coincides with the version of the incident given by the Secretary to the Military Prosecutor, Adolfo González. According to his testimony, the Regional Secretary of the Socialist Party, Leonello Vincentti, was killed on the base "with a *corvo*." That explains the screams heard by prisoner Juan Lafferte from the tent where he was held along with a French priest at the Copiapó military base. Lafferte had said at the time, "It seemed that one of the prisoners got cocky." Perhaps Vincentti had a premonition about what was going to happen and tried to resist, as had Professor Mario Ramírez, the regional secretary of the Socialist Party in La Serena.

*****

The family of Adolfo Palleras Norambuena filed a lawsuit for homicide in November 1985. The judge carried out several essential legal steps that clarified some of the points in the Copiapó case before military justice closed the investigation – due to the statute of limitations set by the Amnesty Law of April 1978. For example, the exact time when Palleras was taken away from the Copiapó jail was verified through a prison record that stated: "Wednesday, October 17, 1973, Page No. 250. Paragraph No. 45, at 0030 hours and by order of the Military Prosecutor (verbal) of Copiapó, Army Captain Mr. Patricio Díaz Araneda presents himself before this body so that the prisoner ADOLFO PALLERAS NORAMBUENA be handed over to him by said court, and he was handed over to him in the presence of noncommissioned officer Army Major Mr. Orlando Luke Smith, who signs hereunder for verification willingly."[8]

However, the military prosecutor of Copiapó also informed the judge, "Having reviewed the documentation of this military prosecutor's office, we find that there is no record of having initiated any proceedings against Adolfo Palleras." That is, Palleras was not even tried for any alleged crime. At the end of 1985, the military prosecutor added copies of four memorandums that he found in the documentation, as follow:

1. A memorandum dated October 16, in which noncommissioned officer Orlando Luke, at that time the warden of the jail, reported, "Given the lack of security and excess of prisoners at this facility, it is believed that the most dangerous prisoners may be holding night meetings in order to devise an escape."

2. A memorandum dated October 17, written by the Military Prosecutor, Major Carlos Enriotti Bley, instructs La Serena's military prosecutor to transfer "the following list of prisoners, due to their high-risk status and the limited space in the public jail and in Engineering Regiment No. 1 in Copiapó, to La Serena jail."

3. A memorandum dated October 16, in which Commander Oscar Haag Blaschke requests a common grave for the dead.

A translation of memorandum 3 follows:

Chilean Army
1st Division
Atacama Engineering Regiment No. 1

Copiapó, October 16, 1973
From: the Head of the Atacama Zone in State of Siege
To: The Administrator of the Cemetery of the National Health Service

This administration will provide every facility necessary for the burial in a common grave of the following individuals who died in an escape attempt:

(A list of names follows)

LT. COL. OSCAR HAAG BLASCHKE
Commander of the Zone under State of Siege

4. A memorandum dated October 17, in which Captain Patricio Díaz Araneda reported the incident to Commander Haag.

A translation of memorandum 4 follows:

Chilean Army
1st Division
Atacama Engineering Regiment No. 1
Subject: Report on the escape and execution of prisoners.
Reference: Document FISMIL No. 201 dated October 17, 1973, to the Military Prosecutor of La Serena.
Copiapó, October 17, 1973
From: Captain Patricio Díaz Araneda
To: The Regiment Commander

1) Pursuant to the order issued to transfer to the Military Prison of La Serena 13 (thirteen) prisoners due to their participation in extremist acts, I am informing you that on October 17, 1973, at approximately 0100 hours the following events took place:

a) When I received the order to go to La Serena, I ordered truck P:A:M:5354 prepared for me, along with a driver and three guards, to transfer the prisoners to the place ordered.

b) Departure from headquarters was carried out at approximately 0115 hours.

c) Before we reached the top of Cuesta Cardones and due to malfunctions in the truck's electrical system, the vehicle had to be stopped and parked on the shoulder. The electrical malfunction produced the complete shutdown of the truck's lights.

d) When the malfunction occurred, the driver, two guards, and the undersigned proceeded to look for the cause of it, leaving a guard on board to take care of the prisoners.

e) At a moment when the guard was not paying attention, the prisoners proceeded to push him out of the truck and attempted their own mass escape from the scene.

f) In view of this and seeing that the order to stop did not produce any reaction from the escaped prisoners, I shot a warning shot in the air, and since this also had no effect, I gave the order to shoot at them, all thirteen of them dying as a result of the shots.

g) The personnel who were in the truck working as guards immediately recovered the bodies, which were then brought to the military compound to conduct the appropriate procedures.

2) These events are reported to the Commander of the Regiment, since the high-risk nature of the escaped prisoners did not permit any other solution.

3) For your consideration and judgment.

Yours truly,
Patricio Díaz Araneda
Captain

What happened with the dates in those four official letters — from the warden, the military prosecutor, Commander Haag, and Captain Díaz Araneda? Was it a simple mistake? Could the confusion be the result of an inept attempt to cover up what really happened? To make matters worse, the whole story of the transfer of prisoners to La Serena was, in fact, denied by Commander Ariosto Lapostol because prisoners could not be sent to another region without the prior authorization of the head of the zone in a state of siege who would receive them. Colonel Lapostol had no doubts in this regard when I asked him to clarify these events, saying, "At approximately 1930 hours on October 16th, Commander Haag called me from Copiapó to ask me to receive a group of prisoners. I responded that that was impossible, that I did not have space."

*****

This confusion of dates even caused some of the communications media to say that everything had happened on the night of October 15 or on the morning of October 16, which helped General Arellano's defense when his son stated, "Those prisoners were already dead when my father arrived in Copiapó. Moreover, no one told him what had happened, and he only found out when he returned to Santiago while he was listening to Radio Moscow. From then on, he began to listen to the Chilean news program on that radio station every day."

The first discrepancy: General Arellano left La Serena at 6:00 p.m. on October 16, and he arrived in Copiapó after 7:00 p.m., according to Commander Lapostol's statement. That is to say, General Arellano was in Copiapó when the 13 prisoners were killed, a little after 1:00 a.m. on the morning of October 17.

Second discrepancy: If the massacre indeed happened before his arrival — it is inconceivable to think that this event would not have been reported to the delegate of the commander in chief, especially if said delegate came with the express mission of "expediting trials and harmonizing standards in the matter of the administration of justice." Anyone who has minimal knowledge of the army knows that this would have been impossible. Furthermore, why hide the massacre from General Arellano if the slain men were only prisoners who tried to escape and "paid dearly for their insolence?"

According to General Arellano's defense attorney, "In Copiapó, four death sentences had been decreed, signed by Commander Haag. My father acknowledges that he approved them, that he did not oppose their implementation. These were the death sentences of García, Castillo, Tapia, and Lira."

Four death sentences? New names: Ricardo García Posada, Maguindo Castillo Arredondo, Benito Tapia Tapia, and Lira? While I was trying to find out which person named "Lira" General Arellano was referring to, I found a brief passage in the book, *La historia oculta del régimen militar* (*The Hidden History of the Military Regime*), that mentioned the prisoners of Copiapó. The text states, "One of the prisoners, the personnel manager of the El Salvador mine, Francisco Lira, had been rescued from jail by a friend. When he was traveling in a bus on his way to Santiago, he heard on the radio that his companions had been killed by a firing squad."[9]

Regarding the other three, let's begin with Ricardo García Posada, Economic Commission for Latin America and the Caribbean (ECLAC) official, engineer, economist, and general manager of the El Salvador copper mine (COBRESAL). His wife, Rolly Baltiansky Grinstein, gave a complete account of the facts before human rights defense organizations.

"When the coup occurred, Ricardo was in the mine, and he spoke on the telephone with the closest military authority, police Major Luis Alarcón Gacitúa, stationed in Potrerillos, 40 kilometers away from [the city of] El Salvador. The major told him that he was still loyal to the constitutional government and, therefore, asked Ricardo to remain calm. However, a little later, the El Salvador post's police officer, Captain Ormeño, demanded that Ricardo hand over the company. Ricardo told him that he had spoken with his superior and that he wanted a meeting to clarify any misunderstanding. Ormeño refused, saying, 'I'm the one who gives the orders.'

"On September 12, when Ricardo found out officially about the death of President Allende, he asked the workers to leave the place and turned over the facility to engineer Orlando González, the executive with the highest rank among those present. Ricardo went to Potrerillos and handed over his position to police Major Luis Alarcón. But at that moment, Lieutenant Soto entered the office, saying that the Copiapó military garrison was issuing arrest orders to all officials of the company who were present there 'for having stolen money and having fled to the mountains in the direction of Argentina in vehicles belonging to the company.' There was generalized laughter, and Major Alarcón made a phone call to Copiapó to deny that report as a rumor. Then Alarcón told them [Ricardo and the others from COBRESAL] that they would have to remain, for the time being, under house arrest.

"Ricardo, along with the journalist Fernando Orduña, was sent to the Directors' House of the camp. Later, they sent me and our two small children, ages three and seven, to the same place. Suddenly, on September 14th, the police transferred Ricardo to the public jail in Copiapó. I visited him there two times, three minutes each time. He was never notified to appear before any court. I decided to contact a lawyer, Mr. Frigolett, because I naively believed what the military authorities of the zone had said, that there would be a trial and, therefore, a proper defense.

"On October 15th, I was told that the case would be heard in Potrerillos, according to procedures in time of war; that the prosecutor would be police Major Alarcón; and that Captain Ormeño and Lieutenant Manlio Córdova would act as aides. The military judge would be the head of the zone, that is, Commander Haag."

Rolly Baltiansky's narrative continued: "I went to Potrerillos, and Major Alarcón told me that he would ask for 'a sentence of three years for Ricardo for the mere fact of having been general manager of the company.' Feeling relieved with this information, I returned to Copiapó. On the morning of October 16, I went to visit him in jail. He wasn't there. Then I headed for the base, where I was told that he wasn't there either. However, while I was speaking with a military official, I happened to see my husband walking in the regiment's courtyard; his hands were tied, and two soldiers guarded him. I called out to him, trying to get closer, but he gestured to me that he couldn't speak, that I should leave. It was the last time I saw him alive.

"On October 18, a list of 13 people killed for trying to escape appeared in the Copiapó newspaper, *Atacama*. His name was not listed. Feeling upset, I asked for an interview with an army major named Enryotti." (At the time, she understood his name to be Andreotti). Mrs. María Tapia, wife of another prisoner, labor leader Benito Tapia, went with her to see the major. "When I was demanding more news on the whereabouts of our husbands, he lowered his eyes, saying that he would be sending us information in writing that afternoon.

"The hours dragged on and on. I became desperate and decided at around 6:00 p.m. to go to the lawyer I had hired, Frigolett, to ask him to do something. Just at the moment when the lawyer was telling me, 'Nothing will happen to your husband; remember that he worked for the UN,' María Tapia came in with an envelope in her hand, eyes open wide, shouting, 'They killed them!'"

The paper inside the envelope contained the following notification:

Copiapó, October 18, 1973

Pursuant to a sentence decreed by the court-martial on October 17, 1973, and approved by the Hon. Government Junta, October 18, at 0400 hours, the prisoners Ricardo García Posada, Benito Tapia Tapia, and Maguindo Castillo Arredondo were executed by firing squad.

The condemned will be given to their relatives at the local morgue for burial, and the remains are prohibited from leaving the cemetery, in accordance with the penal regulations in force for these types of cases.

Burial will take place without any ceremonies and with the presence of no more than five persons, and no later than at 1900 hours today.

Council Secretary

Rolly Baltiansky's account continued: "At that moment I shook the lawyer, and I shouted at him, 'You were supposed to defend him — why didn't you?' And he answered, shaking and falling onto a sofa, 'But Madam, they give me hours and days to defend criminals, but in the case of your husband, they didn't even give me one minute.'

"I ran to the cemetery, but I was not permitted to view the remains. That day the curfew was moved up to 2000 hours; therefore, I was forced to leave the cemetery. The following morning, I went to the cemetery very early, and Ricardo's body had already been buried. You could only see their names on a piece of wood. Then the crosses, just like the graves, disappeared. To this day we do not know where they are buried."

The widow, Rolly Baltiansky, who was serving as a UN official in Mexico, added, "In the *Atacama* newspaper, two days after the shooting, it was published that he [Ricardo García Posada] was sentenced for inciting violence and for trying to paralyze the mine, which is rather difficult since he was in prison as of September 12, 1973," the day after the coup. Baltiansky received two different death certificates. The first one, presented in 1973, states that the cause of death was "military execution." The second, obtained several years later, says "impact of bullets."

A friend of Ricardo's, the geologist Patricio Villarroel, was arrested on that October 18, hours after the execution. He told Ricardo's widow that, on the base, everybody said that a military group that came from Santiago in a helicopter was responsible for the executions: "They came from Santiago, and don't forget one name: Arellano Stark."[10]

*****

The other two employees of COBRESAL executed in Copiapó were labor leaders Benito Tapia and Maguindo Castillo, and they were killed just like Ricardo García Posada. Almost all the evidence indicates that, in this case, the Commander of the Regiment, Lieutenant Colonel Oscar Haag, who blamed General Arellano for the other 13 deaths, assumed responsibility for these three deaths. This is how the executions were reported to Commander in Chief of the first Division, headquartered in Antofagasta, General Joaquín Lagos Osorio.

In fact, General Lagos had received Haag's report when, on October 31, 1973, the Armed Forces Command (Comando de las Fuerzas Armadas — COFFA), a body Lagos did not know existed, asked him for the list as well as the number of people executed in his jurisdictional zone.[11]

General Lagos' report stated:

I. Copiapó
a) By decision of the Commander of Copiapó: 3
b) By the Delegate of the Commander in Chief of the Army
(General Arellano): 13

What happened in Copiapó is that the military tried to hide the facts behind the false report of the prisoners' alleged escape attempt and behind the confusion of dates and reports. Furthermore, Lieutenant Colonel Haag did not report to his superior in a timely fashion. As General Lagos told me years later, neither General Arellano nor Colonel Arredondo, when they arrived in Antofagasta, "said anything about what they had done, especially the previous night, in Copiapó."

The Copiapó episode of the Caravan of Death needed to be clarified with Commander Oscar Haag Blaschke himself. When I contacted him in 1988 to request an interview, I received the following signed letter:

> When the events occurred in mid-October 1973, I had the rank of Lieutenant Colonel, and I was working as Commander of the Regiment and Head of the Zone under State of Siege of Copiapó.
>
> At that time a special commission was in the Regiment, presided over by a high-ranking officer with higher attributions than the ones I had. This is undeniable because it is public knowledge.
>
> As to these events, my only participation, as head of the Zone Under State of Siege, was to carry out the identification of the bodies by specialized personnel from the local Civil Registry and Identification office, which issued at that time the appropriate death certificates to the families for legal purposes.
>
> After the aforementioned was over, I ordered the immediate burial of the dead in the Copiapó cemetery. Now, regarding the statement that I made to the press as head of the zone, which was published the next day in the *Atacama* newspaper in Copiapó, that corresponded with the information that was given to me at the time.
>
> Oscar Haag B.

Despite Colonel Haag Blaschke's terse, Teutonic style, his statement is clear: the massacre of the 13 prisoners in Copiapó was perpetrated by General Arellano's entourage, and Haag could do nothing to stop it because it was "a special commission . . . presided over by a high-ranking officer with higher attributions than the ones I had."

Colonel Haag ends his letter saying that he drafted and disseminated the military proclamation that stated that the 13 prisoners were killed while trying to escape because that was what was reported to him by the same "special commission."

Notes

1. From research conducted in Copiapó by the journalist María Eugenia Camus for *Análisis*, November 19, 1985.

2. Camus, 1985, *Análisis*.

3. As stated by the author, this article appeared in the newspaper *Atacama*, published in Copiapó on October 18, 1973. *Ed.*

4. Camus, 1985, *Análisis*.

5. Judge Advocate translates in U.S. military ranking to military prosecutor, and that is the way the term has been translated throughout this edition. The speaker is referring a man who was the secretary of Major Carlos Enriotti Bley, military prosecutor, mentioned at the beginning of this chapter as one of the members of the court-martial.

6. Statement before human rights defense organizations.

7. Statement before human rights defense organizations.

8. Book of Records of the prison's armed guard. This record was released by Prison Warden No. 1, Alejandro Rojas Araya, who was in charge of the prison facility, to the judge of the Second Criminal Court of Copiapó on November 25, 1985.

9. Ascanio Cavallo Castro, Manuel Salazar Salvo, and Oscar Sepúlveda Pacheco, 1990, *Chile, 1973-1988: La historia oculta del régimen militar* (Santiago: Editorial Antártica).

10. Camus, 1985, *Análisis*.

11. Point No. 37 of the official testimony of General Joaquín Lagos Osorio.

CHAPTER 7

What Are We Going to
Do Now, General?

From Copiapó, on Wednesday, October 17, at approximately 10:00 a.m., General Sergio Arellano Stark phoned General Joaquín Lagos Osorio to let him know that he would arrive in Antofagasta the next morning, on October 18. "He was asking permission to enter my jurisdictional zone because he was coming by helicopter, by order of the Commander in Chief of the Army, to apply more uniform criteria for the administration of justice," Lagos said.[1]

General Arellano, whose formal title was Delegate of the Government Military Junta and the Commander in Chief of the Army, had to be very careful with protocol. Although General Arellano was acting as the representative of General Augusto Pinochet, who held the highest governmental/military power, General Lagos, Commander of the First Division, had more seniority than Arellano, which made Lagos his superior according to military protocol. In the telephone call, General Arellano did not tell Lagos that he had been designated as Pinochet's "delegate," nor did he mention it when he arrived in Antofagasta. Arellano ignored the point until the end of his visit, according to General Lagos.

"He said he would arrive in Antofagasta the following day, October 18, 1973, at approximately 1000 hours and that they needed quarters for 10 people. I told him to land at the headquarters of the Esmeralda Regiment and that he could stay at my house. When I asked him who was accompanying him, he mentioned, among others, Lieutenant Colonel Sergio Arredondo González, who had been the executive officer when I commanded the Coraceros Regiment. This is the reason why I told him that Commander Arredondo could also stay at my house," General Lagos claimed 13 years later.[2]

After the telephone conversation, General Lagos instructed Public Relations Chief Major Manuel Matta Sotomayor and his aide, Captain Juan Zanzani Tapia, who worked in the governor's office, to prepare for the arrival of the delegation.

"That same morning I received a telephone call from General Oscar Bonilla, minister of the Interior, who mentioned the possibility that the

Antofagasta Bar Association might defend those people with pending charges," stated General Lagos, who immediately arranged a meeting with the leaders of the Bar Association at his office.

Around noon that day, the Bar Association's leading members arrived, including President José Luis Gómez Angulo, Directors Mahomud Tala Rodríguez, Ignacio Rodríguez Papic, Carlos Marín Salas, Horacio Chávez Zambrano, and Luis Fernandois. General Lagos stated General Bonilla's request, explaining to them that they were seeking "to achieve a proper administration of justice, guaranteeing respect for all procedural rules to ensure that the people charged would be appropriately defended. Everyone, without exception, accepted my request and thanked me for this measure."

After that meeting, General Lagos had an interview with the attorney from the capital, Gastón Cruzat Paul, and with Luis Fernandois, a lawyer from Antofagasta. Cruzat represented the family of the prisoner Eugenio Ruiz-Tagle Orrego, and he requested that Fernandois conduct the defense before the court-martial. "I told them that, according to the agreement recently made with the Bar Association, there was no problem with their request," Lagos pointed out.

On Thursday, October 18, at approximately 10:00 a.m., General Lagos went to the Esmeralda Regiment to welcome General Sergio Arellano Stark and his entourage: Lieutenant Colonel Sergio Arredondo González, Majors Pedro Espinoza and Marcelo Moren Brito, and Lieutenants Juan Chiminelli and Armando Fernández Larios. Captain Emilio de la Mahotier piloted the helicopter.

Lagos recalled, "On his arrival, I asked General Arellano to tell me the reason for his visit. He answered that he brought an order from the Commander in Chief of the Army, General Augusto Pinochet Ugarte, to regularize the standards applied in the administration of justice, which seemed reasonable to me — given the situation and considering that this reinforced what General Bonilla had requested the day before."

General Arellano also asked for a meeting with the military garrison's personnel, the officers and permanent staff, saying that he had been entrusted with a special assignment by the commander in chief of the army. When Lagos asked him for details, Arellano answered that it involved the behavior of the garrison's personnel in the country's current situation. Lagos replied that Pinochet himself had recently been to Antofagasta and had dealt with the personnel extensively on that issue and that both he and his unit commanders had consistently insisted on this point as well. However, Arellano insisted, so Lagos set up a meeting in the Mechanized Unit

Training School, where he introduced Arellano to the staff. Lagos remembered that meeting:

"General Arellano focused his presentation on the conduct of the military, which should be exemplary, avoiding any abuse of power. At the end, I told him that his presentation had contributed nothing new. Then we went with General Arellano and Commander Arredondo to have lunch at my house, and the rest of delegation went to the Hotel Antofagasta, where a reservation had been made. Before going to lunch, I told the Division Chief of Staff, Colonel Sergio Cartagena, to make the necessary arrangements for the afternoon, as the general would work in my office in the division, and I would work in the governor's building. I also asked him to order the division's military attorney, Lieutenant Colonel Marcos Herrera Aracena, to show General Arellano the summary cases that had been decided and the ones that were still being processed, so that they could see them together and relate them to the new procedures brought by General Arellano, also so that a memorandum could be drafted for me to analyze later.

"During lunch, the conversation centered exclusively on the situation in Santiago, and neither General Arellano nor Commander Arrendondo said anything about what they had done the night before in Copiapó, which was an area under my division. (In fact, the Commander of the Copiapó unit, Lieutenant Colonel Oscar Haag Blaschke, also had not reported anything to me.) We finished lunch and went to work, General Arellano to my office in the division and I to the governor's office."

In the afternoon, General Lagos was informed that General Pinochet was flying from Santiago toward Iquique and that his plane would make a maintenance stop in Antofagasta. He notified the local heads of the navy, the air force, and police, as well as General Arellano.

"At approximately 6:30 p.m., we were all in the airport hangar, but General Arellano was missing. The chiefs of the armed forces and police of Antofagasta asked me why General Arellano wasn't with us but instead was with his own people on the landing strip, approximately 100 meters from where we were. I told them that I had not noticed and did not know the reason for that behavior. At the same time, I explained to them the reason for his trip, repeating what General Arellano had told me. When the commander in chief's plane arrived, I greeted him and reported that Antofagasta was absolutely peaceful. After greeting the other generals,[3] along with General Arellano, who had joined us by then, I informed him [General Pinochet] of the conversation that I had had with General Bonilla and my meeting with the directors of the Antofagasta Bar Association. That conversation was witnessed by the generals of Antofagasta as well as by General Arellano."

General Pinochet knew that he would see Arellano and his entourage in Antofagasta. Proof of this is that Pinochet especially sought out Colonel Sergio Arredondo to give him the good news that he had appointed him director of the Cavalry School, a position that normally fell to a colonel of that branch.

When General Pinochet's plane left, General Lagos offered to take General Arellano back to the city in his car. "Because of this, Commander Arredondo, who was standing there, asked me if he could borrow the vehicle that was assigned to General Arellano. I assumed he was going to visit his brother who lived in Antofagasta to tell him that General Pinochet had named him director of the Cavalry School. Therefore, I agreed to the request and sent greetings to his brother, who I knew."

On the way from the airport to Lagos' house, the car carrying the two generals was driven in a normal manner, with the driver respecting all the traffic lights and signs.

"General Arellano was surprised. He told me that that was stupid, that you had to run all the lights and make the escorts clear the way. I told him that I thought it was unnecessary and even arrogant. It wasn't even justified for security reasons, since we were living in a climate of peace in Antofagasta," General Lagos assured me, remembering details of what had happened that day on October 18, 1973, in an interview we had almost 16 years later.

When they arrived at General Lagos' house before dinner, Lagos asked Arellano how he thought the administration of justice was going in Antofagasta, in view of the instructions he brought from his superior. Lagos said, "He told me there was nothing important to mention and that the next day we would talk about the details he had already discussed with the military attorney. While we were having dinner, Commander Arredondo phoned, and I answered. He apologized, saying that he wouldn't be on time to eat with us. I believed that he was at his brother's house. Before we finished dinner, General Arellano expressed concern that he had not been with the people who worked with him that day. They were staying at the Hotel Antofagasta. I told him not to worry, that I would personally drive him over to see them at the hotel. Today, I remember that he didn't mention that concern again, and by the time we retired to our rooms, Commander Arredondo still had not arrived."

"The next day, October 19, 1973, after breakfast, which was served in our rooms, after 0800 hours, we were ready to go to the Esmeralda

Regiment's heliport for General Arellano's departure to Calama. The military attorney of the division, Lieutenant Colonel Marcos Herrera Aracena, arrived to get some signatures from General Arellano. According to what General Arellano himself said, it was for work carried out the previous day. After General Arellano's helicopter left for Calama, I was not told about anything being out of the ordinary. I went to the intelligence office in the governor's building, I would estimate, at approximately 1000 hours on October 19, 1973."

No, Lieutenant Colonel Arredondo had *not* gone to see his brother the night before. And General Lagos discovered this in a dramatic way as soon as he reached the governor's building. Major Manuel Matta Sotomayor, chief of public relations, asked to speak to him. Matta came into the office with a contorted face, General Lagos recalled:

"'What are we going to do now, General?' asked Major Matta.

"'Do about what?' I said, intrigued.

"'But what? Don't you know, General, what happened last night?' Matta asked with a mixture of amazement and consternation.

"'What are you talking about?' I asked.

"'But . . . you really don't know, General?' Major Matta stammered.

"'No, I do not know what you are talking about. Say it immediately, Major!' I demanded, irritated.

"Then he told me that during that night, the General's entourage took 14 detainees, whose cases were in process, from the place where they were being held to a ravine called the Quebrada del Way and killed all of them with submachine gunfire and repeater rifles. After that, they took the bodies to the Antofagasta Hospital morgue, and since it was very small and all the bodies didn't fit, most were left outside. All of the bodies were mutilated, with approximately 40 bullet wounds each. At that time, they were lying out in the sun so that everyone passing by could see them.

"When I heard about this horrible massacre, I was stupefied, and I felt enormous indignation for these crimes perpetrated behind my back in my area of jurisdiction. I gave orders to the military and civilian doctors to reassemble the mangled bodies and to notify the relatives so that the bodies could be returned to them in the most respectable and expeditious manner. While I was doing that, I received a telephone call from my wife at home, who demanded an explanation of what had happened because there were more than 20 women standing in front of our house, crying loudly. They were asking for the reason why their husbands, sons, or brothers had been killed, and they begged her to intercede so that the bodies would be returned to them. I briefly explained to my wife what had happened, that I had just that moment been informed, and that I would do everything I could to return the bodies in the most dignified way possible. Then my aide came in, Captain Juan Zanzani Tapia, who was telling me that the directors of the Antofagasta Bar Association were urgently requesting to speak to me. I asked them to come in immediately, despite the mood I was in.

"The directors of the Bar Association said that they were sorry they could not comply with my request from the previous day because of what had happened the night before, when 14 prisoners had been murdered without judicial sentences. I told them that I had just found out what had happened at that very moment, that everything had been done behind my back, and that I had not called the court-martial or signed any sentences. I thanked them for their cooperation, and I told them that this would perhaps be the last time I saw them, because I would turn in my resignation from the army to the commander in chief of the army because of these events.

"That day was very hard for me: arranging for and organizing the transfer of the bodies to the relatives. I recall that I even asked Father José Donoso, whom I had appointed chaplain of the jail, to tell some of the relatives about the execution of their loved ones. I tried to telephone General Pinochet, which turned out to be impossible because he was traveling between Iquique and Arica. I urgently wanted to tell him what General Arellano and his entourage had done.

"On the afternoon of that day, I held a meeting with the unit commanders of the Antofagasta Garrison in my office in the division. The following people attended: Chief of the General Staff, Colonel Sergio Cartagena (now deceased); Colonel Adrián Ortiz G., Director of the Mechanized Unit Training School; Lieutenant Colonel Enrique Valdés P., Commander of the Artillery Unit; Lieutenant Colonel Lagos Fortín, Commander of the Infantry Unit; Lieutenant Colonel Victorino Gallegos, Commander of the Telecommunications Unit; and Lieutenant Colonel Juan Bianchi G., Logistics Unit Commander. My first question to them was whether they had any knowledge of what had happened the previous night. They were all silent. Then I asked who had provided the vehicles to transport the prisoners to the Quebrada del Way and then the bodies to the morgue. Colonel Adrián Ortiz G., Director of the Mechanized Unit Training School, told me that he had done so. 'Under whose orders?' I asked him. But this time he didn't answer me. I told them that I was the one in charge and that only with my authorization could vehicles be moved, especially if they were going to be used in this fashion.

"I reproached them for their total lack of loyalty and added that I was not taking any actions because the following day I would present my resignation to the commander in chief of the army, who was on his way back from Iquique to Santiago. Unanimously, they asked me not to resign, given the country's present circumstances. But I told them that I did not accept this abuse and that these crimes had tainted the army and the country and had been carried out without respect for the law."

General Lagos later expanded upon this point of his testimony: "The silence of the unit commanders was probably due to their surprise. They did not understand my question because they were all convinced that I knew everything, that I actually knew all about General Arellano's mission. So they didn't understand what was happening to me. And I, furious, did not understand what had happened. Imagine my state of mind! A general of the Republic had been my guest for a few hours and, behind my back, had ordered the murder of 14 detainees, prisoners who for the most part had given themselves up voluntarily, trusting in me. I was responsible for those prisoners, according to the Geneva Convention! In military school and in war games, we were taught to respect the Geneva Convention regarding the treatment of prisoners. We had to protect them from every violent act, and we had to make every effort to be good 'lawyers' if we were assigned to serve in their defense in the court-martial. It was outrageous — they had massacred 14 defenseless prisoners behind my back!"[4]

*****

The night of the 18th of October 1973, on General Joaquín Lagos' appointment book, was marked with blood, while a veil of grief covered the homes of the families and friends of the 14 victims of this horrible slaughter, as General Lagos, chief of the zone under state of siege, characterized it.

All of the death certificates were the same:

Date: October 19, 1973.
Time: 0130 hours.
Cause: acute anemia, wounds caused by projectile.

Publicly, General Lagos decided to lie to keep what he called his "authority over the citizens." First, he separated the victims into groups, to try to give the impression of separate executions. Then, in four cases, he used the charge that they were extremists. The press at the time reported the following regarding these four men:

El Mercurio, Santiago, October 21, 1973

MASS MURDER PLOT UNCOVERED IN ANTOFAGASTA

The execution of Mario Silva Iriarte, Eugenio Ruiz-Tagle Orrego, Washington Muñoz Donoso, and Miguel Manríquez Díaz was carried out. These individuals were all implicated in the formation of the so-called "industrial belts." The official communiqué of the Public Relations Office of the Chief of the Zone Under State of Siege reported that "the executions were ordered by the Government Military Junta to accelerate the process of Marxist purification and to focus efforts on national recovery."

La Defensa, Arica, October 25, 1973.

FOUR EXTREMISTS SHOT

Antofagasta, 25. Four extremists were executed at dawn pursuant to the sentence of the court-martial of the city: Mario Silva Iriarte, Eugenio Ruiz-Tagle Orrego, Washington Muñoz Donoso, and Miguel Manríquez Díaz. The four were captured on September 12 when they tried to put into practice a sinister Marxist plan, a part of Plan Zeta to attack and murder members of the armed forces. Therefore, they have paid with their lives for their nefarious and bloody scheme to murder their countrymen.

In the case of three others, the following was reported:

El Mercurio, Santiago, October 24, 1973

THREE EXTREMISTS EXECUTED

A communiqué from the Public Relations Office of the Chief of the Zone Under State of Siege stated the following: "By decision of the Honorable Government Junta, three people were shot by firing squad at dawn on the 20th: Luis Eduardo Alaniz Álvarez, Danilo Alberto Moreno Acevedo, and Nelson Guillermo Cuello Álvarez, all of whom were engaged in political activities and terrorist conspiracy."

In the cases of the other seven men, the chaplain of the jail gave the news to the relatives.

*****

Who were these victims in Antofagasta? The first seven, listed below, were publicly identified as terrorists in order to justify their deaths:

- **Mario Silva Iriarte**: 38, married, five children, attorney, general manager of the Chilean Development Corporation (Corporación de Fomento — CORFO) in the north of Chile and regional secretary of the Socialist Party. He appeared voluntarily before the new military authorities.
- **Eugenio Ruiz-Tagle Orrego**: 26, married, one daughter, engineer, general manager of the state-owned cement company (Industria Nacional de Cementos, S.A. — INACESA), active member of the leftist Catholic Unity Popular Action Movement (Movimiento de Acción Popular Unitaria — MAPU). He appeared voluntarily before the authorities.
- **Washington Muñoz Donoso**: 35, government representative in the private beer brewery corporation (Compañía de Cervecerías Unidas). He was arrested at his home.
- **Miguel Manríquez Díaz**: 24, married, one son, professor, employed by INACESA, active member of the Socialist Party. He was arrested at his home.
- **Luis Eduardo Alaniz Álvarez**: 23, journalism student at the Universidad del Norte, active member of the Socialist Party. He appeared voluntarily before the new military authorities when his name appeared in the military proclamation.
- **Danilo Moreno Acevedo**: 28, driver for the state-owned CORFO, labor union leader, active member of the Socialist Party. He appeared voluntarily before authorities. The military court sentenced him to three months' imprisonment and closed the case (process number 396-73) because he was already dead.
- **Nelson Cuello Álvarez**: 30, employed by CORFO, active member of the Socialist Party. He appeared voluntarily before authorities.

The names of the other seven men executed in Antofagasta are provided below. Their families were notified by the prison chaplain:

- **Mario Arqueros Silva**: 45, governor of Tocopilla, active member of the Communist Party. He was arrested at his home.
- **Dinator Ávila Rocco**: 32, a worker in the María Elena mine of the state-owned Chilean Mining and Chemical Company (Sociedad Química y Minera de Chile – SOQUIMICH), active member of the Socialist Party. He was arrested at the mine. A military court sentenced him to two months' imprisonment after he was dead (process number 398-73).
- **Marcos de la Vega Rivera**: 46, married, three children, engineer, mayor of Tocopilla and active member of the Communist Party. He was arrested at his home.
- **Norton Flores Antivilo**: 25, social worker, employed at state-owned SOQUIMICH, active member of the Socialist Party. He was arrested at his home.
- **José García Berríos**: 66, labor union leader for Antofagasta's dock workers, active member of the Communist Party. He was arrested at his home.
- **Darío Godoy Mancilla**: 18, high-school student, active member of the Socialist Party. He was arrested at his home.
- **Alexis Valenzuela Flores**: 29, labor union president at SOQUIMICH, labor union leader for the United Federation of Chilean Workers (Central Única de Trabajadores de Chile – CUT) in the north of Chile, councilman of Tocopilla, active member of the Communist Party. He was arrested at his home.

Normally, the paucity of the information for this sort of list has two causes: either the families' fear prevents them from contacting human rights defense organizations, or the families are exiled, so that contact becomes impossible.

To try to understand what happened in Antofagasta, it is important to look more closely at the actual story of some of these individuals, for example, Tocopilla's Mayor, Marcos de la Vega, age 46, a building contractor, who was married with three children. The story told by his sister is heartrending:

"After the coup, the people told him to leave Tocopilla, to go somewhere safe. But Marcos would answer, 'Why should I leave if I haven't stolen a peso, if I haven't taken anyone's job away, if all the books in the mayor's office are up-to-date, if I haven't done anything bad?' Thus, he worked until September 16th in his office. That day the newspaper published that all the authorities of Tocopilla would be arrested. So he came home in the afternoon, asked for thick clothing, ate, asked for a hot cup of *mate,*[5] and he sat down to wait for them. The police surrounded the house, entered with submachine guns, and took him away. They treated him very badly. One day the wife of Governor Mario Arqueros went to speak with a military prosecutor, and she saw Marcos pass by with a bloody mouth. She told the prosecutor, and precisely at that moment she saw her husband go by in the same condition. On October 14th we saw him [Marcos] in the Tocopilla jail. He embraced us firmly, and he asked us for a field bed because he was being taken to Antofagasta the next day. From then on, we took clean clothes to him every day in Antofagasta. But on Saturday the 20th, they rejected my clothes at the jail. And then on Sunday the 21st, one of the guards told us that the chaplain wanted to talk to us. He told me he was dead. We couldn't believe him because Marcos was not ill. On Monday the 22nd, we went to the morgue, telling ourselves that they were wrong and that there must have been some mistake."[6]

But there was no mistake. Marcos de la Vega, mayor of Tocopilla, was there. "They gave us his blood-soaked clothes in a plastic bag. We could only see his face and one hand that had a wound as if a nail had been driven through it. The truth is that several bodies had the same mark on their hands. It was a deep wound. One officer became angry because we had bought a coffin with glass. He wanted the coffins to be completely sealed. They didn't allow us to have a wake. We had to go from the morgue directly to the cemetery. We begged them to let the cortege pass in front of our house, but they did not allow it. The obituary that I paid for in person to go in *El Mercurio* did not appear. When we got to the cemetery, it was full. The people were running from one burial to another. And in Tocopilla, when the news spread, people ran out into the streets crying. They had to shoot into the air to get them back into their houses. After the burial, our mother lay down on her bed, and she died of grief five months later. My father tried to hang himself — he was so desperate. One of Marcos' daughters would scream that we should all go out and make a formal complaint so that we could all be killed. In the beginning, his three children seemed brave, and they would say publicly that their father had been killed because he was a communist. Then they went into a depression phase. The little girl talked all day with her invisible father. They fled to Holland in 1976."

The case of Miguel Manríquez Díaz is also very moving. He was 24, married, the father of one child, and had graduated in physical education. He was a socialist and worked in the National Cement Industry plant (Industria Nacional del Cemento — INACESA). Miguel was arrested on September 24 in his house. His family could not see him since he was held in solitary confinement, and his father only found out about his death two days after it had happened: "While I was in the chapel of the San Luis School, accompanying the relatives of a friend who had died, Father José Donoso came up to me and told me that my son had been shot."

Miguel Manríquez' father described his son's body as he viewed it in the morgue: "His hands were tied with wire, the kind used for electricity, and around his neck he had a black handkerchief. I momentarily thought that he had been blindfolded." When he went to get his son's personal effects in the Antofagasta jail, he saw that the notary, Vicente Castillo, who worked with the court-martial proceedings, was standing at the door. When he passed by, the notary said to him, "This is terrible; this is terrible!"[7]

Another chilling story is that of Mario Silva Iriarte, manager of CORFO-Norte. He was a lawyer, age 37, a socialist, married, and the father of five children. On the day of the military coup, he was assigned to go on a special mission to the CORFO headquarters. He heard his name in a military proclamation, and he left for Antofagasta immediately. His wife, Graciela Álvarez, remembered, "He arrived on the morning of September 12. He told me he had decided to give himself up to the authorities because he had nothing to hide. We went to the governor's office at approximately 8:00 in the morning, and he was arrested. In the afternoon, along with other prisoners, he was taken away. I will never forget his gesture when he left: he raised a closed fist. They put him in an open military truck that moved slowly through the streets so that people could see the prisoners. They took him to the Cerro Moreno Air Base, where I saw that he was shackled, barefoot, surrounded by guards who pointed their submachine guns at him. Then they transferred him to the jail, and he told me that several times they had simulated a firing squad. I tried to speak with the military prosecutor, Lieutenant Colonel Marcos Herrera Aracena, but I was only able to see him on October 19. Then he told me that my husband had been shot at dawn that day.

"To think that he gave up voluntarily because he believed in the professionalism of the military — he never imagined they were capable of mass murder," Graciela Álvarez reflected.

She continued, "General Lagos gave us permission to bury him in Vallenar. The casket came sealed. We couldn't see his body. We went directly to the cemetery in a pickup truck and van lent to us by CORFO. We were not authorized to hold a funeral or put up a headstone."[8]

The grief-stricken family of attorney Mario Silva Iriarte was forced to abandon the house assigned to the general manager of CORFO immediately. They continued to be discriminated against. Their summer house in Chañaral, for example, purchased in 1968, was expropriated by decree. Three years later, there was a new assault on the memory of their father and husband in a report sent to the Organization of American States (OAS) by the military government. The report was published as follows in *El Mercurio* newspaper:

El Mercurio, Santiago, June 9, 1976.

The first military tribunal of Antofagasta tried Mario Silva Iriarte, in court case process number 349-73, for the following crimes:

a) Illegal association,
b) Endangering external security and the sovereignty of the state,
c) Embezzlement of public funds, and
d) Fraud and illegal extortion .

His participation in these crimes was proved convincingly.[9]

Lies on top of lies. Just after Mario Silva Iriarte was murdered, General Lagos had publicly explained his "execution," saying that he was captured while he was trying to implement a plan to assassinate soldiers. In addition, three years later, the military government informed the country and the world that he was also a common thief. The grieving, desperate family's hands were tied. What could be done in those years? In 1979, attorney María Inés Morales Guarda asked the military prosecutor to verify whether Mario Silva Iriarte had been tried. The First Military Tribunal's answer was negative. Moreover, it was verified that in case process number 349-73 (the government report to the OAS) Mario had not been included. That process number was actually for another case in which three prisoners were sentenced to five years of internal exile.[10]

The family of Eugenio Ruiz-Tagle Orrego, manager of INACESA until the military coup, also had to endure the same kinds of repeated lies. Eugenio's mother, Alicia Orrego, remembered, "Eugenio gave himself up on September 12 to the new authorities after his name appeared in a military proclamation. From that day on, he suffered physical abuse and was never allowed to speak with his lawyer. In fact, lawyers Cruzat and Fernandois spoke with General Lagos, and he promised to rescind Eugenio's incommunicado status. I reached Antofagasta on October 18 at night. The next morning, I was told at the jail that I could see him on the following day. When I arrived [on the 20th], I was told that he was incommunicado."

The authorities did not dare tell Alicia Orrego that her son was already dead. She found out through one of the official communiqués that appeared in the press on October 21. "They didn't let me go into the morgue. I was only able to see my son's body already in a casket, with the window part sealed. I cannot give first-hand information about the physical torture that he endured. I didn't see his body, but the attorney and the employee of the funeral home both cried when they told me about it. I can speak about his neck, his face, and his head. What they described is etched with fire in my memory forever. He was missing his left eye. The lids were swollen, but he had no wounds or cuts. They took out his eye with something in cold blood. His nose was broken, pierced, swollen on the inside, and detached as far as one of the nostrils. His lower jaw was broken in several places. The mouth was a swollen bloody mass, and you could not see his teeth. On his neck, he had a long, wide cut that was not very deep. The right ear was swollen, cut, and torn from the lobe upward. He had signs of burns or, perhaps, a superficial bullet wound in the right cheek that was very deep. His forehead had small cuts and bruises. His head was turned at a strange angle, which made me think that he had a broken neck. I know he had two bullets in his body, one in his shoulder and the other in the stomach."[11]

*****

Eugenio Ruiz-Tagle Orrego's family was traditional and conservative. He was the black sheep because of his decision to join the leftist Unitary Popular Action Movement (Movimiento de Acción Popular Unitaria — MAPU). His mother did everything possible to use the family's influence to help her son. In fact, from General Lagos' testimony, it is clear that two important lawyers told him on October 17, 1973, the day before Eugenio's murder, that they would take over his defense. And a few days after the killings, on November 1, 1973, General Lagos stated that while he was in Santiago meeting with General Pinochet, the general "gave me a letter from the attorney for the family of Eugenio Ruiz-Tagle Orrego, Mr. Gastón Cruzat Paul, which registered a complaint regarding the death of his client and censured the attitude of the division military attorney, Lieutenant Colonel Marcos Herrera Aracena."

On General Pinochet's desk was the official report of the deaths that had been requested the day before from General Lagos by the Armed Forces Command (an organization that Lagos had never heard of). In the report, just as in the Copiapó case, General Arellano's responsibility was recorded in writing. The following is a verbatim report regarding Antofagasta:

II Antofagasta:
a) By decision of the Commander in Chief of Antofagasta: 4
b) By the Delegate of the Commander in Chief of the Army (General Arellano): 14

General Joaquín Lagos Osorio decided to end his military career. It was clear that he could not be relied upon for the "work" that the military power demanded. In February 1974, General Lagos was transferred to Santiago, and eight months later he was retired. Thirteen years after the murders, in 1986, General Lagos raised some questions about certain points contained in his previous testimony and said, in a sworn statement, "There are still the following questions in my mind: Why did General Arellano do everything behind my back? Why wasn't a court-martial convened, an institution in which all the people charged have the right to a lawyer?"[12]

General Arellano's defense holds that with respect to the events of Antofagasta, "The facts narrated by General Lagos are quite reliable because my father knew nothing about what happened in La Serena and Copiapó. In addition, Lagos knew nothing about what happened in his jurisdiction because his subordinate, the military governor of Copiapó, did not inform him about the death of the 13 prisoners. His [General Arellano's] activities in Antofagasta were the ones described by General Lagos: a meeting with personnel of the military garrison (officers and permanent staff), lunch in Lagos' house, a review of the cases with the officer who was the military attorney, a trip to the airport to greet General Pinochet, and supper and lodging at General Lagos' house. And at 8:00 in the morning of the following day, after having breakfast, he left without knowing what had happened in Antofagasta while he slept. General Lagos says that a little before leaving the house, the military attorney showed up 'to get some signatures.' He [General Arellano] did sign some papers that were only instructions drafted the previous day, which had been typed after the meeting they had held. These working memoranda were signed in General Lagos' house, and they obviously stayed in the files of the division." This is what attorney Sergio Arellano Iturriaga asserted.

Notes

1. Deposition by letter, requisition No. 23620, of General Joaquín Lagos Osorio, given July 3, 1986.

2. Deposition by letter, requisition No. 23620, of General Joaquín Lagos Osorio, given July 3, 1986.

3. The generals in charge of the army, air force, and national police in Antofagasta.

4. On August 12, 1949, after three months of work, the diplomatic conference that reviewed the Geneva Convention of 1929 Relative to the Treatment of Prisoners of War was signed by the nations of the world. Its objective: that humanity would never again have to live through the barbaric transgressions that occurred during the Second World War in the treatment of Jewish prisoners.

On September 12, 1973, the day after the military coup in Chile, the government Junta dictated Decree Law No. 5, through which it declared that the state of siege it had declared the previous day should be understood as "a state or time of war" only with respect to military justice. Said decree-law was published by the *Official Gazette* on September 22, 1973, and, from that moment on, political prisoners became prisoners of war. This was officially communicated to the prisoners by the chiefs of the camps where they were detained, at the same time that the International Red Cross began its relief work on these cases.

Some of the articles of the Geneva Convention pertaining to this case are the following:

Part 2 General Protection of Prisoners of War

Article 12 Responsibility for the Treatment of Prisoners

Prisoners of war are in the hands of the enemy Power, but not of the individuals or military units who have captured them. Irrespective of the individual responsibilities that may exist, the Detaining Power is responsible for the treatment given them. . . .

Prisoners of war may only be transferred by the Detaining Power to a Power which is a party to the Convention and after the Detaining Power has satisfied itself of the willingness and ability of such transferee Power to apply the Convention. When prisoners of war are transferred under such circumstances, responsibility for the application of the Convention rests on the Power accepting them while they are in its custody.

Nevertheless, if that Power fails to carry out the provisions of the Convention in any important respect, the Power by whom the prisoners of war were transferred shall, upon being notified by the Protecting Power, take effective measures to correct the situation or shall request the return of the prisoners of war. Such requests must be complied with.

Article 13 Humane Treatment of Prisoners

Prisoners of war must at all times be humanely treated. Any unlawful act or omission by the Detaining Power causing death or seriously endangering the health of a prisoner of war in its custody is prohibited, and will be regarded as a serious breach of the present Convention. In particular, no prisoner of war may be subjected to physical mutilation or to medical or scientific experiments of any kind which are not justified by the medical, dental or hospital treatment of the prisoner concerned and carried out in his interest.

Likewise, prisoners of war must at all times be protected, particularly against acts of violence or intimidation and against insults and public curiosity.

Measures of reprisal against prisoners of war are prohibited.

Part 3 Captivity

Article 17 Questioning of Prisoners

Every prisoner of war, when questioned on the subject, is bound to give only his surname, first names and rank, date of birth, and army, regimental, personal or serial number, or failing this, equivalent information.

If he willfully infringes this rule, he may render himself liable to a restriction of the privileges accorded to his rank or Status. . . .

No physical or mental torture, nor any other form of coercion, may be inflicted on prisoners of war to secure from them information of any kind whatever. Prisoners of war who refuse to answer may not be threatened, insulted, or exposed to unpleasant or disadvantageous treatment of any kind. . . .

The questioning of prisoners of war shall be carried out in a language which they understand.

Section 3

Article 120 Death of Prisoners of War

. . .The detaining authorities shall ensure that prisoners of war who have died in captivity are honourably buried, if possible according to the rites of the religion to which they belonged, and that their graves are respected, suitably maintained and marked so as to be found at any time. Wherever possible, deceased prisoners of war who depended on the same Power shall be interred in the same place.

Deceased prisoners of war shall be buried in individual graves unless unavoidable circumstances require the use of collective graves. . . .

Article 121 Prioners Killed or Injured in Special Circumstances

Every death or serious injury of a prisoner of war caused or suspected to have been caused by a sentry, another prisoner of war, or any other person, as well as any death the cause of which is unknown, shall be immediately followed by an official enquiry by the Detaining Power. . . . If the enquiry indicates the guilt of one or more persons, the Detaining Power shall take all measures for the prosecution of the person or persons responsible.

5. *Mate* is a beverage like tea, brewed from a leaf similar to holly, popular in Argentina, Chile, and other South American countries.

6. From testimonies recorded by the Vicarate of Solidarity (Vicaría de la Solidaridad) and the Chilean Human Rights Commission (Comisión Chilena de Derechos Humanos).

7. From testimonies recorded by the Vicarate of Solidarity and the Chilean Human Rights Commission.

8. From testimonies recorded by the Vicarate of Solidarity and the Chilean Human Rights Commission.

9. General Lagos publicly released this information in the three newspaper reports from *El Mercurio* and *La Defensa* cited earlier in this chapter, based on the official military proclamations.

10. Internal exile meant that the prisoner was transferred to a very remote location. Sometimes the military dictatorship would send dissidents to mountain villages in the north, areas in the extreme southern tip of Chile, or even to small islands that were practically uninhabited.

11. Testimonies recorded by the Vicarate of Solidarity and the Chilean Human Rights Commission.

12. Deposition by letter, requisition No. 23620, of General Joaquín Lagos Osorio, given July 3, 1986.

CHAPTER 8

Everything Is Ready, General

The helicopter that transported General Sergio Arellano and his entourage arrived in Calama at approximately 10:30 a.m. on Friday, October 19, 1973. The Commander of the 15th Infantry Calama Regiment, Colonel Eugenio Rivera Desgroux, was notified of General Arellano's arrival the day before by the Division Commander, General Joaquín Lagos Osorio, who had received him in Antofagasta. General Lagos did not tell him why General Arellano was coming, so Commander Rivera thought it might be related to the case of Major Fernando Reveco Valenzuela, of Calama, who had been under arrest in Santiago since the beginning of October (see Chapter 3, this volume).

With those first thoughts, Colonel Rivera began our long interview and continued to explain the Caravan of Death's dramatic episode in Calama.

"Why did you think that the visit of General Arellano was related to Major Reveco's arrest?" I asked.

"Because I was convinced that Arellano was a military judge in Santiago, given the fact that he was commander in chief of the Second Division," he answered.

"But Arellano was not a judge at the time. He was in charge of Troop Command. The Commander in Chief of the Second Division was General Herman Brady."

"That's right. I was wrong. I really thought he had that position. When you leave Santiago you more or less know what is happening in the capital, but I was wrong about Arellano. And the fact is that General Lagos did not tell me what Arellano was coming for. I made the preparations to receive him with a program and all of that," Commander Rivera answered.

"Did you know him?"

"Yes, very well."

"Did he act normally when he arrived in Calama?"

"No. He was very strange. We were wearing our service uniforms, dressed appropriately to honor a general. But when the door of the helicopter opened, all of them came out with steel helmets, uniforms full of ammunition clips, and submachine guns."

"A helicopter with combat soldiers."

"Yes, in combat mode. We, on the other hand, had a military band and were in perfect formation to render honors. It was very strange — look, we practically never use steel helmets. This helmet is like a plastic chamber pot inside, covered with another one made of steel. It is tremendously heavy and uncomfortable. It's only used in combat."

"You thought it strange that General Arellano was dressed like that?"

"But not only because of his combat uniform. He was also very tense, in total contrast to the way we greeted him, as a friend and our chief. He seemed surprised at the honors we gave him. Here is an interesting detail. I had been assigned to receive him at the base. In retrospect, I understand why he tried to pass through the city unnoticed. But at that time, the order to prepare a heliport was impossible to follow. We were in the middle of repairing the sewers, installing electricity, providing drinking water, and leveling the interior courtyards."

"So you had no level courtyard able to receive a helicopter?"

"Correct. The Regimental Command told Antofagasta that the helicopter could not land there and that they should land at the airport. As soon as he arrived, General Arellano rejected a big part of the program I had prepared and told me that he had come to review and accelerate the trials."

"When did he tell you that he came as delegate of the commander in chief?"

"In the office, he showed me the paper that said that he was a delegate of the commander in chief, signed by General Pinochet."

"And what did that mean to you?"

"That this made him supreme chief and military judge. That's the way I understood it. He became the judge from that moment on. In fact, he asked me for all the cases, both those that had been sentenced and those that were pending. He reviewed them, and he congratulated me."

"Were you with him while he did so?"

"Yes, he reviewed them in my office between 11:00 a.m. and 1:00 p.m. Then he asked that a court-martial be established at 2:30 p.m., after an official lunch that I had planned in his honor, with police officers and the regiment."

"Did General Arellano participate in the court-martial?"

"No."

"Did you?" I asked Colonel Rivera Desgroux.

"No."

"Who took part in it?"

"It was presided over the first time by National Police Prefect, Colonel Abel Galleguillos. The members were Major Luis Ravest, Captains César Zabala and Víctor Santander, and the lawyer Claudio Mesina Schultz. As prosecutors, Lieutenant Colonel Oscar Figueroa and Police Major Osvaldo Arriagada. The lawyer was Claudio Mesina Schultz. Lieutenant Álvaro Romero was secretary, the actuary was the noncommissioned officer Jerónimo Rojo, and the typist was Rosalba Flores."

"And what happened to the members of General Arellano's entourage?" I inquired.

"When we were waiting in the hall for the beginning of the court-martial, Commander Arredondo appeared and asked whether he could interrogate the prisoners in the jail."

"Whom did he ask for permission?"

"I think it was General Arellano because he was the one who authorized him."

"Didn't you think that the request was strange?"

"No, because I didn't know what task General Arellano and his team had assigned to him. The truth is that I didn't leave Arellano for a second, not even to go the bathroom. Bear in mind that we had known each other for several years, we had been together in military school, and we had gone to Arica together. So, while the court-martial was taking place, we walked together through the regiment's facilities. Moreover, everything was very informal when we went to Chuquicamata, at approximately 3:30 p.m. I drove with General Arellano at my side and the driver behind. We went in two or three Jeeps."

"Didn't you think it was strange that four officers of the entourage stayed on the base: Commander Sergio Arredondo, Major Pedro Espinoza, Major Marcelo Moren Brito, and Lieutenant Armando Fernández Larios?"

"No, because of what I just said. They stayed to interrogate the prisoners in the jail. Now that you mention Fernández Larios, I remember that they introduced him as an 'outstanding combatant in the assault of La Moneda.' I was struck that someone so young was a part of General Arellano's General Staff."

"You stated that all of you returned to the base at approximately 8:00 p.m. and that when you drove in, 'The officer of the guard told me that the court-martial had already finished its activities and that the officers were in the mess hall waiting for General Arellano's farewell dinner'?"[1]

"That is right."

"There is something I don't understand, Colonel. Why didn't the officer report to you what had already happened? Why didn't he tell you that the court-martial had finished abruptly because the prisoners could not be present in court, given the fact that they had already been executed?"

"Maybe it was my fault. I was driving, and my question to him was, 'What's going on in the court-martial?' The officer on guard answered, 'It is already over, and the officers are in the mess hall waiting for the dinner.' I immediately sped up."

"Is it possible that the officer on guard had not realized that General Arellano's General Staff might have left with officers and soldiers of the base to go to the jail to get the prisoners?"

"He must have known. I insist that it could have been my fault — I am high strung by nature, and perhaps I didn't give him time to inform me. Or perhaps the problem was so serious that the poor kid, a second lieutenant, did not dare tell me. Because he must have taken part in everything that happened. Because General Arellano's General Staff first came to look for personnel; then they came to look for tools and some bags for the bodies."

"And all the material, it went through the Guard?"

"Yes, of course."

"Colonel, if the officer on guard knew and the court-martial had already met on the base and had found out about the execution of 26 prisoners, the whole base must have known. The dinner, was it normal? Did you see concerned, tense faces, at least among the members of the court-martial?"

"Since I didn't imagine that something like this could have happened, I did not perceive anything abnormal."

"How can you explain that none of your subordinates approached you to tell you during that dinner? How do you explain that your second-in-command, Commander Figueroa, or the regiment's chaplain didn't tell you?"

"I think that, given my personality, I did not give him the opportunity to tell me. I'm very high-strung. Maybe Commander Figueroa wanted to tell me, and I didn't understand."

"When?"

"Just before we went in to dinner, at the door of the officers' mess club. He addressed General Arellano and told him, 'Everything is finished, General. You must sign the pertinent documents.' And he gave him some papers. I then offered him the use of an office so that he could review and sign the documents. He answered, 'It's not necessary, Commander, I'll sign right here.' And he signed them on a small table in the mess hall. Then he looked at me and said, 'Implement the decision tomorrow.' When he heard him say that, Commander Figueroa told him, 'Everything is ready, General.' Arellano only said, 'Good.'"

"Do you believe that Commander Figueroa tried to tell you in that way?"

"Could be, but I didn't understand. For me it was only this: whatever Arellano ordered was done. Because every military chief is responsible for what he does."

"Do you believe that, from your second-in-command downward, everyone interpreted that you were aware of the executions, since you were physically with Arellano all day?"

"Could be."

"And that explains why no one informed you about what they assumed you knew."

"Could be."

"It's difficult for civilians to understand."

"For me, everything was developing normally until that moment. There were no complaints: the food was on time, good food, and the waiters were there with appropriate uniforms at the right time. Everything was quite proper. In fact, I was very calm because everything that happened in the regiment was Arellano's responsibility, because he was the chief at the time."

"That's why you didn't ask Figueroa what documents he brought to be signed?"

"Sure. It wasn't my place to ask."

"Did only General Arellano sign?"

"Just Arellano, and he signed them in front of me. The truth is I never read those documents."

"What happened after dinner?"

"We went to the airport to say goodbye to General Arellano and his group. The helicopter took off at approximately 11:30 p.m. to Antofagasta."

"Why Antofagasta?"

"Because that was the itinerary. He had left his luggage in Antofagasta."

"What happened after the helicopter left?"

"Commander Figueroa, whom I had noticed acting very strangely — he seemed very tired after the dinner — came up to me and told me, in spurts, that in the afternoon something very serious had occurred. That the court-martial had to be suspended because when they called the defendants, he was told that they had all been shot following the orders of Colonel Sergio Arredondo."

"How did you react?"

"I could not believe it was true. I didn't understand anything. I gave orders to return to the base immediately, and I called a meeting of officers to receive complete confirmation of what had happened. When I entered the base, I found a tremendously tense situation. Some of the men were even in a state of shock. Among the noncommissioned officers, there was pain and consternation because the brother of a corporal had been shot. I waited until 12:30 a.m. for the officers to meet, but finally I decided to convene the meeting at 7:00 in the morning the next day."

"Why?"

"Because at that time, Captain Carlos Minoletti and other officers and personnel of the engineering company had not returned. On orders from Colonel Arredondo, they were burying the bodies out in the *pampa* (countryside, desert). Besides, everybody was very agitated."

"Did you find out the details of what had happened?"

"I asked Commander Figueroa to summarize the events. He told me that the court-martial had summoned the persons charged at approximately 5:00 p.m., and he was told that, on orders from Colonel Arredondo, 26 people had been taken from the Calama jail to Topater Hill and had been executed there. In view of this, the president of the court, Police Colonel Abel Galleguillos, ordered the session adjourned.

"Commander Figueroa added that when he left the court, he thought he should clarify what had happened. He found out that, with the authorization given by General Arellano, Colonel Arredondo and his team went to the Calama jail with a reinforcement of officers and soldiers from the base, took 26 prisoners, and then transferred them to Topater Hill. There, Colonel Arredondo's team interrogated the prisoners and proceeded to execute them.

"When the executions were over, Colonel Arredondo ordered Captain Minoletti, commander of the Engineering Company, to use personnel from his unit to bury the bodies in the pampa.

"Finally, Commander Figueroa decided that it was imperative for him to document the events. On the advice of attorney Claudio Mesina Schulz, he drafted death sentences for the men who had already been executed. And those were the documents signed by General Arellano in front of me in the hall of the officers' mess club."

"They killed them on Topater Hill?"

"Yes, it is a hill very close by, two or three blocks away from the base, on the other side of the Loa River, a location that had a good backdrop for shooting."

"You have stated that you only read the names of the 26 people murdered in those documents."

"Yes, I did it the following morning because I had to prepare the military proclamation."

"But why didn't you take those documents and read them?"

"Because I didn't want to involve myself in anything that was outside my responsibility."

"Weren't you even curious?"

"How could I be curious with all the problems that were coming down on me!"

"That's why you didn't want to see them?"

"No, I did not touch or see them. Because it wasn't my problem. It was clear to me that the entire aberration was not my responsibility. It is a military concept: The chief is responsible. And if I became aware of the matter, I would have to get involved."

"What happened to those documents?"

"The military attorney's office sent them to the military court in Santiago, according to procedure."

"Did you then decide to prepare the text of the military proclamation?"

"I ordered Major Luis Ravest to draft the military proclamation with Figueroa, the executive officer. Before making it public, I called my superior, General Lagos, in Antofagasta at approximately 9:00 in the morning."

"How did you tell him what happened?"

"Very cautiously because we were using a public telephone. We did not have a direct intercom. I told him what had happened half in code. I told him, 'The visit went through here, and an enormous number of people have fallen. I'm going to make this public through a military proclamation that says that while they were being taken to Antofagasta, there was an escape attempt, and the birds fell.' He told me not to do such a foolish thing."

"Why lie?"

"Me?"

"Yes, you. Why did you want to lie?"

"Because I could not accuse a superior officer. I had to protect General Arellano as a general, and, second, the army had to be protected from this aberration, and, third, I also had to protect the Military Junta because it would be a tremendous blow if their delegate had indeed committed such an atrocity."

"So, you had to lie?"

"Right. It was the result of an analytical discussion I had with my officers and my General Staff: What do I do, how do I say it? There had to be a compassionate lie to be able to fix at least part of this. My wife becomes outraged whenever I say this. But I couldn't make the truth public, the mass murder."

"What did General Lagos order you to do?"

"Not to make the military proclamation public. To communicate it privately, family by family, and to ask one responsible member of each family to sign for it in acknowledgment."

"Did he say anything to you about what happened in Antofagasta?"

"Yes, he told me that they had just reported that something similar had occurred in Antofagasta. That he was going to inform General Pinochet, who was passing through there that day."

"The fact is that you considered what happened a mass crime?"

"That's right."

"Did you investigate which persons in your regiment had participated in this crime?"

"No, I never investigated who participated."

"Why?"

"Look, in the morning meeting that day with my officers, if I recall correctly, I started out by saying, 'Gentlemen, we don't have any responsibility in these events. I don't want to know anything about this matter because it is not our responsibility.'"

"You understood that General Arellano was a delegate of the commander in chief of the military Junta and that he was carrying out that mission by superior orders?"

"That's what the paper he showed us said, that he was empowered to take over."

"Therefore, you never imagined that General Arellano was violating the orders that he had received?"

"To me, he was carrying out a mission, and, according to disciplinary regulations, he should do so according to conscience and according to the law."

"And if he fails to do so, he is responsible."

"That's right. He is responsible."

"Colonel, why was your lie incoherent? You wanted to cover up the crime with the story of the escaping prisoners, but you also ordered that 'shot by firing squad' should be written on the death certificates."

"I ordered it like that because I couldn't continue lying. All I could do was mitigate it a bit. And when Dr. Luis Rojas Delzo, the military doctor who was director of the Calama Hospital, asked me, "What do we write?" I said, 'Shot by firing squad.' I didn't think about it twice. I never imagined at the time that this contradiction was going to cause me so many problems, that it would make me appear to be a traitor to the army."

"Didn't you ask General Lagos for some instructions regarding what to do with the bodies? You knew the families were going to request them."

"No, because they were already being buried when I found out what had happened. That must be very clear. The bodies were being buried, starting at 6:00 or 7:00 p.m. When I arrived for the evening meeting, I postponed it because some officers were burying the bodies and others were there, out of control. Officer Hernán Núñez even suffered a nervous breakdown. He was later chief of Civilian Organizations of the military government. I was told that he had to undergo some violent forms of treatment so that he would react, because he had participated in the slaughter and they had ordered him to finish off someone, I don't know who."

"Let's see, let's go over the facts. You know that the bodies had already been buried, you know that they buried them in bags, but you're also sure that some of your personnel who buried them know where they are."

"Yes, Captain Minoletti directed that operation."

"Didn't you ask General Lagos what to do?"

"No, because I was the superior officer in the zone."

"But General Lagos decided to reassemble the mangled bodies and hand them over to their relatives in Antofagasta."

"When I proposed the possibility of handing them over, I was told that they were scattered on the pampa and that they were all butchered. The officers of my General Staff, Figueroa, Ravest, and others told me this."

"Butchered?"

"Yes, butchered. I was told that so-and-so would take out his *corvo* (curved knife, scimitar) and would insult each prisoner while he ran him through. This happened especially with Haroldo Cabrera."

"So it wasn't only bullets, but also corvos?"

"Yes, knives."

"Did you confirm with the doctor the condition of the bodies?"

"Yes. I remember he told me, 'Colonel, the bodies cannot be returned because they are dismembered, mutilated.' I proposed the possibility of returning them in sealed caskets. He told me, 'No, because they will open them. Just imagine how we will look if they see them!'"

"So you also lied when you offered to return them a year later to the families?"

"Yes, that's right. Another compassionate lie. Because I knew from experience that in the north bodies do not decompose. They remain intact but dry."

"You offered to return them, knowing that you wouldn't do it?"

"Please, put yourself in my place. Early on Monday the 22nd of October, 1973, my wife saw a great number of people in front of the door of the governor's office, the majority in mourning — horrible! She was very shocked. I arrived a few minutes later in my combat Jeep. And those people began crying, demanding that I return the bodies and that I explain what had happened. Earlier, on Saturday the 20th, the bishop had asked me to return the bodies and asked my permission to say a mass. However, I did not permit it. With much sadness, I told him, 'Monsignor, I cannot. Just imagine my problem here.'"

"Did you speak with the families?"

"I made everyone come in. The widows, as is the custom here in the north, wore long black veils. It was truly a dramatic scene. I began to try to explain the matter. Since I'm from the country and I have the experience of the Chillán earthquake (where my father, three brothers, and some other relatives died, whom I buried personally), I spoke for a long time about my grief, but the people insisted that I return the bodies. I couldn't tell them that it was impossible because of the state they were in. Because just as you have said, I had the power to locate them and unearth them. But I couldn't.

According to military regulations, I should have said: 'General Arellano, your order was to bury them in the pampa, but now I exhume them because I think it was an error on your part, given the situation I now have here.' There were moments when I thought about disobeying his orders, but my advisers' advice was, 'If we already have a scandal like this, when they see the bodies, everything will blow up.' That is why I committed myself to return them in a year, knowing that I couldn't, because the north's climate would not erase what was done to them in the massacre.

"At the end of 1974, when I was out of the army, a lady who was a widow of a worker from ENAEX asked me to keep my promise. I spoke with General Rolando Garay, who was then chief of the First Division, and with Colonel Eduardo Ibañez Tellerías. They agreed to look into the matter. Bishop Oviedo said that he also tried to do so. But nothing was accomplished."

"What did you do afterward? Did you complain to the highest level?"

"No. I had already complained to General Lagos on October 20, 1973, and then again when he asked me for the list of the people who had been shot, and I sent that to Santiago. There I clearly stated the names of the people shot by General Arellano's entourage."

*****

Thus, using Colonel Eugenio Rivera Desgroux's list, General Joaquín Lagos Osorio reported what happened in Calama. The following is his report:

III Calama:
a) By decision of the commander of El Loa: 3
b) By the Delegate of the Commander in Chief of the Army (General Arellano): 26

Twenty-six prisoners were slaughtered with firearms and corvos. That was Colonel Rivera Desgroux's statement, and his version coincides with the one given by a high-ranking officer in 1987, who had been in the Calama Regiment in 1973. Journalist Pablo Azocar interviewed him, and, as the officer was on active duty, he asked that his name be withheld.[2]

General Arellano's group, according to this officer, asked for the help of several lieutenants and soldiers of the Calama Regiment: "They asked for more people because they were going to get the prisoners to interrogate them. They said they needed security. And since those men then became a part of the entourage, they, therefore, became eyewitnesses to what happened."

"What was the first thing that the entourage did in Calama?" Azócar asked the officer.

"They asked to review the cases of all political prisoners. Some of the cases had been finished; others were about to be closed. Then Arellano asked that all the cases be reviewed. We were in the middle of that review when the entourage went to the jail and took 26 prisoners 'to interrogate them,' they said. Nevertheless, they took them from the jail at approximately 5:00 in the afternoon on the 19th, and one hour later they proceeded to execute them. So the situation was that while the cases were under review, the people were already dead."

The high-ranking officer added, "What we didn't know was whether that team was following the orders of General Arellano or whether it acted on its own. Because it's practically unthinkable that a group of officers would independently kill 26 people. And, besides, the Caravan had already passed through La Serena (October 16), Copiapó (October 17), and Antofagasta (October 18), where the same type of executions were carried out. This makes it highly improbable that this was a case in which they acted on their own."

"Do you have any information as to the way the executions were carried out?"

"According to the information we received later in the army, in some cases they even acted sadistically. Several were not shot but were killed slowly. Some of the witnesses became sickened by the executions. It was horrible. A typical example: They would fire a shot into the victim's legs, and then another shot closer to the heart, and that way they killed them little by little. There were even knives used. Armando Fernández Larios, who was in the group with Pedro Espinoza, Sergio Arredondo, Marcelo Moren, and Juan Chiminelli, was particularly cruel in that sense."

"Who got sick when they witnessed the executions?"

"Lieutenants Núñez, Moreno, and Díaz. They returned to the base literally sick. There we found out that they had all participated in that manner. 'Now it's your turn,' they would say, and they would pass around the weapons. Colonel Rivera and Commander Figueroa almost died when they found out what had happened. They were indignant — they just couldn't believe it. They even recalled at that moment that one of the people executed, Carlos Berger, was going to be freed the next day, after completing half of his 61-day sentence. This was confirmed when the cases were reviewed. Something similar happened to Silberman's driver, Carlos Piñero, whose only fault was having been the driver of the general manager of Chuquicamata mine. He was also to be freed in a few days."

Journalist Azócar's interview continued: "One witness (Grimilda Sánchez, who was imprisoned in the same place) stated that the platoon was led by Officer Marcelo Moren. Does this agree with your information?"

"Yes. Marcelo Moren was the one who acted as the chief despite the fact that Colonel Arredondo was present there and had a higher rank."

"In what state were the bodies after the killings?"

"We were told that some were unrecognizable. They shot them all over their bodies. They particularly took it out on Haroldo Cabrera, whom they apparently hated because he was hostile. They made him die slowly. The death of David Miranda Luna was heroic. He refused to be blindfolded. He was an old labor leader, a man who had been a communist since he was born. When they went to blindfold him, he said, 'No.' He said they should shoot him just as he was, that his conscience was very clear and that it should bear heavily on their consciences that they were killing an innocent man," the high-ranking officer said.

*****

Another important witness regarding what happened in Calama at that time was the Apostolic Church administrator, Monsignor Juan Luis Ysern. I spoke with him in the Archbishopric in Santiago, and he calmly narrated what he remembered, "I found out what happened in a way that left me very grief-stricken. I couldn't even speak. Some of the soldiers who participated in the firing squad were left there as guards that night, to watch over some of the prisoners who were on the base. The fact is that the soldiers spent all night talking about what had happened on the previous afternoon. And the prisoners could hear everything. They weren't able to sleep a wink; they tormented themselves, asking, why am I alive?"

"Did the prisoners tell you that?"

"One of the prisoners had them call me in early the next day and told me. I couldn't say anything; I couldn't reveal the source because that prisoner's life was at stake. I was left with tremendous sorrow, but I didn't dare say anything. At the prison exit, someone was calling my name, and it was Checura, the former governor of Calama, who was also a prisoner there.

When he saw me, he knew. He started crying, and I couldn't hold it any longer. Both of us began crying, embracing, just like little kids."

"What details were known, Monsignor?"

"The story was very general. It was a massacre. Yes, that's right, a massacre. We were all very afraid. I didn't dare to acknowledge that I knew about it, and I went home. Suddenly, a woman arrived at my house, a widow or mother; I don't remember. I pretended that it was the first time that I heard about this situation. And then, I went to speak with Colonel Rivera, who was area chief, and I requested the bodies of the executed people."

"How was Colonel Rivera?"

"He was very moved. He even asked me, 'What do I do, Monsignor?' I answered, 'In your case, I would have already tendered my resignation.' Then I became afraid of what I said, because, heavens, if good people and conscientious people resigned, cruel people would be put in charge. So almost simultaneously, I said to him, 'No, no, wait, don't tender it.'"

"Did he tell you what had happened in detail?"

"Yes. He told me that when he returned from Chuquicamata with General Arellano, the general had signed papers that had been given to him without giving them any importance, and when Arellano returned the papers, he had said, 'Carry out the order tomorrow.' And the executive officer said that everything had already been done. Colonel Rivera had even repeated, 'Mission accomplished, General,' without really knowing what it was all about. And they went to supper, and then they went to the helicopter to say goodbye. Just after the helicopter had left, Colonel Rivera found out what had happened. He arrived at the base and found his officers anguished, hysterical, just like little kids, and some were even vomiting. It was a real blowout inside the army.

"Colonel Rivera wanted to hold a meeting with the officers but couldn't because Captain Minoletti was burying the bodies. He had to wait until the next day. And when I went to talk to him about the problem of the bodies, he didn't know what to do. We looked for solutions together. They were already buried out in the desert, and Colonel Rivera had nothing to do with that."

"Was the possibility of exhuming them ever discussed?"

"Yes, and we examined the possibility of having a common grave in the cemetery and moving everyone there, so that the relatives would at least know where they were. Colonel Rivera asked me to organize the relatives so that they might go talk to him. I made a handwritten draft and gave it to one of the grieving relatives. I told them to organize and to go talk with Colonel Rivera. I didn't want to continue as mediator because they were already in direct contact. Later, I was surprised to learn that the idea of making a common grave in the cemetery was not going forward, that he had given them a certificate for the return of the bodies in one year."

"Today Colonel Rivera says that was a compassionate lie."

"I thought he had the intention of going through with it. What he himself called a compassionate lie at that time was what was published in the newspapers. He wanted to defend General Arellano, General Pinochet, and the whole thing. That's why he repeated the same excuse of that time, that they had been shot while trying to escape."

*****

Up to this point, the statements fit perfectly in the tragic puzzle of Calama. In contrast, General Arellano's son, speaking on his behalf as his defense attorney, asserted the following:

"My father arrived and reviewed the cases in the morning. Three death sentences had already been carried out early in October, and there were a dozen prisoners being held for the case of the explosives plant. That was most serious problem in Calama: a loss of explosives had been detected in Chuquicamata, a fact that seemed doubly dangerous because that's where the ENAEX explosives factory was. Military leaders were convinced that an attack was being planned against that plant.

"After lunch, General Arellano went with Colonel Rivera to Chuquicamata. They spent the whole afternoon in the field, studying the security problem. When they returned, a dinner was planned for the entire garrison. A little before going into the dinner, my father found out about the massacre that had occurred that afternoon. The truth is he does not remember who told him or informed him about it. The fact is that he showed his shock in front of all those present. He severely reprimanded Colonel Arredondo, the highest-ranking officer left in Calama, and asked him what had happened.

"'They rebelled, and we had to shoot them,' Arredondo said."

"'Put it in writing!' General Arellano ordered."

"'But, General,' Arredondo stammered."

"'In writing — draw up a document immediately!' ordered Arellano again.

"Colonel Arredondo drew up the document describing the death of the prisoners who had 'mutinied,' while they were being transferred to be court-martialed. This document was photocopied and was added to all the cases of the people who had died. The fact is that this document was added to only 23 cases; three were missing. I saw that document, and it was signed by Arredondo," I was assured by attorney Sergio Arellano Iturriaga.

He added, "In that same discussion, my father found out that 14 prisoners had died in Antofagasta. He does not remember how he found out. He then decided to return to Antofagasta immediately to clear up everything that had happened with General Lagos."

General Arellano's defense states that it was in Calama where he found out for the first time about the massacres in Calama and Antofagasta. Following the logic used by the defense, we must make a correction: He did not find out about the "massacres" but about the deaths of prisoners for trying to escape or "mutiny." And if Colonel Arredondo accepted the responsibility for what happened, signing a document that was then added to the other cases, this acceptance did nothing more than to use a lie to cover up the mass crime.

Colonel Eugenio Rivera stated that the episode of the public confrontation between General Arellano and Colonel Arredondo did not take place. Under oath, he said he only saw General Arellano sign some documents and that later his executive officer informed him about the content of the papers: death sentences to "document" the situation of those who had already been executed. And General Arellano's defense held that he "did not sign sentences, but rather the instructions for Colonel Arredondo's document that was going to be added to each case."

However, the different versions of these events does not negate the central fact: Twenty-six prisoners were killed without any legal procedures being followed. Colonel Rivera stated that, when he found out about the "massacre," he decided not to investigate what had happened. "I don't want to know anything about this matter because it is not our responsibility," he had said to his officers. And General Arellano stated that he found out about the 40 deaths perpetrated by his entourage — 14 in Antofagasta "for trying to escape" and 26 in Calama for rebellion — and did not order an investigation to clear up what really had happened. He was satisfied with the document signed by Arredondo. But did he think such macabre "coincidences" were possible? That for two consecutive days his General Staff had to kill all the prisoners they were interrogating because they tried to escape?

Didn't he have the power and the duty to investigate right there, in Calama, what had happened?

*****

There were 26 victims in the episode that Monsignor Ysern characterized as "a coup within the army." Who were these 26 men? Nothing is recorded in the files of human rights organizations about some of them, as in the cases of Carlos Álvarez Acuña, David Garrido Muñoz, Víctor Ortega Cuevas, Roberto Rojas Alcayaga, Jorge Yung Rojas, Hernán Moreno Villarroel, and Luis Alfonso Moreno Villarroel, the last two probably brothers.

Very little is known about the others. Carlos Piñero Lucero was the secretary and driver for the Cobrechuqui general manager's office. Luis Hernández Neira, a worker in the mine, was arrested at his house on September 30. Rafael Pineda had been fired from his job after the coup and was arrested when he was about to board a plane for Valparaíso to look for work. Carlos Escobedo Caris was also a driver in Cobrechuqui; he was 24, married, and had a newborn son.

As to the murdered workers from ENAEX, the explosives plant, let's first look at the case of the labor leaders. Domingo Mamani López, who was 41, married, and the father of four children, was president of the Employees Labor Union (Sindicato de Empleados). He was arrested at his house on October 12. He was sentenced to 24 years of internal exile (exile within Chile), south of the 38th parallel. He felt ashamed of his "privileged" treatment because his friends Busch and Valdivia had been shot on October 6th, and he had said to his family at that time, "I should be dead just like them." Another labor leader, Bernardino Cayo Cayo, who was 42, married, father of two children, was arrested at the ENAEX plant on October 12, along with nine other workers. The same events occurred in the cases of Geranio Carpanchay Choque (age 28, married, four children); Milton Muñoz Muñoz (age 33, married, one daughter); Ignacio Gahona Ochoa (35 years old); and Rolando Hoyos Salazar (age 38, a socialist), a worker and director of the industrial union. In fact, the case of Hoyos is especially significant. He is the victim (mentioned earlier in this chapter by Colonel Rivera Desgroux) whose brother was a corporal in the regiment. Corporal Guillermo Hoyos Salazar "was sent as the driver of the military truck to Tocopilla at 5:00 p.m. on October 19. He was told to go on that mission because his brother was going to be shot," asserted the widow.[3]

Manuel Hidalgo Rivas, who was 23, had one daughter, and his wife was pregnant, was also an ENAEX labor leader. In the case of Rosario Aguid Muñoz Castillo, who was 26, a worker, married, and Socialist Party member, the complaint filed by his wife, Lidia Olivares (who was in her eighth month of pregnancy) partly explains the mass arrest of ENAEX workers: "On one of the nights prior to the coup, he [Rosario] took part in a watch so the plant wouldn't be taken over by the military. Eleven workers participated in that task." When one of those 11 workers, Francisco Valdivia, the president of the workers' union, was arrested, sentenced, and shot, the rest presented themselves voluntarily to the police to state what had really happened. They were freed. On October 12, when they were entering the lunchroom, they were arrested.

The narrative of Lidia Olivares, the widow of Muñoz Castillo continued: "My husband told me that everybody would be sent to internal exile. But on the 19th, I went to see him at approximately 5:00 in the afternoon, and they told me that he was not in jail. At that time, I saw they were taking five prisoners with their hands pressed behind their necks, between a double file of soldiers. They put them into pickup trucks and then made them lie face down. The soldiers sat on the sides, on the railings."

The next day, October 20, Chaplain Luis Jorquera came to Lidia Olivares' house.

"Are you alone, ma'am?" the chaplain asked.

"Yes, Father, alone," she answered.

"I must tell you that unfortunately your husband was court-martialed and killed," the chaplain said softly.

"No, I don't understand you, Father," she mumbled, without taking her hands away from her swollen abdomen. She was eight months pregnant.

"Ma'am, is there another adult in the house?" the chaplain asked.

"No, Father. What you just told me, what does it mean?" she insisted.

"I'm telling you that your husband was shot by a firing squad," he finally said.

Lidia Olivares said that she felt the room turn upside down, and a painful contraction made her lose her balance. The priest caught her and left her on a sofa, sobbing and moaning, while he ran to get help from the neighbors. Aguid del Rosario was born shortly afterward.

Fernando Ramírez Sánchez, age 26, another of Calama's 26 victims, was a supervisor in La Exotica mine and worked as the secretary of the Socialist Youth in Calama. He was married with two daughters, one of whom had hydrocephalus. This case presents a complete family drama. Three people in this family were arrested. Fernando's father, engineer Luis Busch, was executed by a firing squad on October 6. Luis Busch's widow, Grimilda Sánchez, had received a long sentence and was in a jail cell when the prisoners were taken away on October 19 and loaded into a military vehicle. Among them was her son Fernando.

Mario Argüelles Toro, age 34 and married, was a socialist who owned a small business. He was arrested on October 1, charged with hoarding food, and on October 16, he was sentenced to three years of internal exile south of the 38th parallel. His wife, Violeta Berríos, saw him a few minutes before the military group arrived to take him from the jail: "He already knew that he was going to be exiled to the south for three years and that they would be coming for him at any time. He asked me to bring him warm clothing." She went to the police station to get more information and, a little after 6:00 p.m., a policeman told her to go to the jail because "they are taking people out to kill them." She ran, and when she arrived, she heard shots in the distance. She asked the guard what was going on. "It sounds like a cannon," he answered.[4]

The case of another one of Calama's dead, José (Pepe) Gregorio Saavedra González, is especially moving. He had not yet turned 18 and was the president of the Calama School Student Center. When he returned from classes on September 24, he was arrested and taken to the interrogation center in the ENAEX plant. Then he was transferred to the jail. This is his last letter to his mother:

Mama:

Today they took 30 people and exiled them to the South, maybe they will also take the 24 of us who are still left here. They only took the leaders.

When you come tomorrow, bring me thick clothes and canned goods and another pair of shoes. Ask Rojo if it's true that they're taking us away; then you can prepare yourselves to bring the necessary things.

Tell all my friends to come and say goodbye, just in case. Maybe they'll take us to Dawson Island,[5] across from Punta Arenas. Tomorrow Tuesday — visit — all of you please come.

A kiss from your son,
Pepe

P.S. Cigarettes, lots of cigarettes.

Pepe's mother had run the concession stand at the noncommissioned officers' (NCOs') mess hall on the base. That's why he asked her to contact NCO Gerónimo Tomás Rojo, who was working in the military prosecutor's office. As it turned out, Pepe would not need the thick clothes, canned goods, or cigarettes to get him through his sentence of 541 days' internal exile south of the 38th parallel. Since Pepe was the youngest child, his older brothers tried to keep their parents from finding out what had happened, but their mother eventually found her 17-year-old son's death certificate.

Another victim of the death squad in Calama was Alejandro Rodríguez Rodríguez, who was 47, a socialist, married, and had five children. He had been mayor of Calama and leader of the Confederation of Copper Workers (Confederación de Trabajadores del Cobre — CTC). He worked in Chuquicamata and was arrested on September 14, when he responded to a military proclamation summoning him to the governor's office. He never had a trial.

Also killed in this group was Haroldo Cabrera Abarzúa, age 34, finance vice-manager of the Chuquicamata mine. A socialist, he was trained as a commercial engineer and had four children. During the 1989 interview I conducted with Major Fernando Reveco Valenzuela,[6] president of the court-martial of Calama and the person in charge of the military occupation of the mine, the case of Haroldo Cabrera came up as follows:

"Were many of the officers very harsh?" I asked Major Reveco.

"Yes. They asked for the death sentence for the most innocuous misdemeanors. There was one person who had a good reason to want these men to disappear. He had been an intelligence officer, and he handled dollars when they were very scarce. It surprised us all; we even discussed his case with the deputy commander and wondered where he got those $100 bills he was flashing around. That's why he wanted to kill the prisoners immediately, because he wanted to cover up his corruption."

"Who gave money to this officer?"

"The finance office of the Chuquicamata mine, which Haroldo Cabrera had been in charge of. It seems that they assigned him [the intelligence officer] a monthly quota of dollars. And he told them that nobody could know about this because it was to finance intelligence work, to pay Chilean agents in Bolivia. That's why he wanted these men to die before they talked. On the night of the coup, he began to promote the idea of killing them. It seemed strange to us, and we talked about it with the second in command."

And Major Reveco went on to say, "On the night of the coup, Haroldo Cabrera sent for me, and we met. There, he told me that he was in anguish about the whole matter, that he had given the intelligence officer approximately $1,000 for intelligence work and that this could be evidence that he had never acted against the regiment."

Thus, on September 12, Assistant Finance Manager Cabrera turned himself in to Colonel Rivera, confident that everything would be cleared up quickly. Major Fernando Reveco remembered the trial and the court-martial clearly: "That was a more serious case. We discovered that there was a grenade factory in the garage of his house. He swore he had rented the garage to someone and that he did not know what was going on in there. The truth is that he had no need to rent out the garage, and while it is true that Cabrera was very loving with his family, it was very strange that he would have explosives right next to his wife and children. That partly convinced us, in the court-martial, and that's why we gave him a very stiff jail sentence, many years, but not the death penalty." Haroldo Cabrera's death certificate, exactly like that of the other 25 prisoners, stated:

Date: October 19, 1973
Time: 1800 Hours
Cause: Destruction of the thorax and cardiac region.
Execution by firing squad.

In Calama, the Caravan of Death also executed David Miranda Luna, assistant manager of Cobrechuqui mine, secretary-general of the Mining Federation, and a communist leader. He was 48, married, and had four children, the youngest five years old. He had only been working in the mine for eight months at the time of the military coup. Through a military proclamation, the new authorities summoned him, and he reported in. However, on September 17, he returned home for a few hours under house arrest, and a military patrol arrested him again. His wife, María Magdalena Michea, saw him in jail. She remembered their encounter as follows:

"'What can I bring you, sweetheart? Should I bring a lawyer?'

"'No, no, what do I need a lawyer for if I can defend myself?'

"'But it could be good to hire a lawyer,' I had insisted.

"'What do I need a lawyer for, sweetheart, if this is not going to be long? Look, I'm getting out of here soon. So don't do anything.'"

María Magdalena then decided to go to Santiago to see how those of her children who lived there were doing. A telegram from her oldest son [David, Jr.] urged her to return quickly. She recalled, "We arrived, and there was David sitting on a sofa, calm and somber. I asked him why he hadn't gone to wait for us. He didn't answer. I asked what he had heard about his father. He didn't say anything; he was silent. I insisted. Then he stood up, he embraced me hard, and he said, 'They killed him, Mother, they killed him.'"

María Magdalena couldn't believe it. Desperate, she ran to see the military chaplain. When she found him, María recalled that he told her, "'Look, it's true. Unfortunately, in your husband's group, one guy rebelled before reaching La Piedad, and they all went wild.'" Since she never saw her husband's body, she couldn't believe that he was dead for a long time. And, in her search for information, she was able to talk with a soldier from the Calama Regiment. "He told me that General Arellano was screaming at the regiment's colonel, that he was scolding him because he had not ordered them killed earlier. If that general hadn't come here, this slaughter wouldn't have taken place, because the colonel, whose name was Eugenio [Rivera Desgroux], was very kind to us. If there had only been the military from here, this wouldn't have happened. They came here from Santiago to kill."

Finally, we come to the last victim we have information about, the Director of El Loa radio station, Carlos Berger Guralnik, a young journalist and lawyer, who was married to lawyer Carmen Hertz and was the proud father of Germán, who was a few months old at the time. Major Fernando Reveco, who presided over the court-martial, remembered him as "tall, good looking, elegant. We charged him because the radio continued to broadcast after the order to shut down the station. We gave him a few days of jail time, 61 days. No more, because it was a misdemeanor."

Carlos Berger and his family had arrived in Calama only 25 days before the military coup, as he was to become director of the El Loa radio station. At a critical moment, he decided that he should collaborate, in his capacity as radio announcer, to help the area of Calama, a rugged area of miners, recover a climate of tolerance and respect. His widow, Carmen Hertz, recalled:

"Carlos was arrested in my presence, at the El Loa radio station, by a large armed contingent on the day of the coup at 11:00 a.m., because he refused to stop radio broadcasts. Both in Chuquicamata and in Calama, there was no armed resistance, and the mine continued to operate normally, which was confirmed by Colonel Rivera and Major Reveco in their testimonies. Carlos was sentenced to 61 days in prison in the Calama Public Jail for what was characterized by military justice as 'a misdemeanor.' Moreover, he was notified of the sentence. Because I'm a lawyer and because I went every-where with my little boy since I didn't have anyone to leave him with, there was no problem visiting Carlos every day, first at the base and then in the jail.

I could even characterize the treatment given to me by the guards and officers as cordial and deferential.

"Since there was good will and we were not from the area," Carmen continued, "the only thing we wanted to do was to return to Santiago quickly, so on October 18, I asked the military prosecutor to commute the days left in Carlos' sentence for a fine. He agreed verbally, but he pointed out that the petition had to be made formally. At noon on the following day, October 19, I brought him the necessary documents. Nevertheless, the prosecutor told me that he couldn't accept my request, pointing out that the situation had changed, without giving me any additional information. He only alluded to the fact that that day a helicopter had arrived in the city with a group of officers from Santiago, under the command of General Arellano Stark. It was the first time I had heard the name of that general.

"Since I couldn't understand what was happening, what this new situation meant and what consequences these things might have, I went to the jail to tell Carlos. It was approximately three in the afternoon. I found him extraordinarily nervous and worried because they had taken half of the prisoners from the jail, hooded and shackled, to an unknown place. Even in the jail I also noticed different measures. For example, they didn't let us go into the courtyard where we had always gone, but rather to a special room. I stayed with Carlos until approximately 5:00 p.m. He was tanned, wearing his jeans and his shirt, carrying his pipe. We said goodbye with a kiss. His last kiss.

"I went up to Chuquicamata where I lived, and about two hours later I found out that the rest of the prisoners left in the jail had also been taken to an unknown destination. I called the warden of the jail on the telephone, because I couldn't go down there due to the curfew. He told me not to worry because all the political prisoners had been taken to the base to give routine statements. He didn't know anything else. I kept calling every half hour until approximately 12:00 p.m., and the answer was always the same: 'They'll be arriving soon; they'll be arriving soon. Don't worry.' First thing in the morning, I went down to Calama. In the governor's office, I ran into a horrible scene: There were public officials crying, hysterical, and a colleague, the governor's secretary, embraced me disconsolately and told me, 'Carmen, they shot all of them!' I asked her what she was talking about. And she added, crying, 'They shot Carlos — they shot him yesterday.' I couldn't understand anything. I thought that everyone was crazy and that it couldn't be true. He had only one month left in his sentence! There was even a good chance of immediate freedom! It had to be a mistake.

"I went to the base immediately. When I arrived, I noticed a really tense and chaotic atmosphere: Different military officials were running everywhere, and it was very difficult to get someone to see me. An officer named Shejman told me that the prisoners, including my husband, had been transferred the night before to Santiago to different detention centers. When I heard this contradictory story I began to take steps, which ended with an interview in the afternoon with the Governor, Colonel Eugenio Rivera. He told me to wait at home, that he would find out and would send me the exact information about my husband's whereabouts."

At about 8:00 p.m., during the curfew, according to Carmen Hertz, the call came. The caller, without identifying himself, asked to speak with Eduardo Berger, Carlos' brother, who was a doctor at the Chuquicamata Hospital. So he picked up the phone. The voice said to leave the house and go to the corner. And then he hung up. Carmen insisted on going with her brother-in-law. They went outside, and at the corner next to the sidewalk was a military Jeep. Inside were two soldiers and a priest: Lieutenant Alvaro Romero, NCO Jerónimo Rojo, and Chaplain Luis Jorquera. This was the "commission" named by Colonel Rivera to inform the families. Carmen said she would never forget the scene because it was so frightening: "One of the soldiers stood up inside the Jeep and began to read a text. I remember the part that said, 'When the prisoners were being transferred to Antofagasta, they tried to escape, and they were all killed.'"

It couldn't be. He's dead? And his body? No ma'am, the bodies won't be returned. It's a mistake. It must be a mistake. Safe-conduct to travel to Santiago. The highway all night. No, it can't be. Why, there he was in jail, wearing his jeans, his shirt, holding his pipe. No, it can't be. Santiago early at dawn, be careful with the military patrols, be careful when they shout halt. And there Carmen was, at Carlos Guralnik's mother's house, Dr. Dora Guralnik's. Carmen recalled the moments before she broke the news to Carlos' mother: "I had to tell Dora what had happened. And while I spoke, I shivered and shivered. I couldn't stop shivering. It was true. Carlos was dead. In Santiago, I got the death certificate: destruction of the thorax and cardiac area — execution by firing squad. Time: 6:00 p.m. Just one hour after I said goodbye to him in the jail. Just one hour later."

*****

Carmen Hertz and her son Germán then left for Buenos Aires. Carlos followed them in their dreams: "I dreamed about him every day. I would run into him at the airport, at the station, and he was alive, always arriving and arriving." And while Carmen Hertz took refuge in her dreams, the relatives of other victims had similar experiences. David Miranda's widow, Magdalena Michea, wrote letters to the Chacabuco concentration camp. It must be a mistake, she reasoned, David couldn't be dead; she hasn't seen the body. And while she wrote, Pepe Saavedra's father couldn't find solace for the loss of his only son, his youngest child, only 17. Almost mute to the world, he concentrated on building a wooden fence for the house — every day for one year, without using a single nail. Meanwhile, the sons of Rolando Hoyos said that their father was still alive. Luis Gahona's sister refused to go to mass or to any activity that reminded her of what had happened because she chose to believe that Luis was still alive somewhere.

Not to see the bodies, not even to know that their loved ones were buried in a mass grave in the cemetery — as in La Serena and Copiapó — made the families' mourning for the men killed in the Calama tragedy even deeper. During 12 years of silence, many families walked through the desert, looking for clues, for traces of the bodies. After 1985, when what happened was finally made public, the search intensified.

In April 1986, lawyer Luis Toro, of the Vicarate of Solidarity, located the person who seemed to be the closest witness. Mario Raúl Varas Varas testified before a judge from Antofagasta, and they went together to the place where the bodies had been buried. This place had also been pointed out in a judicial statement by a young female amateur archeologist. She had found the burial site in 1980, and she was puzzled to find bones dressed with contemporary clothing instead of clothing from 1973. But by 1986, the corpses had been removed, and they have never been located.

Mario Raúl Varas' testimony follows: "When the undersigned was a service manager of SENDOS[7] in Calama, in October 1973, I sent an electrician named Díaz, who worked for my company, to a place in the filter plant on Topater Hill to install some telephone wires. This was at about 8:10 in the morning in October; I don't remember the exact date. The electrician returned, running into my office at approximately 9:30 a.m. and told me the following:

"'Mr. Mario, when I was on top of the pole, I saw a bulldozer moving earth and carrying in its shovel parts of a bunch of dead people, and the same shovel would then bury them. I got scared, and I took off toward the hills, and I came right over to tell you.'"

Mario Raúl Varas explained, "I immediately went to the place (the telephone pole), and I saw this machine smoothing down the area so as not leave signs of the little mounds.

"That same day in the month of October 1973, many people went to the governor's office that was headed by Colonel Eugenio Rivera Desgroux, shouting for their husbands and brothers."

Mario Raúl Varas says he then drew a map of the place and gave it to Bishop Carlos Oviedo. Let us review the facts of Varas' statement: The electrician Díaz, up on the telephone pole, saw how the bodies were being buried with a bulldozer. Varas, the manager of SENDOS, pointed out that it was in the morning, which would have been the morning of October 20, 1973.

In my interview with Colonel Rivera Desgroux, I touched on this point. "Colonel Rivera," I asked him, "there is a testimony that states that the bodies were buried the day after the massacre. And you insist that it happened that same night."

"I don't know any more than what I've said. When I found out what had happened, I immediately returned to the base, and I wanted to meet with my officers. But Captain Minoletti Arriagada and other officers were not there because, according to what I was told, they were burying the bodies on the orders of Colonel Arredondo. I was also informed that the bodies were mutilated, butchered," Rivera Desgroux assured me.

"Colonel, after the Calama massacre, did you ever see General Arellano again?"

"Yes, at the beginning of 1974, in Santiago."

"Did you mention the matter of Calama?"

"No, but at the end of March, Military Attorney Vega, who worked with General Arellano, came to my office. He told me, 'Look, Colonel, I have a tremendous problem; I'm missing the cases of the people who were shot in Calama.' I said to him, 'Oh, how strange! But General Arellano already knows about that. Many of those people were shot without a trial.' Vega left, and we never again spoke about the matter."

"When did you leave the army?"

"In 1974. I was punished for everything that happened: for trying to defend Major Reveco, for writing 'executed by firing squad' in the death certificates, for everything. Formally, I was not promoted to general. But basically [I was punished] because I was no longer 'trustworthy.'"

"After what happened in Calama, did you know that General Lagos submitted his resignation to General Pinochet?"

"Yes, Colonel Lagos told me," Colonel Rivera replied.

"Did you think about resigning from the army at the time?"

"No. My wife always asks me why I didn't resign then. But I was a professional soldier, and I thought that what happened did not affect me, that it was General Arellano's responsibility."

"You went to work for ENAEX?"

"Yes, in October 1974."

"To work at ENAEX (the National Explosives Company) one year after the military coup, you must have had the approval of the security services?"

"It's an independent state enterprise."

"But it would have been very unlikely for Colonel Oppitz to have given you a job without approval from above. And you even became chief of security. That means that you were not untrustworthy. You said they felt you weren't trustworthy."

"Well, Colonel Oppitz asked General Arellano about the idea of hiring me, and Arellano approved."

"In one of your statements, you said that General Arellano was 'also a military judge in Valdivia and Concepción at the same time.' Do know anything about what happened in those two cities?"

"Two or three people told me about Valdivia. But about Concepción I had firsthand information, and I knew that General Washington Carrasco had stopped General Arellano cold, avoiding a massacre."

"You have no doubts regarding General Arellano's responsibility for the massacres?"

"No, I attribute to him all the responsibility, according to our regulations, because he was the superior officer. General Arellano can say that Colonel Arredondo acted on his own initiative, but militarily he [Arellano] has no possibility of avoiding his responsibilities as chief."

"Colonel, let's go to the heart of what happened. One possibility is that you, the superior officers who were in the provinces, were not mentally prepared to wield the heavy hand with the chiefs of public services, political leaders, and well-known leaders of the Popular Unity government, with whom you had social relationships that were more or less harmonious, even friendly in many cases. The mission of the helicopter's entourage was to give you — the army — an exemplary lesson in repression that was sorely needed."

"Look, we proceeded, from the moment we were ordered to act on the day of the coup, according to our philosophical, humanistic, and military beliefs and in accordance with our military traditions. I think you are right, that there was a need for us to become more violent because many commanders adopted initiatives that tended to normalize the situation to try to obtain the total support of the population toward the military regime. I had been a governor before, and people would come up to me with complete trust. That is why I felt that I should keep the same attitude. I tried to apply the *Code of Military Justice* in the time frames specified [under its section] on 'Time of War.' That's why at the end of September or beginning of October, almost all of the cases were ready in Calama."

"Did your officers change, did your regiment in general change, after the helicopter left?"

"Yes, they were affected by what happened because they were clearly aware of the tremendous mistake and the discredit it brought upon the army."

"Did you perceive fear among your officers?"

"I remained the same."

"But you left — what about the ones who stayed in the army?"

"Yes, you're right, judging by what has happened during all these years."

As a matter of fact, Major Fernando Reveco Valenzuela, president of the Calama court-martial until October 2, 1973, was obviously interested in what happened in his regiment when he was imprisoned in Santiago.[8]

He stated, "I've gathered official and unofficial versions. I spoke with Luis Aracena Romo, who was later second in command of the regiment, and he told me that when Arellano's entourage arrived, their arrogance was incredible. Even a second lieutenant, such as Fernández Larios, would not salute his superiors. They didn't even recognize rank. From all the various accounts I heard, one thing is very clear: the members of the entourage terrified the regiment."

"The families of the victims have held that Arellano's mission was to give a terrifying example of repression to the left so that citizens in general would know what to expect. Wouldn't you add that what happened also sought to terrify the military themselves, to force them to be much tougher?"

"Of course. General Arellano's mission was directed inward, toward members of the military. That was the objective, because General Pinochet did not know what army he was leading; he did not know how many favored the constitutional line of [his predecessors] Generals Schneider and Prats. Pinochet had to make everyone follow the same hard line, whatever the cost," Major Reveco finally affirmed.

Notes

1. Judicial statement by letter, requisition No. 1092 on November 19, 1986.

2. This interview by Pablo Azócar was published in the Chilean magazine *APSI*, issue No. 198, on April 27, 1987.

3. Testimonies presented to the Chilean Catholic Church's Vicarate of Solidarity (Vicaría de la Solidaridad).

4. Testimonies presented to the Chilean Catholic Church's Vicarate of Solidarity.

5. Dawson Island, on the southeast side of the Strait of Magellan, between the mainland and Tierra del Fuego, is the island where former President Allende's government leaders were held after the coup. *Ed. and Paul E. Sigmund.*

6. See Chapter 3 in this volume.

7. The National Sanitary Works Service (Servicio Nacional de Obras Sanitarias — SENDOS).

8. The following statements are from the interview Patricia Verdugo conducted with Major Reveco. See Chapter 3, endnote 2.

CHAPTER 9

General Pinochet Said...

G eneral Arellano's son, his defense attorney, testified that the general did not know anything about what happened in Cauquenes until the case became public in 1986, that he found out about the events in La Serena and Copiapó later, while listening to Radio Moscow.

Regarding what happened in Antofagasta and Calama, he added that General Arellano found out that same night of October 19, 1973: "Since this was the jurisdictional zone of General Joaquín Lagos, commander in chief of the First Division, my father decided to return to Antofagasta that same night to explain what had happened," asserted attorney Sergio Arellano Iturriaga.

First, let's examine the various statements about what happened the next day, Saturday, October 20, 1973, in Antofagasta. General Joaquín Lagos Osorio left very early for the governor's office and, knowing that General Arellano and his entourage were back in Antofagasta, Lagos ordered that the helicopter could not leave without his permission.

The following is General Lagos' account:

"At approximately 9:00 a.m., General Arellano called me from the Esmeralda Regiment to thank me for all the kindness I had shown him. Angrily, I responded that his thanks did not matter to me and that he should come to the governor's office immediately to explain his behavior and the massacre carried out by his entourage behind my back. I also told him that he should not try to leave. A few minutes later, he arrived at the governor's office, accompanied by Lieutenant Colonel Sergio Arredondo, whom I did not allow to enter my office despite his insistence.

"I confronted General Arellano and reproached him for his criminal attitude. I expressed my indignation at these crimes committed behind my back in a place under my jurisdiction. He apologized, saying that Commander Arredondo had acted on his own initiative without his authorization. I was extremely incensed by this subterfuge — declaring himself almost innocent by assigning the responsibility to a lower ranking officer, when he was the chief of that entourage — General Arellano himself. I told him that I could not find words to characterize what had happened, that he had trespassed on my authority and responsibility, killing people who were being held pending their trials. These people had the right to be treated according to military justice procedures, which, even in times of war, guarantee by law: a trial before a military prosecutor, defense of the accused, and, finally, a court-martial and sentence by a military judge (myself, for these cases), who had to make decisions in good conscience. I added that what had been done constituted a monstrous as well as a cowardly crime because defenseless people had been brutally killed with no sentences given by a military judge."

General Lagos' testimony continued:

"Faced with this situation, General Arellano answered me, saying that he would assume all responsibility. I reiterated that I deplored his dishonorable attitude toward the army, the country, and toward me and said that this event was known not only by the people in Antofagasta, but also by the rest of the country and those abroad. And then, he reached into his sleeve, taking out a document he gave me to read: the document, from the commander in chief of the army [General Pinochet], named General Arellano as his 'Officer Delegate' to review and expedite the cases. Because of the state I was in, I did not read that document with due attention — I was very upset that he had not shown it to me when he arrived and was doing so only now, after they had killed 14 prisoners. If he had shown it to me before, that is, when he arrived, I would have given an order to all the unit commanders, informing them of the powers that were invested in General Arellano, as, with this order, the commander in chief of the army had stripped me of my responsibility and delegated it to General Arellano.

"I ordered him and all of his people to leave my jurisdictional zone, because, based on what I knew now, I had no other alternative but to inform the commander in chief of the army of these events. That very afternoon [General Pinochet] would be returning to Santiago, making a stop in Antofagasta. I gave orders to let the helicopter that carried General Arellano and his entourage go on to Iquique."

The foregoing was taken from General Lagos' written deposition[1] that covered his conversation with General Arellano. When I interviewed him in 1989, 16 years after the events, I asked him to explain this episode.[2]

"General Lagos, what does 'Officer Delegate' mean in the army?"

"Look, the regulations stipulate several special categories. There is the 'Officer Messenger,' who carries and delivers very important messages. There is the 'Orders Officer,' who delivers very important documents and is authorized to comment on them with the superior who receives them. And finally, there is the 'Officer Delegate,' a very special category that we — internally — call the 'heroic drug.'"

"Why, General?"

"Because the officer delegate is named to replace a commander who is acting poorly, one who is not faithfully obeying orders from superior powers. The officer delegate strips the powers from the acting commander, and he acts as the superior officer of the questionable commander."

"Were you acting poorly?"

"That day I found out that my superior officers were questioning my actions. Until then, I thought I was doing very well. Except for the painful obligation of having signed four death sentences during the days right after the military coup, I was proud that there was a climate of peace in Antofagasta."

"And the political prisoners?"

"We tried to keep them under the best possible conditions and see that they would receive trials with all the legal guarantees. I knew the military coup had as its goals imposing order and governing with justice for all Chileans."

"General Lagos, in your statement you said that you reprimanded General Arellano for his 'criminal behavior.' Was it really like that?"

"Of course! I told him he was despicable, a murderer. That what he had done deserved a firing squad in a public central square. That's what I screamed at him."

"Until General Arellano showed you the document signed by General Pinochet that named him 'Officer Delegate.'"

"At that point, I couldn't go on, except to reproach him for not having shown it to me earlier. In fact, later I found out that he had shown it to two other officers in my Division and that he had given a copy to the military attorney, Lieutenant Colonel Marcos Herrera Aracena."

"That explains why everyone else believed that you knew about General Arellano's mission."

"Yes, I believe so."

"And all your officers, moreover, knew that General Arellano was staying in your house, that he ate with you. Therefore, they must have assumed that you agreed with the mission."

"I believe so."

*****

General Arellano's lawyer, his son, gave the following version of the same events: "My father slept at the Esmeralda Regiment's base in Antofagasta, and early in the morning on October 20, he and Commander Arredondo went to the office of General Lagos, commander in chief of the Division, who, in that position, was the military judge of the aforementioned region. In that meeting, they almost came to blows. General Arellano insisted that Commander Arredondo should participate in the meeting, so that General Lagos could tell him personally what had happened. Nevertheless, Lagos refused, using his power as senior general and arguing that my father was the hierarchical superior of that entourage.

"Finally, my father reminded him that he [General Arellano] was only obliged report to the commander in chief since he was his delegate. To remind him, he showed the document that named him 'Delegate of the Commander in Chief.' The document was addressed to General Forestier, commander of the Sixth Division, who was awaiting him in Iquique. That meeting [between General Arellano and General Lagos] was dramatic. Therefore, feeling very bitter because of all that had happened, my father continued his trip to Iquique, where he expected to find General Pinochet, which did not happen," stated lawyer Arellano Iturriaga.

However, General Lagos did speak with General Pinochet that Saturday, October 20, 1973. General Lagos recounted their meeting in his testimony: "That afternoon I went to the Cerro Moreno Airport, along with the chiefs of the air force, navy, and police, to greet the commander in chief of the army. My wife also went to the airport with the commander in chief's wife, who was staying at our house. She had come to Antofagasta earlier to visit with her relatives, and they also went to the airport."

That is, Lucía Hiriart de Pinochet had learned the details of the events in Antofagasta because the victims' families had come to the Lagos' house, where she was a guest, and they had begged for an explanation of what had happened and for their loved ones' bodies to be returned to them.

General Lagos' account continued: "I asked the chief of the air force to prepare a room in the hangar beside the place where the commander in chief's plane would stop. When he [General Pinochet] arrived, I greeted him and told him that I urgently needed to speak with him. Initially, he answered that he needed to continue his trip as soon as possible; however, given my insistence and after spending some time with his relatives, he told me that he would give me five minutes. Immediately, I invited him to come with me to the room that had been prepared, where only the two of us met because I thought that this was an army matter.

"I informed the commander in chief of the army about everything that had happened in Antofagasta and about Calama. That morning Colonel Eugenio Rivera Desgroux, from Calama, had informed me about the executions that General Arellano and his entourage had carried out in that zone the night before, stating that General Arellano had overstepped his powers. I also told him [Pinochet] that these events had caused the worst possible harm at the national as well as international levels and had done serious damage to our country. For these reasons and because I could not accept these procedures, I asked him to relieve me of my position in Antofagasta because General Arellano's actions had made me lose my influence over the people and the division under my command — and because they went against the standards of respect and justice that had been established since September 11, 1973. Therefore, I thought I could not continue in the army, and I asked him to put through my resignation.

"General Pinochet said that he would never have thought that General Arellano would do this. He agreed with me, moreover, about the damage that these deaths would cause; he told me that I would be transferred to Santiago in the near future but that for the time being I should remain at my post. Under the present circumstances, he said that I should personally try to deal with public opinion regarding this serious situation that had occurred.

"I would like to state that this meeting, which was going to last five minutes, lasted more than one hour. At the end of our meeting, General Pinochet asked me for a telephone to speak with General Arellano in Iquique. He did not locate him, but he left the following message with the person who answered: 'That General Arellano should do absolutely nothing more, that he should return to Santiago first thing tomorrow morning, and when he arrives come to talk to me.' Afterward, General Pinochet continued his trip to Santiago."

In his defense, General Arellano asserted that he never received the above message from General Pinochet. He stayed in Iquique that weekend, October 20 and 21, and took special precautions with the members of his entourage so that there would not be a repetition of the same events: "He left them detained in the officers' mess hall." That is why, his defense maintained, nothing happened in Iquique.

According to General Arellano's attorney, Sergio Arellano Iturriaga, General Arellano returned to Santiago on October 22 and asked for an emergency meeting with General Pinochet. "They had two or three meetings to speak about the matter, very harsh and difficult meetings. My father [General Arellano] demanded that General Pinochet investigate what had happened, but he always answered evasively."

On October 24, Minister of the Interior General Oscar Bonilla announced, "The military Junta today decided to suspend all summary executions and, at the same time, warned that this adopted measure does not mean that those who violate the law will be unpunished."[3]

According to General Lagos, on October 31, 1973, a new organization called the Armed Forces Command (Comando de las Fuerzas Armadas — COFFA) sent a telex to him, requesting that he report "the number and names of those executed within my jurisdictional zone."

In his written deposition to the Criminal Court of Antofagasta, General Lagos stated:

"I made the report separately for Copiapó, Antofagasta, and Calama in the following manner:

I Copiapó
a) By the decision of the Commander of Copiapó: 3
b) By the Delegate of the Commander in Chief of the Army
   (General Arellano): 13

II Antofagasta:
a) By the decision of the Commander in Chief of Antofagasta: 4
b) By the Delegate of the Commander in Chief of the Army
   (General Arellano): 14

III Calama:
a) By the decision of the Commander of El Loa: 3
b) By the Delegate of the Commander in Chief of the Army
   (General Arellano): 26" [4]

Immediately, General Pinochet called General Lagos, saying that he was to present himself in Santiago the next day, November 1, with the documents of the people executed in his jurisdiction. General Lagos described his November 1 meeting with General Pinochet: "On that occasion, because of the events perpetrated behind my back, I reiterated that I wished to be relieved of my position, both in Antofagasta as well as from the army, because I did not want to be part of those events in the eyes of the country, the army, or my family. I did not get an answer to my petition, and he [General Pinochet] ordered me to return to Antofagasta."

That same night, General Pinochet's aide, Colonel Enrique Morel Donoso, came to the place where General Lagos was staying with Lagos' report. He communicated Pinochet's order: "That the main report (*Oficio Conductor*) should not specify what was done by General Arellano and that only a general list should be written." The next day, November 2, General Lagos went to General Pinochet's office, which at the time was in the Diego Portales Building, where, he reported, "there was an officer who redrafted the main document, according to the orders given by the commander in chief of the army. After delivering the redrafted document, I returned to Antofagasta to take over my post." This account is part of the written deposition of July 3, 1986, by General Joaquín Lagos Osorio for the Criminal Court of Antofagasta.

However, to return to my interview with General Lagos in 1989, I asked him at the time, "General Lagos, you characterized what happened as a crime. When you returned to Antofagasta, did you order a summary proceeding; did you initiate any investigation to find out everything that had happened in your jurisdiction during General Arellano's stay?"

"I didn't ask anything; I didn't investigate anything. Please understand! Any such action would have been an act against the army, against the commander in chief. Against whom could I have opened the summary proceeding? I did my duty as far as reporting to the appropriate persons and requesting that my resignation from the army be accepted. I could not do any more."

"General Lagos, 14 prisoners were murdered in Antofagasta, 13 prisoners in Copiapó, and 26 prisoners in Calama. In total, 53 political prisoners in the zone under your command. What happened to you? How did you feel?"

"It was and is such a huge pain, an indescribable pain. To see what you have venerated your whole life ruined: the concept of command, doing your duty, respect for your subordinates, and respect for the citizens who give us the weapons to defend them and not to kill them."

"General Lagos, my sources say that you were left very much alone after you decided to answer a judicial summons in 1986 and clarify what really happened."

"Yes, it's true. I was left alone because people are very cowardly. But I was left with the most important thing: the support and love of my family and of my true friends."

"Are you sorry, General, for your decision to cooperate with the justice system?"

"No. I've acted with dignity, as a soldier should. That's the way I was educated, to be an honorable and clean man, to preach by my example. I assume all the risks implied in that."

*****

General Joaquín Lagos Osorio resigned from the army. His resignation became effective almost one year after the events of 1973, and, as a civilian, he returned to Antofagasta to become head of the INACESA plant.

However, what happened with General Arellano? Why didn't he resign? I asked the General's son, "If General Arellano asserts he was innocent, that his entourage went over his head and, worse yet, incriminated him in the murder of more than 70 prisoners, why didn't he resign immediately, as General Lagos did?"

"It's because my father wanted to clarify the tragic episodes. He couldn't resign. If he had left, it doesn't take much to foresee the wording of the communiqué that would have publicly explained his resignation or his alleged expulsion, blaming him for what had happened. My father believed that he would not be able to counteract that version, given the moment the country was living through: All the press operated under military censorship, and public dissent was not tolerated. Moreover, my father did not want to appear to be attacking his own government, even at his own expense. Even now, he doesn't want to do it at the army's expense."

According to General Arellano's defense, the explanation of what happened begins with the identification of the members of his entourage and continues by following the trail of their later activities. Attorney Arellano Iturriaga did not overlook "the possibility of a trap laid by the newly created office of DINA, as a mission that could have as its main objectives: 1) to get rid of another general who could get in the way of General Pinochet's total takeover of power and 2) to make an ostentatious demonstration that there was a command that went above the traditional structures of the army that would operate like the German Gestapo within every regiment but without using different uniforms."

Let's look at what we know about the four officers on General Arellano's General Staff.

Colonel Sergio Arredondo González

From being chief of the General Staff of General Arellano, he went on to become director of the Cavalry School (Escuela de Caballería), a promotion that General Pinochet himself communicated to him in Antofagasta, on October 18, a few hours before the execution of the 14 prisoners. Between the years 1976 to 1978, he was military attaché in Brazil. A friend and classmate of Colonel Manuel Contreras, Arredondo might have headed Chile's National Intelligence Directorate in Brazil (DINA-Brazil) and was an important person in DINA's international arm.

When Arrendondo returned to Chile in 1978, he worked as industrial relations manager for the privately owned National Ceramics Company (Fábrica Nacional de Loza — Fanaloza) for nearly a year. Then he assumed a position in the ministry of justice, followed by a return to Brazil as representative of state-owned Codelco-Enami in São Paulo.[5] It was at that time in Brazil, in January 1986, that attorney Carmen Hertz personally lodged a complaint against him with Brazilian human rights organizations and requested his expulsion from the country as an undesirable person. The Brazilian press interviewed him and described him as "dark-haired, tanned, tall, and very elegant." When asked about the Caravan of Death's killings, he told the *Jornal do Brazil*, "If those shootings really happened, they could only have been authorized by the military commanders of the local garrisons. They were the top authorities because we were living in a state of war. The truth is, I don't recall it that well, because a lot of time has gone by. However, it is possible that there were one or two legal executions. It may have happened, but to bring it up now is only due to a spirit of revenge," he said, in *portuñol,* a dialect that combines Spanish and Portuguese.

Colonel Arredondo admitted that he had traveled in a helicopter with General Arellano to the north and south of the country, saying, "They were professional visits, visits to garrison commanders. The revolution in Chile was stronger in Santiago. We had, as experienced officers, the obligation of communicating the news and recommendations to the garrison commanders from the interior, and we could not use the telephone or telex. We would go personally. I don't recall if we traveled to La Serena, Copiapó, Antofagasta, and Calama between October 16th and 19th. These were stages that are forgotten in time. But in none of these trips did I have any knowledge of firing squads or even of trials of political prisoners. They were, as I've said before, merely professional trips."

Although the Brazilian government rejected the petition for his expulsion, Colonel Arredondo returned to Chile very soon after that. In August

1987, attorney Hertz presented a lawsuit against him in the United States, when she found out that Colonel Arredondo was a member of the Chilean horseback riding team in the Pan American Games in Indianapolis. The deputy sheriff of Marion County, Indiana, Gary Tingle, said, "They tried to find him, but it was impossible." And journalist Hércules Zamorano, of Santiago's *Las Últimas Noticias* newspaper, confirmed the reason why he had not been found: In the official events bulletin for the games, ". . . his name appears misspelled. Other sources indicate that his identification card appears with the name González, (his mother's name), and that he had left the country under the name Sergio González." Apparently, Colonel Arredondo González returned to Chile before he was notified of the lawsuit for "violation of human rights" against him.

A member of the Polo Club, Colonel Arredondo was the protagonist of a scandalous episode during an international equestrian meet in Chile. It so happened that General Joaquín Lagos Osorio, also an international training judge, was invited to the same event by the Equestrian Federation. Without warning, Lagos was verbally attacked by a screaming Arredondo:

"Stool pigeon! Disloyal! Get that bastard out of here!" Arredondo shouted, alluding to General Lagos' testimony, which had been made public a few days before.

General Lagos remained calm and stayed for the event.

Lieutenant Colonel Pedro Espinoza Bravo

Espinoza Bravo had belonged to DINA since its inception. In 1976, he was DINA's chief of operations, and, because of his participation in the plot that culminated in the September 1976 murder of former Chilean Foreign Minister Orlando Letelier in Washington, D.C., the United States asked for his extradition in 1978. Based on a case with ample evidence, he was charged with giving direct instructions to the agents who took part in the criminal mission. At that time, Espinoza was commander of the Pudeto Regiment in Punta Arenas. He was held under arrest for nine months in Santiago's Military Hospital until the Supreme Court rejected the U.S. petition for his extradition. At an unspecified date, he was sent to South Africa with an unspecified position in the military mission. He was brought back to Santiago in February 1987 and was promoted to the rank of brigadier general. In 1995, he was imprisoned along with DINA's Director, General Manuel Contreras, for his participation in the murder of Foreign Minister Orlando Letelier.

Major Marcelo Moren Brito

Moren Brito was deputy commander of La Serena Regiment until the day before the military coup. According to the regiment's Commander, Ariosto Lapostol Orrego, "I put him in charge of the troops that I was ordered to send to Santiago on September 10, 1973." Moren Brito participated in the bloody military occupation of the State Technical University. "Then he left the captain in charge of the troops, without telling me, and put himself at the disposal of General Arellano," Lapostol added.

Testimonies given by his superiors characterized him as "a hothead and violent" from the time he was a cadet. As a member of General Arellano's General Staff, Moren Brito became known for his cruelty toward his victims. He had belonged to DINA since its inception and served as commander of the clandestine detention center known as Villa Grimaldi. A large number of the prisoners under his control at Villa Grimaldi have never been seen again — their names appear under the chilling designation: "disappeared."

In late 1977, Moren Brito retired from DINA (renamed the National Information Headquarters[6] by then) at the same time that General Contreras left as the organization's head. Moren Brito retired in June 1985, with the rank of colonel.

Lieutenant Armando Fernández Larios

Fernández Larios was introduced in the regiment as "a combatant in the assault of the La Moneda Palace." He stated later that he was not a part of General Arellano's General Staff but was assigned to his personal security. He was also assigned to the personal security of the spokesman for the military Junta, Federico Willoughby. Fernández Larios had belonged to DINA since its inception. In 1976, he traveled outside Chile three times with false documents and different aliases: Alejandro Rivadaneira Alfaro, Alejandro Romeral Jara, and Armando Faúndez Lyon. In 1978, the U.S. Justice Department charged him for his participation in the murder of former Foreign Minister Letelier. He was held under arrest for nine months in the Military Hospital in Santiago until the Supreme Court rejected the U.S. petition for his extradition. Then he was promoted to the rank of army major, and he continued receiving his paycheck although he did not have a specific job assignment. In 1983, he was named as a participant in the assassination attempt against former Commander in Chief of the Army, General Carlos Prats and his wife (Buenos Aires, 1974).

In 1985, when Carmen Hertz presented a lawsuit against Fernández Larios for homicide, he asked a military judge, General Samuel Rojas, to pardon him and not force him to testify. The text of that document, dated November 12, 1985, reads as follows:

1. That in 1973, my rank was that of Lieutenant, and in October of the year in question I was commanded by my superiors to work for the personal security of General Sergio Arellano Stark, not as a member of the General Staff or working team, because I did not hold the rank of officer nor the distinction of being part of the General Staff.

2. That during the time that I carried out the aforementioned functions, I never had the opportunity to participate in the meetings, decisions, or resolutions adopted by General Arellano or his General Staff.

3. The aforementioned situation is brought up because, when the lawsuit was brought against me, the amnesty law was applied in my defense, a fact that I consider unjust since it attributes to me a responsibility in these events.

4. During 1978 and 1979, I was arrested as a result of a similar situation, which unleashed a strong publicity campaign using my name, resulting in damages to me personally, to my family, and to my profession.

5. Whereas for the above reasons and because recent references to my name in different publications make me responsible for the events in Calama, I wish to express that, in view of my rank and my decision-making level at that time, I have absolutely no responsibility in those events.

6. Therefore, pursuant to Article No. 68 of the *Discipline of the Armed Forces Regulations DNL 347*, which states, 'Armed forces personnel that are commissioned or commanding a unit, institute, or establishment or at the disposal of another military authority will be subjected to the disciplinary jurisdiction of the chief or commander under whose orders he is in commission or commanded,' it is not in my competence to assume final responsibility or to present myself to make statements to courts or appear in newspapers and magazines, assuming a responsibility that cannot possibly be in the competence of a low-ranking officer.

7. The aforementioned does not mean the evasion of responsibilities, which I have always assumed in my military career, both those concerning my hierarchical rank as well as those that correspond to my subordinates.

8. Therefore, I request, your honor, that as a military judge and general officer you make every representation to whom it might concern to separate me immediately and publicly from the present situation, releasing me from appearing at any time before any court for these events that are not related to the commission of services imposed on me by my superiors.

What happened with Lieutenant Armando Fernández Larios' petition? In February 1987, when, surprisingly, he gave himself up to U.S. justice to be tried for the Letelier case, the "Document for Petition to be Released" from the army that was submitted to the Vice Commander in Chief of the Army, General Santiago Sinclair, was made known. In point 17 of that document, dated January 21, 1987, Fernández Larios said:

> In November 1985, I saw myself possibly involved in the unfortunate events that occurred in October 1973, when I was under the command of General Sergio Arellano, an entourage that I was a part of only as one of the general's personal security lieutenants, having no decision-making or acting power during the period the commission lasted. Therefore, once this [these events] appeared in public light, I went to speak to General Arellano. He only told me that he knew nothing, that he was very nervous, and that it was a colonel who was guilty. I went to the Vice Commander in Chief of the Army, substitute General Mr. Valdés, and I requested that the army please exonerate me from responsibility in these events, since he well knew that due to my rank and position I had nothing to do with the events that happened. I received as an answer that the army of 1985 had nothing to do with the actions of the army of 1973. Moreover, I was forbidden to make public statements and, much less, hire an attorney. I requested my discharge from the institution, and it was rejected. There are two witnesses to this conversation, Colonel Castro, secretary-general of the army, and Brigadier Mujica, General Valdés' advisor. Disagreeing with this, I submitted a document to General Samuel Rojas Pérez, military judge, in which I explained my deplorable situation and requested that I be disassociated immediately and publicly from all the aforementioned events. From this written communication, I received as an answer the following:
>
> a) Secret communication No. 1.000-09-05 of November 13, 1985, from the Commander in Chief of the Second Army Division, to the Deputy Commander in Chief of the Army, whereby it is stated that the document is submitted to you, since the undersigned (General Rojas) lacks authority.
>
> b) Secret communication 1.000-10-06 of November 13, 1985, from the Commander in Chief of the Second Army Division to Major Armando Fernández Larios, whereby it is stated that the military judge does not have the necessary authority to decide my petition and that he has informed the Deputy Commander of the Army. I am sending you, along with this document, photocopies of the previous document, and the ones they sent as a response to my petitions.

Major Fernández Larios described the content of those documents in a less formal way, during an interview he gave to the prestigious U.S.

journalist and former Editorial Director of National Public Radio, John Dinges.[7]

"When my name also appeared in this case, I said, 'No, enough!' I went immediately to the Ministry of Defense and said, 'Well, what's happening here? Why do I appear in this? I was a lieutenant, and the others were colonels, generals, and commanders. Why are they getting me into this?' And once again, I heard, 'Don't worry, don't worry, this is going to go away. Don't you know what the amnesty law is? Well, the amnesty law protects you, take it easy.' I said, 'I don't want to use the amnesty law. I want my name to disappear from this matter! You know what Arellano and his people did, so why am I involved?' But they said, 'No, no!' The same thing. And when I went to speak with Arellano at his office (I had first called him on the telephone, but he told me that he could not see me in his office), I walked in and I told him, 'General, you have to get me out of this matter.'"

"Did you want him to say that you had nothing to do with the shootings?" Dinges asked.

(Takes a breath). "Of course, he had to do it! He knew I had nothing to do with the deaths of all those people! Well, Arellano, who is an imposing man, takes a little bottle of Valium and shows it to me, saying, 'Look, Fernández, I'm very nervous, and I have to take two of these little pills twice a day. I'm very tense, and I can't help you.' I said to him, 'What? Well, you can be very nervous, but what do I care? Get me out of this matter because you know I have nothing to do with it!' He answered, 'No, no, I can't do anything.' At that moment, I saw that general as a sugar cube — if you threw one drop of water on top of him, he would dissolve into nothing," Fernández Larios asserted.[8]

And in an interview given to Santiago's newspaper *El Mercurio*, Lieutenant Fernández Larios added this information: "I was chosen at random when I was in the Infantry School by General Arellano to be his bodyguard. I was a 23-year-old second-lieutenant. I did not participate in any shootings or confrontations. I wasn't even in General Arellano's office when his team discussed these matters. I only made sure everything was OK."

After these statements were published in the press, General Arellano stated, "I did not choose Mr. Fernández in 1973 for any function, and by the way, I did not know him. He was assigned to my General Staff just like the other members, and his functions matched that assignment. Moreover, I did not participate in meetings to discuss armed actions in the northern zone with Lieutenant Fernández or with any other officer. On the contrary, I required the highest degree of professionalism from all officers in the First Division, in order to avoid any abuse of power. Regarding Fernández' visit to me at the end of 1985, he stated his feelings of abandonment and specifically asked me to make a statement saying that when the tragic events that occurred in Calama in October 1973 took place, he was with the group of officers who accompanied me to the Chuquicamata mine. I responded that I was not able to say that, and in the judicial investigation that I expected to be carried out, I would limit myself to report those facts I was certain about, with the aim of contributing to establish the truth of what had happened and the corresponding responsibility."

Thus, with a trail of crimes behind him, Major Armando Fernández Larios asked for his discharge from the army at the same time that he was flying clandestinely out of Chile to give himself up to U.S. authorities. In number 18, the final point of his document petitioning to be discharged from the army, Fernández Larios said:

"After nine years, I still have not received any satisfaction on my just petitions to be able to prove my innocence in all of the events in which I was involved only because I was an officer trained to receive and obey orders from my superiors. Based on the 18 reasons contained in this document, I request that I be discharged immediately from the institution so that I can, privately, as a civilian, make it clear to my family and to myself that my name has nothing to do with the bloody events, which are opposed to military professionalism, whose responsible parties are none other than those individuals who have the highest ranks in the army. I hope that this discharge is useful, so that in the future, a junior officer is not blamed for the actions of the High Command of the Army."

Major Armando Fernández Larios was sentenced by a U.S. court to 27 months in prison. General Pinochet characterized him as "a deserter."

To the story of the four officers on General Arellano's General Staff, the story of his own aide must be added. In 1973, then Lieutenant Juan Viterbo Chiminelli Fullerton was assigned to the Support Command of the army. Afterward, he joined DINA and became part of the General Staff with responsibilities in the External Operations Department. Along with Colonel Pedro Espinoza Bravo, Chiminelli appears as a signatory on the deed of one of the "mother-companies" of DINA, the Pedro Diet Lobos Company. Chiminelli was caught spying in Peru in a serious incident that caused the expulsion of Chilean Ambassador Francisco Bulnes in January 1979. He retired from the army with the rank of lieutenant colonel.

*****

The sinister DINA is a common factor among the four officers in Arellano's Caravan entourage and even his aide. Lawyers who have worked to defend human rights, specifically in this case, have asserted that these five officers were brought into DINA after carrying out the macabre mission — precisely because they had demonstrated executive capacity in the "dirty war." According to the human rights lawyers, "The criminal history of three of them, Espinoza, Moren Brito, and Fernández Larios, has been public since 1978." In other words, the attempt to shift some responsibility onto DINA for the Caravan's actions was nothing more than a last-minute excuse. But General Arellano's defense insisted that DINA already existed in October 1973 and set a trap to "eliminate" him.

The fact is that after General Arellano executed his tragic mission as General Pinochet's "delegate," he was not eliminated — from life or from the army. Despite the differences he may have had with General Pinochet from before the coup, his military career followed a normal course: He was promoted to division general, and, at the beginning of 1974, he was named commander in chief of the Second Army Division (from La Serena to Talca) and, with that authority, he acted as the military judge of the zone.

I asked General Arellano's son, his defense lawyer, "Your father was commander in chief of the Second Division between 1974 and 1975. Since he was chief of that area, also military judge, how do you explain that he did not take the responsibility to investigate what his entourage did, at least in La Serena, a city under his command?"

"I don't know. I do not have an explanation," Arellano Iturriaga told me.

In March 1975, General Arellano was transferred to the Joint Chiefs of Staff. And at the end of that year, he retired. In 1976, as a civilian, General Arellano accepted a job offer.

"The owner of the Fanaloza company, Antonio Martínez, decided to set up a board of directors composed of former soldiers, and he called my father. General Javier Palacios, his friend, was also there," lawyer Arellano stated.

"If your father had terminated every relationship with Colonel Sergio Arredondo González after he discovered that he had ordered the massacres behind his back, how do you explain that they worked together in Fanaloza in 1978?"

"It was General Palacios who recommended Arredondo. The fact is that my father hardly ever saw him, and, a few months later, he asked Antonio Martínez to fire him [Arredondo] because he wasn't a good worker, which is true. He could not use what had happened in the North to get him fired from his work," Arellano Iturriaga responded.

General Sergio Arellano Stark did not agree to be interviewed by me, despite my repeated requests for more than one year. He only gave an interview to *El Mercurio*, in March 1986, and very few lines were devoted to the case and then only to reassert his innocence.

If I had interviewed him, I would have asked him several questions to try to clarify the following points:

1. Considering the repeated massacres or executions that violated every legal procedure in time of war, one can infer that:

   a. These occurrences were not isolated or fortuitous events that could be attributed to the excesses of a subordinate.

   b. Therefore, the executions appear to be a perfectly planned sequence of events by a higher command. Which one?

2. Considering the later military/government careers of all of those who participated in the mission, one can infer that:

   a. The perpetrators were not punished by the High Command of the Army, and,

   b. On the contrary, they continued to be promoted within the institution. Why?

3. Regarding the later military careers of at least three high-ranking officers (General Lagos, Colonel Lapostol, and Colonel Rivera), one can infer that:

   a. Their decision — to assign responsibility and clarify, privately or publicly, that what happened was the responsibility of the commission that had come from the capital — was not backed by the Army High Command, and

   b. They were, therefore, punished with the virtual end of their military careers. Why?

4. Regarding the order given by General Pinochet that General Lagos rewrite his report, specifically to delete "what was done by General Arellano," one can infer that there was:

   a. A decision of hierarchical superiors to cover up what had happened insofar as army records were concerned, and

b. A decision taken by superior officers that what had happened did not merit punishment. Why?

5. Regarding the activities of General Arellano while his General Staff proceeded to carry out massacres — having lunch in the dining room of the Social Club of Cauquenes with Commander Castillo Whyte, talking with Commander Lapostol in the gardens of the base in La Serena, eating and sleeping in General Lagos' house in Antofagasta; and visiting the Chuquicamata mine with Commander Rivera Desgroux — one can infer that:

   a. Either the general had a mission, for which he did not need the cooperation of his General Staff; therefore, he was not interested in knowing what they were doing, or

   b. The general was lying to made sure he had good alibis for a hypothetical future investigation, as he was far away from the scenes of the crimes. What is the truth?

6. Regarding the composition of General Arellano's General Staff, one can infer that:

   a. They were not legal advisers who justified their presence as support in the mission designed to "review cases"; nor did they have special backgrounds enabling them to cooperate in the task of "coordination" with local governments.

   b. Therefore, the general's mission was to carry out the executions of prisoners outside any legal process. In fact, two of General Arellano's staff members, Moren Brito and Fernández Larios, stood out for their cruelty and coldness in actions carried out at the time of the military coup in downtown Santiago, an area commanded by General Arellano Stark himself. Is there any other explanation?

7. Regarding General Arellano's testimony that he learned about the deaths in Calama but did not find out about the criminal actions of his General Staff on October 4 in Cauquenes, on October 16 in La Serena, on October 17 in Copiapó, and on October 18 in Antofagasta, one can infer that:

   a. Either there was an inexplicable conspiracy of silence among the members of his General Staff and the High Command of each regiment and each division, a conspiracy that, in some cases, is still in force, three cases of conspiracy (in La Serena, Copiapó, and Antofagasta) having been reported by Moscow Radio and another one by the Chilean press in Cauquenes in 1980.

b. Or that General Arellano lied, and those who are telling the truth are General Joaquín Lagos, Colonel Ariosto Lapostol, Colonel Oscar Haag, and Colonel Eugenio Rivera. Who should we believe?

Notes

1. The foregoing text comes from General Joaquín Lagos' written deposition of July 3, 1986, presented to the Criminal Court of Antofagasta.

2. The following statements were made by General Joaquín Lagos during an interview with Patricia Verdugo in 1989.

3. On October 25, *El Día* newspaper in La Serena, ran the following headline covering the width of the front page: "Executions Suspended."

4. General Joaquín Lagos' written deposition to the Criminal Court of Antofagasta, July 3, 1986.

5. Codelco-Enami refers to the National Copper Corporation (Corporación del Cobre — CODELCO) and the National Mining Company (Empresa Nacional de Minería — ENAMI), both state-owned.

6. The National Intelligence Directorate (DINA) was renamed the National Information Headquarters (Central Nacional de Informaciones — CNI).

7. A professor at Columbia University's School of Journalism, John Dinges co-authored with Saul Landau *Assassination on Embassy Row* (New York: Pantheon Books, 1980), a book about the murder of former Chilean Foreign Minister Orlando Letelier and U.S. citizen Ronnie Moffitt in Washington, D.C.

8. Interview by John Dinges, *APSI* magazine, No. 193, February 1987.

CHAPTER 10

Five Massacres and an Amnesty

The pilot of the Puma helicopter for the trip through northern Chile that took on such tragic dimensions was Captain Emilio de la Mahotier. At first he refused to grant me an interview, saying, "You must go through the Public Relations Department of the army." But, finally, he agreed to answer some of my questions.

"Do you remember that trip to the north in October 1973?"

"Look, I've logged almost 8,000 flying hours, and for me that trip wasn't any different from many others."

"And did you hear the conversations in the cabin between General Arellano and the members of his entourage?"

"Impossible. Have you ever flown in a Puma? The engines are very loud, and the pilots are in a different cabin from the one the passengers are in. Also, you have earphones on to communicate with the co-pilot and mechanic, and the earphones are inside a helmet. There's a tremendous amount of noise, and it's impossible to hear what the passengers are saying."

"And what did you do during the time that General Arellano and his entourage were in La Serena, Copiapó, Antofagasta, and Calama?"

"The usual routine: make sure that the helicopter was in good working order, inspect it carefully, because a helicopter is much more complicated than an airplane."

"And when did you find out that prisoners were massacred on that trip?"

"Many years later, when the news began to appear in the press, it was really very uncomfortable to see my name linked to these events. For me, they were simply passengers. The truth is that I don't know what happened, and I very much doubt everything that I've read. It can't be true," de la Mahotier said in closing.

The truth is that the Caravan of Death was the object of comments, speculation, and surreptitious rumors for more than a decade. In the Chilean army, they called it "the good humor caravan." It was only 12 years after this tragedy — which is more complex than it first appears to be — that the "Arellano case" could be written about. And it made front-page headlines. The person who triggered the release of information was the general's son and spokesman, attorney Sergio Arellano Iturriaga, who in July 1985 published a slim volume entitled *Más allá del Abismo: Un testimonio y una perspectiva* (*Beyond the Abyss: One Testimony and a Perspective*).[1] On page 62 of the book, one paragraph unleashed forces that had been hidden until then:

> In October 1973, my father received an order to review numerous cases being heard in the provinces, especially in the north, by court-martial, even though it was only in the beginning of 1974 that he was named military judge because he was commander of the second division. He devoted himself to the task with the advice of three military attorneys named by the commander in chief, giving priority to those cases whose sentences called for capital punishment, which obliged him to travel to various cities. On that thankless mission, he modified the majority of the sentences, ratifying only those cases that were especially serious according to the procedural information. During his stay in Calama, where there was great turmoil due to revelations about a frustrated plot to blow up the Dupont explosives plant, a group of political prisoners was executed without first being sentenced, on the outskirts of the city. Only upon his return, in Antofagasta, my father found out what had happened, but soon after, Radio Moscow involved him in the events. The amoral standards of political warfare were applied in different ways by both sides.

Attorney Arellano assured me that he wrote that paragraph, as published in the book, without consulting his father. If that indeed was the case, we must infer that, in referring to such a serious matter, he relied upon what General Arellano had told him and repeated to him for 12 years. Substantially, it means that General Arellano only told his family that 1) he reviewed cases in the provinces, 2) he did so accompanied by three military attorneys designated by General Pinochet, 3) only in Calama were prisoners executed "without first being sentenced," and 4) only upon his return to Antofagasta did he find out what had happened in Calama.

At the beginning of October 1985, three months after the book was published, Colonel Eugenio Rivera Desgroux publicly refuted attorney Arellano Iturriaga, in a letter published by the magazine *Análisis*.[2] Immediately afterward, General Arellano himself decided to intervene, claiming that these were "slanderous statements," that he had no "criminal responsibility" in the events, and that he would "cooperate in every way necessary" with the judicial system to clarify them.[3]

For the first time since the military coup, a general and colonel publicly confronted each other over this serious case that violated basic human rights. With this opening, the first thread of the hidden tragedy was revealed. And many people — relatives of the victims, lawyers, and journalists — decided that the time and the opportunity had come to unite forces to solve the puzzle. Information began to appear haphazardly: the identity of the victims, the identity of the alleged perpetrators, and the dramatic search for the bodies in Calama.

On October 19, 1985, 12 years after the events in question, attorney Carmen Hertz, widow of Carlos Berger, filed a criminal lawsuit for "aggravated homicide" against General Arellano and officers Marcelo Moren Brito and Armando Fernández Larios, the only members of the entourage who had been identified thus far. Faced with this new turn of events, General Arellano reiterated his decision to cooperate with the judicial system and publicly stated, "I will not invoke the amnesty law, so that the whole truth might be known and those responsible be punished."

But the judge of the Second Criminal Court of Calama, Gloria Solís, declared herself without legal competence to investigate the case, arguing that jurisdiction lay with military courts because military officers were involved. On October 29, 1985, the military judge of Antofagasta, General Carlos Meirelles Muller, accepted the case and immediately applied the amnesty law to it. The text of his ruling is as follows:

> Accepted jurisdictional capacity declined by the judge of the Second Criminal Court of El Loa [Calama] in light of the information contained in the complaint as filed and of the legal foundations of the resolution of that court, whereas:
>
> 1) That, pursuant to the merit of the petition of lawsuit pp. 7 and following, the deduced penal action seeks to make effective the responsibility that, in the crime of homicide of Carlos Berger Guralnik, would fall on Sergio Arellano Stark, Marcelo Moren Brito, and Armando Fernández Larios, perpetrated on October 19, 1973, date of death being confirmed with the death certificate on page 1.
>
> 2) That, according to Law Decree No. 2.191 of 1978, published in the *Official Gazette* on April 19 of the same year, amnesty was given to all persons who, as perpetrators, accomplices, or accessories after the fact were party to criminal acts during the period between September 11, 1973 and March 10, 1978.
>
> 3) That criminal responsibility is extinguished, among other reasons, pursuant to what is expressly established in article 93 of the Penal Code, by reason of the amnesty.
>
> That article 107 of the Code of Penal Procedure states that, "before proceeding with penal action, in whichever way the trial had begun, the judge will examine if the information or data given permit establishing that the criminal responsibility of the person charged is annulled." In this

case, previously addressed by an official decree on this point, proceeding with the trial is rejected, and whereas, in the dispositions in article 17 No. 6 of the Code of Military Justice, it is stated: that it is unfounded to begin proceedings for the events which make up lawsuit on pp. 7 and following because the criminal responsibility of the persons that are charged has been annulled.

Signed: Brigadier-General Carlos Meirelles, military judge; the military attorney, Justice Major Armando Alfaro; and the titular Secretary of the Court, Martín Guerra.

The amnesty law was applied 10 days after the lawsuit was filed. Lawyer Carmen Hertz asserted, "From reading the decision, one can deduce that the military judge admits the criminal responsibility of the three officers mentioned in the lawsuit and understands that it is annulled through application of Decree Law 2.191."

She added, "The judge read the lawsuit and did not carry out any of the requested procedures. We found out that he traveled to Santiago the last weekend of October. Upon his return, on Monday the 28th, it was rumored that he already had the decision in his hand, something that he himself ratified during the press conference the following day, where he announced that he was dismissing the case and archiving all the materials."

General Meirelles did not deny his hurried trip to Santiago prior to the application of the amnesty law. A few days later, the team of lawyers in charge of the case received the following account from a reliable source who had personally attended that top level meeting in Santiago. What had happened?

First of all, when faced by the lawsuit presented by attorney Hertz, the military prosecutor of Calama submitted all the information about Carlos Berger to the military judge of Antofagasta, General Carlos Meirelles Muller, including the following documents:

- The police report dated September 11, 1973, stating that Carlos Berger was arrested at 11:20 a.m., inside Calama's El Loa Radio station, carrying a Pasper revolver, and was taken to the Calama Regiment.
- The statement by Carlos Berger, signed by hand, where he says that he bought the revolver in the flea market and he had it because he had been threatened and because he worked the night shift at the radio station.
- The order of admission of Carlos Berger to the public jail with visiting rights.

- The request for the liberation of Carlos Berger and the ruling that rejected it.
- The opinion signed by Colonel Eugenio Rivera, proposing a sentence of 60 days.
- The response to the charge and the ruling by Colonel Rivera, military judge, sentencing him to 60 days in jail.
- The minutes dated October 19, 1973, that point out that, once the court-martial had convened, 26 prisoners appeared, with Carlos Berger listed in third place among them, all accused of treason to the fatherland. That as the prisoners were being transferred from the jail to the base for interrogations, they mutinied and were killed at 6:00 a.m. The only legible signature is that of Officer Alvaro Romero Reyes, secretary of the court-martial.

The same source who gave this account to the team of lawyers handling Carmen Hertz's case also confirmed that the above dossier was known to General Meirelles, military attorney Gustavo Alfaro, officer Martín Guerra, and the secretary.

Two days after receiving the lawsuit in Antofagasta, General Meirelles was called to Santiago. He traveled there accompanied by the military attorney. A meeting took place in the Diego Portales Building; among the attendees were Generals Santiago Sinclair, Fernando Salazar Lantery (working in intelligence and adviser to Pinochet), Enrique Valdéz Puga, Aureliano Tello, Sergio Barros Recabarren, Eduardo Avello Concha (general attorney of the army), Fernando Lyon Balmaceda, military attorney Osvaldo Vial, Ivan Alvear Ravanal (lawyer for DINE-CNI),[4] and a lawyer for the CNI named Villalobos Bolt.

The same informant added, "General Valdés argued [at the meeting in Santiago] that, with this lawsuit, the Vicarate was endeavoring to put the army on trial, and neither the government nor the army would stand for anything similar to what happened in Argentina, that this matter had to be stopped immediately. The CNI people were in favor of carrying out the appearance of an investigation, in order to neutralize the effects of both the lawsuit and news reports about the case. Other generals were opposed to a pseudo-investigation, saying that the files should be destroyed and that the amnesty law should be applied immediately. Another one proposed bringing together all the accused, including General Manuel Contreras. Another general refused, arguing that it would be worse, because Fernández Larios was totally unbalanced and had already said that if he wasn't protected, he would tell everything. An intelligence officer said not to worry, that his boys would take care of everything and, if it came to it, he could be declared insane. Later, General Canessa joined the meeting.

If the above account of this meeting and the terms of the debate are true, it is obvious that the proposal for stopping the matter with the amnesty law indeed triumphed. (Was the Carlos Berger file itself destroyed?) Attorney Hertz immediately appealed General Meirelles' sentence before the court-martial and said, "We hope that General Arellano also appeals this ruling, in which he appears guilty." However, General Arellano did not appeal, but he challenged the decision, stating that since the amnesty was applied without prior investigation, he had been "implicated by a resolution decreed by virtue of the aforementioned law, which would only be applicable to those who have committed criminal acts, but it does not follow that one can apply or extend this law to those who have not committed any criminal act. The resolution, instead, involves a virtual incrimination that I cannot accept, given that, as I've stated publicly, it deals with events in which I had no participation at all and which, to the extent that they may constitute criminal acts, should be duly investigated."[5]

In the meantime, the person who had signed Decree Law 2.191 of 1978, as Minister of Justice, attorney Monica Madariaga (General Pinochet's cousin), decided to intervene to explain that the amnesty law should not be applied without first investigating and determining responsibilities, as follows: "Amnesty is a pardon. It is the conciliatory pardon of all society, which, in the last analysis, is the party affected by the crime and is the owner of all sovereignty, society, which in its generosity, seeks peace in love. But that peace and love cannot disregard justice, which is nourished by truth.... Society pardons when it knows who is being pardoned." Former Minister Madariaga drafted a long legal report that was added to the appeal of the Berger case.

In fact, all the lawsuits crashed against the solid wall of the amnesty law. One after another, as months went by, lawsuits were filed in Cauquenes, La Serena, Copiapó, Antofagasta, and Calama. Some judges immediately declared that they had no legal competence; others decided that they should investigate and did gather some of the proof that we have included throughout this narrative — before military justice intervened to take away the cases, stating that the participation of soldiers was public knowledge. The amnesty law, decreed by General Pinochet to cover up violations of human rights committed between 1973 and 1978, was always ratified by the courts-martial and, more seriously, by the Supreme Court of Chile.

Tenacious lawyer Pamela Pereira, who worked tirelessly on the cases, characterized what happened as "a legal aberration." Amnesty, she explained, "is a cause for final dismissal, but the dismissal establishes that it can only be decreed once the investigation has been exhaustively carried out and the body of the crime and the identity of those responsible has been proved. In this particular case, amnesty was applied without an investigation. Furthermore, we have very serious crimes here and an attempt to force society to forgive them without having precise information regarding the circumstances under which they were perpetrated, who participated, and who gave the orders. Society is forced to pardon [the crimes and the criminals] with a cover-up of the truth that, in my opinion, leads to impunity of the crime."

For his part, General Arellano repeatedly insisted on his total innocence. In an April 1987 exclusive statement to *Hoy* magazine, he said, "I do not seek nor have I sought justification for the legitimacy of the repression within the framework of a dirty war. I have demanded and now continue to demand the truth because without it reconciliation will not be easy. And I wouldn't be able to say this, nor what I have said at other times, if I had been responsible for giving an order like that one."

Carlos Berger's widow, attorney Carmen Hertz, and Mario Argüelles' widow, Violeta Berríos, responded to General Arellano's announcements of his innocence at a press conference held when some of macabre details of the crimes against their husbands were coming to light:

"Mr. Arellano, aware of the cruelty, cowardice, and perversion with which our husbands were murdered, knowing how their bodies were buried in the desert in secret, and knowing about your behavior in La Serena, Copiapó, Antofagasta, and Calama, we ask ourselves: Is it proper for an army officer of the highest rank to assume such an undignified and hypocritical attitude before the relatives of those who were your victims?

"You know the whole truth.

"You know what happened at approximately 6:00 p.m. on October 19, 1973, in Calama.

"You know that you were the general in charge of the entourage, and you cannot evade your hierarchical responsibility.

"You are aware of all the cruelty and violence used to murder our loved ones.

"You know where the bodies of the victims were buried.

"You know why you decided [General Arellano and the entourage][6] to act like that.

"What you might not have known or imagined is that 13 years later you would be confronting an entire nation that looks at you with horror, just as it looks at your subordinates in the entourage, as information about the massacre comes to light, bit by bit."

On May 18, 1987, lawyer Arellano Iturriaga asserted that his father had twice asked the deputy commander in chief of the army office to convene a Military Court with the objective of clarifying the truth and defending his family's honor. But the truth is that in the armed forces the so-called Military Court only functions for military personnel on active duty. And General Arellano must have known that because it was not a surprise when his request was rejected.

Finally, General Arellano's son requested the cooperation of Catholic Bishop Juan Luis Ysern, who had known the tragedy firsthand, since he was the apostolic administrator of Calama in 1973. Bishop Ysern decided that justice could be achieved by bringing the parties together so that they might jointly put together the pieces of this tragic puzzle. "If the case was amnestied, maybe the courts cannot hear it, but this is left to Chilean public opinion — and what matters is that the truth be established," Bishop Ysern declared.

However, the church mediation was brief and unfruitful. Attorney Arellano Iturriaga signed a writ committing himself to obtain his father's personal participation in the meetings, once the procedures had been spelled out and agreed upon. But before the meetings began, attorney Arellano publicly asked Colonel Eugenio Rivera to read the "writ" in which, according to his father's version, Colonel Arredondo accepted responsibility for the execution of the 26 prisoners in Calama on grounds of attempted rebellion. Then he characterized a report on the events prepared by Carmen Hertz as "a major obstacle to progress toward the truth," and he said that, for that very reason, it was "sterile to continue repeating facts and arguments which have already been given, as well as carrying on a dialogue with the deaf in which the truth is lost." Then, on August 7, 1987, General Arellano himself ended the mediation of Bishop Ysern, saying that, given the circumstances, "I thought it absolutely pointless to continue preparing a useless confrontation, and even one of a public nature, that would not lead to any understanding nor the truth that many of us have sought."

As to the existence of a Calama "writ," Colonel Rivera Desgroux responded by saying, "General Arellano has stated, through his son, that he has knowledge of this information. He has even said that he could show the way to get to those documents. If that is the case, and given that the country is clamoring for the truth, why doesn't General Arellano himself reveal to the whole national community, and especially the relatives of the victims, those documents? Why does he wield them as a justification for withdrawing from the process of clarifying the truth, a fact or pieces of information that he might have access to and be able to provide? Are they not precisely the subjects and the points to be clarified in those meetings?"

Attorney Carmen Hertz asked, "That the truth demanded from General (retired) Sergio Arellano Stark, who, I reiterate, to date has not provided it in any legal or moral instance (I do not know about the institutional), may be synthesized from the following questions, which he still will not answer:

1. Did General Arellano act as delegate of the commander in chief of the army on his mission from La Serena to Calama?

2. Who gave the orders in each city to proceed with the executions?

3. Why was the decision made to kill the men?

4. What circumstances surrounded the executions, and where were the bodies of the victims buried?"

The fact is that those two years of dramatic debate, from 1985 to 1987, culminated in a new round of silence and left the Chilean people, having been bombarded by news and statements, to reach their own verdict — for or against General Arellano. In between, there was a revealing public debate among retired army generals.

On November 5, 1985, the newspaper *El Mercurio* published a statement from the Corps of Retired Generals and Admirals of the National Defense (Cuerpo de Generales y Almirantes en Retiro de la Defensa Nacional), distributed by the governmental press agency Orbe, that sought to legitimize the actions of Arellano's entourage. The statement read as follows:

> As a consequence of having taken power and with the higher objective of organizing and giving peace to the country, in which foreign and national subversive elements had formed a vast terrorist organization, a state of internal war and, later, a state of siege were declared from September 11, 1973, until December 31, 1974. During that time, as a painful consequence of the obstinacy of terrorists born in Chile and trained abroad, numerous victims from both sides fell, affecting a large number of homes in our nation.
>
> It causes great concern to those of us who yesterday guided our respective institutions that some ill-informed people have forgotten the past so

easily and are endeavoring to initiate legal actions against armed forces personnel who intervened and put their lives at risk in defense of the sacred right to liberty. Numerous soldiers, sailors, pilots, and policemen have fallen forever in this restoration of peace, and that is why, in their memory, we raise our voices to express on behalf of all the retired generals and admirals our unconditional solidarity with all that they have done until now for our comrades on active duty, since their brave and unflinching action has achieved the domination of sedition and has permitted the country to recover its rhythm of development and progress which now it proudly hails.

Only four generals publicly rejected the statement: General Joaquín Lagos Osorio, General Guillermo Pickering, General Mario Sepúlveda Squella, and General Ervaldo Rodríguez Theodor. General Joaquín Lagos Osorio, commander in chief of the First Division in 1973, resigned from his post as director of the Corps of Retired Generals and made this statement:

> At this very moment, the country is learning the actions taken by a general a few days after September 11, 1973, actions which we — the men who have dedicated our whole lives to wearing proudly the uniform of the institutions of National Defense — cannot support unless those actions are previously clarified in a thorough fashion. As this statement says, I cannot unconditionally be in solidarity with factions like the ones I have just pointed out; my conscience as a man, as a Christian, and as a soldier forbids me to do so. For the prestige of our forces, these events must be clarified, hopefully in court proceedings in which everyone will appear who had knowledge of the events at the time they occurred, so that the country will know the truth and the responsibilities of each person will be defined beyond a shadow of doubt. The aforementioned, I am certain, will contribute decisively to the reunification of all of Chileans.

The other three generals who rejected the statement of the Corps of Retired Generals and Admirals, Guillermo Pickering, Mario Sepúlveda Squella, and Ervaldo Rodríguez Theodor, said that they did not belong to the group and that they did not share the terms of the statement.

Those two years of public debate and elucidation of information showed how deep and raw the wounds caused by the Caravan of Death still were. Press censorship on television channels prevented all Chileans from knowing this drama in depth. However, it is not only a question of tragedy in the lives of the families of the 75 victims.

It is also a tragic mark on the lives of the military who were involved and their families, as I was able to verify in the interviews carried out with those who agreed to speak for this book. I cannot forget the tears of Major Fernando Reveco when he recalled the memory of his own torture by the military or the futile attempt of Colonel Efraín Jaña to hide his pain after describing his prison term and the exile that separated his family. It is impossible to forget the imploring look of Colonel Ariosto Lapostol, who asked at the end of the interview, "What can I do to see them and to ask them for forgiveness?" And the downcast face of Colonel Eugenio Rivera, who sought vainly to hide his shame and pain for everything that had happened. We must not forget the courage of General Joaquín Lagos when he resigned from the army and his profound anger about everything that happened, reflected in his eloquent words: "To see brought to nothing everything that one has venerated for all one's life: the concept of command, obedience to duty, respect for subordinates, and respect for the citizens who give us weapons to defend them, not to kill them."

And, it is impossible to forget the moving efforts of attorney Sergio Arellano Iturriaga to clean his father's hands of so much spilled blood. In the winter of 1998, I told him of my decision to write about the case, and I asked him to act as an intermediary so I might schedule an interview with his father. Finally, he told me that he would act as his father's spokesman. When I saw him, I had no doubt I was looking at another type of victim of this tragedy: the only male child, the bearer of the family name, who grew up feeling proud of his father, who vitally needed to believe in his father's innocence, who urgently needed to proclaim his father's innocence: There he was, seated in front of me, looking for papers, each gesture a desperate flailing for an argument to defend the indefensible.

Finally, pain and desperation defeated Dr. Dora Guralnik, mother of the lawyer and journalist Carlos Berger, who was murdered in Calama. She chose to commit suicide in a tragic leap from the 14th floor of a downtown building in Santiago on June 23, 1988.

Notes

1. Sergio Arellano Iturriaga, 1985, *Más allá del abismo: Un testimonio y perspectiva* (Santiago: Editorial Proyeccíon).

2. Colonel Rivera Desgroux's rebuttal of attorney Sergio Arellano Iturriaga's claims are contained in Chapter 8 of this volume, which deals with the executions carried out in Calama.

3. General Sergio Arellano Stark's statements were widely published in the Chilean press.

4. The National Intelligence Directorate (DINA) became the National Information Headquarters (Central Nacional de Inteligencia — CNI), while the Intelligence Service of the Army (SIM) became the Intelligence Directorate of the Army (Dirección de Inteligencia del Ejército — DINE).

5. General Arellano's answer is contained in the appeals documents filed before the court-martial by attorney Carmen Hertz.

6. The Spanish verb, "decidieron," was given in the plural form; thus this particular accusation may be interpreted as referring to the members of the entourage as well as to General Arellano.

From the Rettig Commission to the Trial of Pinochet

The military dictatorship officially ended on March 11, 1990, the day that General Augusto Pinochet handed over the presidential sash in Congress. Thus, after almost 17 years, we again had a president elected by the Chilean people and a legislative branch of the government that — with the exception of the senators appointed by Pinochet — included 146 legislators elected by popular vote.

The clamor for "truth and justice" in the area of human rights had been getting louder and more forceful during the latter part of the dictatorship, to the point that the opposition political alliance included in its electoral program the "repeal or annulment of the amnesty decree-law." The new President, Patricio Aylwin, in his first public act as president, responded to that popular outcry with, "Yes, truth and justice insofar as possible." What was possible in the first stage of the transition? In politics, what is possible depends on the powers that are engaged in the struggle and their abilities to negotiate. It also depends on the scenario in which that negotiation occurs. And in this case at this time, General Pinochet's presence hovered over Chile like a bird of prey, since he stipulated in his own Constitution that he would stay for eight more years as commander in chief of the army. However, that was not all he had done. General Pinochet had named all of the other commanders in chief and the general director of the police, making their removal impossible by the new president. Pinochet also had named nine senators and imposed an electoral system that overstated the Right's candidates results, so that they would have a majority in Congress.

In this framework, the members of the transition government started with an "invisible gun" pointed toward them on the negotiating table. On two occasions, the weapon became visible: when Pinochet ordered a frightening "Linkage Exercise" in December 1990 and when he carried out a defiant deployment of troops in May 1993 that was called the *boinazo* (a reference to the berets or *boinas* worn by soldiers). In both cases, the former dictator was putting pressure on the government to annul investigations into his family's businesses (among others, the so-called *pinochecks*, in which his oldest son received almost US$3 million for selling weapons to the Chilean army) and to stop the legal investigations of human rights cases.

At the beginning of his term of office, in April 1990, President Aylwin signed a decree that created the National Commission on Truth and Reconciliation (Comisión Nacional de Verdad y Reconciliación), also known as the Rettig Commission, named after the respected jurist who chaired it, Raúl Rettig. Eight persons were named commissioners so that impartiality to all sectors would be guaranteed. The Rettig Commission's principal objective: to investigate the violations of human rights during the military regime; deadline: nine months; mandate: to establish the facts, identify the victims, and omit the names of the perpetrators; reason: it was stated that the Commission could not exercise powers that could only be attributed to the courts. Nevertheless, it was decided that the Commission would submit its information to the judiciary.

What could the judiciary do? On the one hand, the amnesty decree-law was kept in force and, on the other, the courts were open to the possibility of interpreting the law in another way — first, investigate the facts; second, identify the perpetrators of the crimes; and, finally, close the cases through amnesty. Little by little, a thesis was developed that a "disappeared" person was a victim of a kidnapping as long as the remains are not found; therefore, amnesty would not apply, and the case could remain open. According to this interpretation, General Pinochet and his veiled and open threats that "none of my men will be touched" must be included.

For the families affected by the crimes of the Caravan of Death, a faint new hope appeared. They all went to the Rettig Commission to present their cases, and they repeated every piece of information they knew to the attorneys in charge.

*****

On October 10, 1990, three members of the Rettig Commission took a statement from General Sergio Arellano. What did he say? He repeated the version of events given by his son as cited in this book. For example, General Arellano maintained that his military mission had the objectives of "reviewing the status of the cases, on the one hand, to expedite them and, on the other, to ensure that the accused had appropriate defenses." Also, he accomplished that mission accompanied by a General Staff that "was almost completely appointed by other army authorities." In La Serena, he said that he ordered the formation of a court-martial to decide the death sentence of three prisoners. And he left the city believing that the sentences had been carried out. Many years later, he found out that an additional 12 prisoners had been executed.

General Arellano testified to the Rettig Commission that he only found out in Calama, on October 19, 1973, that 26 prisoners "had been executed in a massacre." It was there, according to his statement, that he found out that some of his subordinates had participated, the day before, in the "Antofagasta butchery," where 14 prisoners had been slaughtered.

What had the general done when he found out? He said that he had returned to Antofagasta to clear up the episode with General Joaquín Lagos, but it was impossible because General Lagos "was totally beside himself and would not listen to reason." General Arellano Stark then continued his trip north and, as he stated, "I adopted the necessary measures to control my people." He said that when he returned to the capital, "I reported to General Pinochet about the events, and I requested an investigation to determine what had happened and define responsibilities." However, there was no investigation, and General Arellano said, "I didn't insist on the matter; moreover, I didn't see Pinochet much because he was getting busier by the day."

Finally, General Arellano blamed the DINA for what happened, a thesis that had already been put forward by his son, as reported earlier in this volume. The general said that DINA began to operate on the same day the military coup took place and referred to General Manuel Contreras, head of DINA: "It's better to have Contreras as a friend, and, regarding the events in the north, there was a conspiracy against me." General Arellano did not explain how two DINA officers were innocent (Espinoza and Chiminelli) and how three DINA officers were guilty of that conspiracy (Arredondo, Moren, and Fernández Larios).

*****

The Rettig Commission submitted its report in February 1991. The report gave all the victims of this case an official status. Moreover, since the perpetrators had acted as "agents of the state," the state was to recognize its liability and compensate the families economically. President Aylwin, after receiving the report in La Moneda Palace, was moved to tears when he asked the families' forgiveness on behalf of the Chilean state.

Let us review what the Rettig Commission said about what happened in each city.

Cauquenes

The four young men died a few hours after the Puma helicopter arrived with General Arellano and his people. This entourage "remained in the city until immediately after the executions were verified. Members of the entourage were seen in the city by numerous witnesses." The four young men, the report goes on to say, "were executed by agents of the state without any justification. They were victims of a grave violation of their right to life and their families' legitimate right to bury them."

La Serena

The 15 prisoners died during the visit of "a special entourage that had arrived from Santiago, with the power to review the situation of the local prisoners." The report adds that the Rettig Commission received credible testimony on how the 15 men who were executed were selected "outside any legal process by agents of the state."

Copiapó

At the time of the execution of the 13 victims (October 17, in the early morning hours), Arellano's entourage was in the city. The victims were "executed by agents of the state without any justification, which constitutes a grave violation of their human rights." The bodies were left inside a truck to be buried later, and their relatives were not told where the bodies were buried. The Commission submitted the case to the judiciary, and on July 31, 1990, the remains of these 13 people were exhumed, identified, and given to their families for proper burial.

Antofagasta

The Commission "came to the conviction" that the 14 victims were murdered extrajudicially by agents of the state. The report states, "Before being killed, they were horribly tortured." The first version, given by General Lagos immediately after the events, saying that the executions "were ordered by the government military Junta," is consistent with the fact that the military entourage of General Arellano, delegate of the president of the government Junta, was in the city at the time. Officers of the entourage and officers of the Antofagasta Regiment participated in the execution.

Calama

"The Commission came to the conviction that the 26 prisoners were executed extrajudicially, with cruelty and extreme malice, an illicit act that was the responsibility of agents of the state." The entourage of General Arellano was in Calama "precisely to review the procedural status of the prisoners." In addition, the report adds, "Different reliable reports lead to the conclusion that officers of the Calama Regiment as well as the entourage that came from Santiago participated in the shootings." And the report concludes, "The fact that the bodies were not given to their relatives leads to the presumption of trying to cover up the events."

The Rettig Commission analyzed what happened in a section of its report entitled "The Heightened Repression in October." In addition, it states that after the coup, "the central high command" thought that its approach was different from the one being taken "by the military authorities of some provinces." Since everything was peaceful in the provinces and since the military officers had friendly relations with civilian officials of the deposed regime, the central high command determined that it was necessary to correct that "softness." It was within that framework that the decision of the central high command was made, and "the mission, entrusted to a high-ranking army officer, who traveled throughout the country by air between September and October of 1973, had as its explicit, apparently official aim, to expedite and make the trials of political prisoners more severe, instructing the local authorities to that effect."

Then, the Rettig Commission's report, based on an apparent acceptance of General Arellano's testimony, says that the officers in the entourage seemed "at first sight, to be members of an official group." However, it continues, "This was not necessarily so, because almost all the other members of the entourage came from different sections and units of the army, where they were not under the regular and exclusive hierarchy [command] of the superior officer delegate." In addition, the report goes on to say that all the members of the entourage, except for General Arellano Stark, "will later belong to DINA, several of them holding high positions in said organization and important participation in irregular executions."

In short, the Commission established that the deaths in Cauquenes, La Serena, Copiapó, Antofagasta, and Calama occurred while General Arellano's entourage was "physically present in the cities and at the time all of them took place." The report added, ". . . it is not likely" that the soldiers who participated in the executions could have done so "without higher orders." It stated, "There is no explanation that makes it plausible that it was the local chief who gave the order, while there was in the city a superior with maximum delegated powers or officers of his entourage who could claim to represent this superior officer."

And the final conclusion of the Rettig Commission was that this entourage, "with its official and extraordinary character, with the highest authority — emanating from the office of the commander in chief — who presided over it, with its sequel of shocking extrajudicial executions and with its ostentatious impunity, could not but give the armed forces and police officers but one signal: that there was a single command and it had to be exercised harshly."

*****

General Arellano's Lawsuit Against Patricia Verdugo

In July 1991, following the publication of the first edition of this book in Chile in 1989, General Arellano brought a criminal lawsuit against me, Patricia Verdugo, for aggravated libel in the First Criminal Court in Santiago. I chose Pamela Pereira as my defense attorney. In this lawsuit, General Arellano's attorney, his nephew, Claudio Arellano Parker, held that with my "defamatory" book, I sought the murder of the general and that I had violated the amnesty decree-law by carrying out an investigation that was prohibited even to the courts. The attorney held in the lawsuit that the Rettig Commission "has cleared the name of General Sergio Arellano Stark" and that the commissioners, "in their majority, if not unanimously, came to the conviction of the innocence of my client."

In short, the lawsuit stated that everything written in this book was false: "The gathered testimonies, the opinions, and the conclusions reached by Patricia Verdugo are completely, totally, and absolutely false." This book, the attorney added, had poisoned the minds of Chileans, and, moreover, according to him, I did not have the humility to recognize my error and ask for apologies. The lawsuit requested that I be arrested, that I pay General Arellano compensation, and that all copies of the book be collected from the publisher, bookstores, and from all places where people and institutions might be able to obtain it. In short, the book was to be completely destroyed.

In August 1991, the court accepted General Arellano's petition that the press be forbidden to report on the case. My argument, that if I had publicly affected the general's honor, the matter should be clarified in public, was worthless. The Journalists' Association and 180 leading professionals of the Chilean press asked the judge to lift the censorship of the Arellano case.

Nevertheless, the ruling was upheld. Therefore, I had to defend myself in the dark, so to speak. The plaintiff's attorney said that "the feeling" of the general was that the judiciary should investigate the crimes "in the spirit of seriousness that characterizes our judiciary." Accordingly, "out of respect for the victims and their families," the press should not know about the court proceedings.

I prepared myself for the courts to begin an investigation of the crimes. Our first contribution consisted of clarifying two essential points: the ruling of the Rettig Commission and the accusation regarding the falsity of the interviews gathered in this book. The members of the National Commission on Truth and Reconciliation declared, in short, the same thing that its Chairman, the jurist Raúl Rettig, had said, "The Commission is not empowered to issue verdicts that blame or exculpate specific persons." Moreover, all of the interviewed officers confirmed to Judge Mario Carroza that what they had said to me, as quoted in this book, was the truth.

While these steps were being carried out, General Arellano's son, attorney Sergio Arellano Iturriaga, presented a document in which he mentioned the "three criminals that were assigned to my father's Commission [entourage of 1973]." Everything indicated, according to the general's statement and the report of the Rettig Commission, that Arredondo González, Moren Brito, and Fernández Larios were those "three criminals."

In October 1991, attorney Arellano Parker asked the judge to indict me. The judge refused, and his refusal was characterized by the general's defense as "highly damaging." In addition, Arellano Parker stated that the author of the book had not contributed any evidence "to establish the veracity of her slander." Thus, in October 1991, 18 years after the massacres, my lawyer and I decided to ask the court to call Colonel Sergio Arredondo González and Colonel Marcelo Moren Brito to testify. We did not request the summoning of Fernández Larios because he was in the United States, sheltered by the Witness Protection Program, after completing a sentence for the assassination of former Foreign Minister Orlando Letelier and U.S. citizen Ronnie Moffit, which occurred in Washington, D.C., in September 1976.

Judge Mario Carroza accepted our petition and ordered the interrogation of Colonels Arredondo and Moren Brito, who had never been called to testify before any court regarding the events of 1973. Immediately, General Arellano's attorney argued against the judicial decision, saying that the judge "is ordering the realization of probative steps that have no relationship to the crime (slander) and that, therefore, they are unnecessary, irrelevant, and merely dilatory." The attorney added that I could not pretend to have the right to have the courts carry out an investigation, a right that had been denied to General Arellano when the amnesty decree-law had been applied: "It is illegal, unjust, and illicit that Mrs. Verdugo should have greater or better rights than my plaintiff."

The judge rejected the arguments of General Arellano's defense, which then decided to appeal to a higher court. With that step, they were able to paralyze the investigations. In December 1991, the Second Court of Appeals of Santiago unanimously decided to reject the petition: It found no elements to support the charges against me.

General Arellano then decided to take his case against me to the Supreme Court. Two years later, in December 1993, the highest court of justice in Chile rendered its decision: "Unfounded" — one little word to decide that there was no serious evidence to warrant bringing me to trial. And with that, the case was closed, resulting in the definitive dismissal of the case. The Journalists' Association celebrated, saying that the Supreme Court's decision "confirms the veracity of what was said in Patricia Verdugo's book."

*****

Verdugo's Book Used in Spain as Evidence Against Pinochet

Almost three years later, this book became one of the key pieces of evidence in Spain in the trial against General Augusto Pinochet. In June 1996, the Union of Progressive Prosecutors (Unión de Fiscales Progresistas) submitted charges of genocide against General Pinochet and the Chilean Military Junta to a court in Valencia. Immediately, the Salvador Allende Foundation (Fundación Salvador Allende), headquartered in Madrid, joined the lawsuit, and two advisers of former President Allende, Spaniards Joan Garcés and Víctor Pey, played a crucial role in the events that caused a powerful convulsion in Chilean politics. The fact is that the case went from Valencia to Madrid, since only the National Court (Audiencia Nacional) of the Spanish capital could proceed on the charge of genocide.

After being chosen by lot, Judge Manuel García Castellón, of Spain's National Court, was entrusted to act, and for more than two years he gathered evidence and testimony. In Chile, both the government and the press lowered the profile of the case to the minimum. "It is not important; nothing is going to happen," it was said. "That court [in Spain] has no jurisdiction to investigate a Chilean matter," it was argued. There was mild commotion in Chile when it became known that General Fernando Torres Silva, general military attorney of the army, had voluntarily testified before the Spanish judge. He argued that he had supplied evidence on the historical context in which the military coup occurred, but the truth is that his actions, in fact, recognized the jurisdiction of the Spanish court.

In the second half of 1997, the United States sent clear signals that alarmed some and gave hope to others. U.S. Attorney General Janet Reno announced full cooperation with the Spanish judge, who later traveled to Washington to investigate the files.

I went to Washington, D.C., in October 1997 and interviewed attorney Lawrence Barcella, who had been the prosecutor in the Letelier-Moffit crime. He had just returned from Madrid, where he had voluntarily given some testimony. He assured me that his conscience had troubled him since he had participated in the negotiations between Chile and the United States in 1978. An agreement had been signed to limit DINA agent Michael Townley's confession to the Letelier-Moffit case, leaving aside any reference to other DINA criminal operations throughout the world (the murder of General Carlos Prats and his wife in Buenos Aires and the criminal attempt on former Vice President Bernardo Leighton and his wife in Rome). Barcella returned from Rome with his conscience finally at peace. He was certain that General Pinochet had ordered the crimes, and he said so. Obviously, my interview was not published in Chile. "It isn't news," some argued. "It's dangerous; it can't be done," said others.

At that time, the danger was in angering the lion. It was thought that he had to be kept quiet during his last months, since, in March 1998, General Pinochet was obliged to leave his position as commander in chief of the army to become senator for life in Congress, according to the timetable given in the Constitution, which was enacted in 1980 during the dictatorship. This was a decisive test for the government of President Eduardo Frei, the second president of the transition. Indeed, President Frei's minister of defense awarded Pinochet the Great Cross of Victory (Gran Cruz de la Victoria) medal, praising his contributions to the restoration of democracy, despite the fact that he had just threatened two senators of the government party alliance.

Thus, 1998 began with agitation and ended with a political storm. First, a group of congressmen of the government alliance announced that the alliance would present a constitutional accusation to prevent Pinochet from becoming a senator. The government did everything in its power to prevent this, claiming that there were reasons of state, and the Chamber of Deputies rejected the accusation. Then the Communist Party filed a criminal lawsuit against Pinochet "and others" for the crimes of the dictatorship. General Pinochet responded with a veiled threat when he said that he did not know the exact date on which he would retire as commander in chief of the army.

The crisis seemed to be over. There was even a change in the minister of defense, and Pinochet took off his five-star uniform on March 10, 1998, receiving from the army the title of Meritorious Commander in Chief (Comandante en Jefe Benemérito) a sign of loyalty, similar to "till death do us part" in the Catholic marriage ceremony. Moreover, a little later, he was sworn in as senator for life. Thus, in the first months of 1998, everything seemed to indicate that Pinochet had successfully been able to exchange protective armor. He was now a senator and was protected by congressional immunity for life, with special offices in the Congress for his safety and teams of bodyguards paid for by the taxpayers.

The Case Against Pinochet in Chile

Within that framework, a trial against Pinochet in Chile seemed impossible. The Appeals Court named Juan Guzmán as appellate judge, and the "Caravan of Death case" immediately became crucial in the lawsuit. I had to testify two times before Judge Guzmán, and both times, as I left the Palacio de los Tribunales, I felt that my country was surrealistic: This judge was acting as if he really had the power to investigate the crimes of the most powerful man of the country — and I felt a mixture of astonishment and affection.

I must admit that I was surprised to see the first edition of this book in Judge Guzmán's hands, with many pages marked with little yellow post-it notes and all kinds of annotations. We worked for a long time, examining the case city by city, and at the end, he said goodbye, telling me, "Congratulations, you carried out a very good investigation." Thus, this book (*Caso Arellano: Los Zarpazos del Puma*) became a key part of the case against General Pinochet, making up almost all of the second volume of the case notes.

In October 1998, Senator Pinochet traveled to Europe and checked into the London Clinic for an operation. Soon thereafter, policemen from Scotland Yard arrived and announced that he was under arrest. What had happened? Judge García Castellón, who was in charge of the Chilean case in the Spanish judiciary, had requested that England be allowed to interrogate Pinochet. However, Judge Baltazar Garzón, in charge of the Argentine case, requested Pinochet's arrest and extradition to Spain, having received the latest information about "Operation Condor," which was the name chosen by the regional intelligence "community" in the Southern Cone of Latin America, to coordinate the persecution and extermination of dissidents. General Pinochet had been the supreme chief of DINA and, therefore, he was responsible for "Operation Condor."

Pinochet was kept under house arrest in London for 503 days, focusing the world's attention on the Chilean case. The Chilean government argued, in Pinochet's defense, everything from diplomatic immunity to a lack of jurisdiction by England and Spain. The case against the former Chilean dictator became a symbolic case of people who struggle for human rights and underscored the urgent need to create an international court to try this type of case. In short, a civilized world needs efficient tools to punish dictators who practice genocide, as they are sheltered by the impunity they legislate for themselves in their own countries. Within this context of international debate, the Chilean government raised the argument that Chile could try Pinochet, since Judge Juan Guzmán was already investigating a case that implicated him.

Those 503 days of arrest in London changed Chilean politics. The "untouchable" had been touched, and the heretofore all-powerful was seeking compassion for his deteriorated health. The fog of fear began to dissipate in the deepest recesses of the country. Lawsuits against Pinochet began to pile up, month after month, reaching more than 200 by the end of the year 2000. And the senator for life, after returning to Chile, did not go back to Congress; instead, he was practically locked up in his house while the Courts decided whether to strip him of his congressional immunity so that Judge Guzmán could indict him. On May 23, 2000, the stripping of his immunity was granted for the first time.

The sentence was based on the case that was researched for and elucidated in this book, and, as expected, it became known as "the Caravan of Death case." The judges of the Court of Appeals decided that there were two well-founded suspicions of Pinochet's "culpable participation." The first consisted of Pinochet's having delegated to General Sergio Arellano Stark his function as "Supreme Chief of Military Courts in Time of War." In fact, the document with which General Pinochet named General Arellano "Officer Delegate of the President of the Government Junta and Commander in Chief of the Army" disappeared mysteriously. However, it was sufficient for the Court of Appeals that four high-ranking officers stated under oath that they saw it, and General Arellano himself said he had carried it during his mission. Moreover, a document (reproduced as part of the cover of the original Spanish edition of this book) was in plain view of the judges, in which General Arellano had signed as "Officer Delegate."

The second well-founded suspicion was based on the testimony of General Joaquín Lagos Osorio, who was commander in chief of the First Army Division in 1973. Lagos told Pinochet about the crimes, first verbally and later in a written document. In said document, as reported in Chapter 9 of this volume, General Lagos separated the executions, identifying those that were ordered by "the Delegate of the Commander in Chief (General Arellano)." Actually, General Pinochet had ordered General Lagos to rewrite the document, making only a general list, without specifying the names of those responsible. General Lagos obeyed the order, but he kept the original document, in which General Pinochet made annotations in his own handwriting, a document General Lagos later gave the judge.

In its decision, the Court of Appeals also underscored how strange it seemed to General Lagos that none of the officers of the entourage were punished but that, on the contrary, they were rewarded with promotions. Concerning the victims, Judge Juan Guzmán limited the case to only 19 victims of "aggravated kidnapping." The amnesty law in force and the interpretation given to it by the courts can explain this. That is to say, only those cases in which the murders were proved and the bodies properly identified and returned to the families were amnestied. In the Caravan of Death case, 19 people remained in the category of "disappeared" as of the year 2000 and, therefore, were designated as victims of "aggravated kidnapping," a crime not subject to the statute of limitations. Nor will these cases be subject to amnesty until they are solved and the bodies found.

My journalistic investigation in the 1980s determined that General Arellano's military entourage killed 72 people. The judicial investigation added three new cases in Copiapó for a total of 75. By all indications, another four cases in Linares, 12 in Valdivia, and several more under investigation will be added.

To complete the legal picture, it must be noted that on June 8, 1999, Judge Juan Guzmán decided to charge four members of the retinue and ordered their arrest: General Sergio Arellano, Brigadier Pedro Espinoza, Colonel Sergio Arredondo, and Colonel Marcelo Moren Brito. Then, he charged Major Armando Fernández Larios and requested his extradition from the United States. He also ordered the arrests of Patricio Díaz Araneda, an officer who belonged to the Copiapó Regiment in 1973, and the former military attorney, Daniel Rojas Hidalgo.

By mid-2000, the case comprised 13 public volumes and one classified volume. The thousands of pages of the process show a detailed record of the unflagging task of Judge Guzmán as well as of the macabre work of opening graves in cemeteries and searching for bodies in the Calama desert. Also recorded are all of the exacting details of the meticulous work of the Identification Unit of the Legal Medical Institute (Unidad de Identificación del Instituto Médico Legal): the reconstruction of the skeletons, the identification of the marks on the bones that mean bullet wounds, the comparison of the various skulls with photographs of the victims, and a line-by-line computerized scanning process to establish the identity of each of the victims.

What was the most important evidence that Judge Guzmán obtained when the Court of Appeals decided to strip General Pinochet of his immunity? To summarize the case clearly, it is necessary to divide this painful story and its various details and statements into eight sections: five for the cities of Cauquenes, La Serena, Copiapó, Antofagasta, and Calama and three other sections for the following topics: members of the entourage, mission of the entourage, and General Pinochet's participation in the case.

Cauquenes

The murder of four young men (Lavín, Vera, Muñoz, and Plaza) occurred on October 4, 1973. In his first statement in August 1998, General Sergio Arellano said, "My delegation had no participation because we had been in Cauquenes on October 1, 1973, and, according to information in the press, the events occurred on the 4th. But if something had occurred, it would have been at the instigation of Commander Sergio Arredondo."

During the judicial investigation, Judge Guzmán asked General Arellano, "Arredondo says that he did not go to Cauquenes with the entourage. Why did you think that Arredondo could have instigated the events?"

General Arellano answered, "I insist that the personnel under my orders had no participation in the deaths in Cauquenes. But, in the hypothetical case that this had happened, I think that Colonel Arredondo could have been the instigator because of the fact that he denied that he was in the entourage in the city of Cauquenes, something that is absolutely not true."

In a more recent statement in January 2000, General Arellano said that Arredondo was not part of the entourage for the trip to the south and stated clearly, "I was not in Cauquenes on the day of the events. I was in that city with my Commission on October 1st." However, let us see what the members of his group said. Brigadier Pedro Espinoza stated, "I was in Cauquenes on October 1st." Colonel Marcelo Moren Brito said that the crimes "must have occurred before our arrival in said city." Colonel Sergio Arredondo stated that he was not part of the entourage on its trip to the south. In addition, General Arellano's aide, officer Juan Chiminelli, said that when they were leaving Cauquenes, "We heard about the death of one person, the son of a doctor in the city." Thus, Chiminelli discredited General Arellano's version because he was obviously referring to Claudio Lavín, son of a respected physician in Cauquenes, who was murdered along with three other young men on October 4, 1973. The pilot of the Puma helicopter, Captain Antonio Palomo, was absolutely clear about the date: "We arrived in Cauquenes on October 4th at approximately noontime, landing in the main yard of the Andalién Regiment."

When the judge asked the Commander in Chief of the Third Army Division, General Washington Carrasco, who commanded the zone where Cauquenes is located, how he had found out about the executions in Cauquenes, "which occurred when General Arellano Stark passed through the city," the general answered, "I understand that it was on October 4, 1973, and I received the news a little before General Arellano arrived in Concepción."

The judge asked, "Did the Commander of the Cauquenes Regiment, Rubén Castillo Whyte, have any responsibility in the shootings?"

"I think not, because if he had had responsibility, I would have known about the cases in my position as military judge of the Third Division," General Carrasco answered.

"What was the reason for the executions in Cauquenes?"

"I think I recall being told that those deaths were the result of the prisoners escaping," General Carrasco stated.

Meanwhile, what did Commander of the Cauquenes Regiment Castillo Whyte have to say? From his first to last statement to the judge, he upheld the same version of the events:

"The incidents occurred on October 4, 1973, and that was the same day the helicopter that brought General Arellano and his entourage landed at the Cauquenes base. All of the officers who came in the helicopter wore combat uniforms, even Major Pedro Espinoza, who received the assignment from General Arellano to interrogate Lavín, Plaza, Vera, and Muñoz. And it was Major Espinoza who reported to General Arellano Stark on the result of the mission. Next, Major Espinoza received the order and communicated to the governor's office the fact that General Arellano's order had been complied with."

Moreover, Commander Castillo Whyte gave details on how the prisoners who were going to die were chosen. After the entourage arrived, Castillo Whyte met with General Arellano in the governor's office: "He [Arellano] told me that I should review the cases. I responded that the prisoners were at the Investigations Station and in the Cauquenes jail and that the trials were at a preliminary stage, still without a sentence from the court-martial. After that, he asked me for the records of the prisoners." Then, after examining the records, "General Arellano, marked several names with a pencil, under the column 'crime charged,' and he ordered Pedro Espinoza with Marcelo Moren Brito and Armando Fernández Larios to the Investigations Station and to the Cauquenes jail to investigate and interrogate the selected prisoners."

That was the way in which Lavín, Plaza, Vera, and Muñoz were taken to the El Oriente farm to be murdered. Commander Castillo Whyte added, "By order of General Arellano, I arranged for the bodies to be transferred from the hospital to the cemetery during the night, a mission that was carried out by Lieutenant Jorge Acuña."

The bodies were taken from the farm to the hospital and from there to the cemetery in a truck, whose driver, Marcial Salazar, narrated the chilling details to the judge. Salazar had to lend the soldiers a pot that was used to feed the dogs, so that they could gather up the scattered remains (pieces of skulls, brain matter) that were scattered where the men were slaughtered. "The heads of the murdered young men had several bullet holes, all in the face, and the entire backs of their heads were destroyed," stated Salazar.

The crucial date — October 4, 1973 — was also confirmed by the investigations police of the city, as the victims were taken from their station's barracks. The chief of the station, Mario Baeza, stated that he had gone to the governor's office after lunch: "There I found out that General Sergio Arellano was in the city that October 4th and at that time was having lunch at the Social Club." Baeza went to his station, and there he was told that "soldiers had taken four prisoners from the station. I never knew the names of those soldiers, and I had never seen them in Cauquenes before."

Police Detective Clodomiro Garrido also remembered "the arrival of an officer with the rank of lieutenant, who identified himself as Fernández and was wearing a combat uniform. What most impressed me about him was the fact that he was heavily armed. He had a pistol, revolver, a *corvo*, and a long knife, among others. In truth, he was overly armed."

Retired Detective Exequiel Jara also corroborated the October 4 date and remembered the names Arredondo, Moren, and Fernández as those used by the three military officers to identify themselves at the station. Subdetective Domingo Palma remembered the day when the soldiers in combat gear took the prisoners. In addition, he was able to talk with Claudio Lavín, whom he had known since he was a child. "Lavín asked about the place where he was being taken. He looked worried, and he was almost white with fear," Detective Palma recalled.

To complete the evidence, the attorneys submitted to the court a copy of a legal deposition from General Sergio Arellano Stark, dated November 1994, in a case that was being heard in a court in Linares, "in which he acknowledges having spent the night in Linares on October 3, 1973, after arriving late that night, and [subsequently] leaving for Cauquenes on the 4th of the same month and year." When the judge showed the deposition to General Arellano Stark, the general acknowledged the authenticity of his signature and explained, "This deposition was prepared by the attorney named by the general military attorney, but I did not notice the dates that were there, but only the content of the document, dates that have no bearing on reality."

La Serena

The murder of 15 prisoners occurred on October 16, 1973. When testifying before the judge, General Arellano adhered to the version that he used when he testified before the Rettig Commission in 1990. In short, he stated that he was carrying instructions from the Military Judge of the Second Division, General Brady, to carry out the death sentences of three prisoners (Guzmán, Marcarian, and Alcayaga) and that it was only in 1986, 13 years later, when he found out that there had been 15 victims and that the court-martial he had ordered never convened. He also told the judge that that was when he heard shots inside the base, and he thought that those three prisoners were being shot by a firing squad. Later, when he asked Commander Arredondo about the incident, Arellano said that the colonel "told me that the sentences had been carried out." He also said that three officers of his entourage were responsible for the crimes. "In Calama and La Serena, officers Arredondo, Moren Brito, and Fernández Larios acted on their own. That is my impression," stated General Arellano.

What did the members of the military entourage say? When Colonel Sergio Arredondo was asked about General Arellano Stark's statement, he asserted the following, "The general was always informed of the executions and the number [of people killed] in La Serena, Antofagasta, and Calama. In La Serena, I reported to him the execution of 15 people. He was accompanied by the Commander of the La Serena Regiment, Mr. Lapostol Orrego." Colonel Arredondo added, "It is impossible to think that what happened in La Serena only became known 13 years later."

Meanwhile, Colonel Marcelo Moren Brito told the judge, "I witnessed the shootings, but I did not participate actively. We did not intervene directly in the shootings; we only watched. It is logical that General Arellano knew about the firing squads. I say this because General Arellano was in charge of the mission."

The judge asked, "Could General Arellano believe that there were only three victims and not know about the other 13?"

Colonel Moren Brito replied, "It is unlikely or almost impossible that he did not know, especially given the personality of General Arellano at that time. He was 100-percent soldier — hard, inflexible, lots of prestige, his word was law."

Brigadier Pedro Espinoza told the judge that he was with Lieutenant Chiminelli when he heard the shots in another part of the base in La Serena. "We went to the yard where the shots were coming from, and we saw an indeterminate number of people who were dead. Naturally, I did not know if there had been some decision by the court-martial. One had to presume that that was the case, although I was surprised by the number of people shot."

In fact, Officer Chiminelli said that he was with Espinoza when he heard the shots and that "the rest of the entourage was in the place of the shootings, but I don't know whether they were watching or participating in some way."

The Commander of the La Serena Regiment, Colonel Ariosto Lapostol, testified several times to Judge Guzmán and was finally confronted with General Arellano. In addition to what Colonel Lapostol had already told me (see Chapter 5 of this book), he added some details to complete the picture. He said that General Arellano came into his office on the base and reviewed the records of the prisoners, marking with a red pencil the names of 15 prisoners, the 15 who — according to what General Arellano told him — "should be tried by a court-martial."

Colonel Lapostol added, "In the meantime, Major Marcelo Moren wrote the name of every prisoner in a separate notebook." At that point, Colonel Lapostol told how he had intervened to tell General Arellano that among the 15 people chosen, "there were three people who had already been tried by a court-martial, a court presided over by me, and they were already serving their sentences in La Serena penitentiary. Nonetheless, General Arellano told me that those sentences were very light and that, therefore, it was necessary to try them in a second court-martial."

Colonel Lapostol said that he insisted on this point several times, but Arellano would not budge. Finally, he told him, "General, you preside over the new court-martial." General Arellano refused. Indeed, Colonel Lapostol's statements reflect the anger and pain that Arellano's decision provoked in him with respect to prisoners Guzmán, Marcarian, and Alcayaga. Obviously, the colonel's dignity and judgment as commander were challenged, as he had presided over the court-martial and had confirmed the men's jail sentences.

"It was," Lapostol said, "a moment of great tension. Finally, I requested permission to leave." What could he do when he was confronting a general who came vested with supreme power, officially representing General Pinochet? Colonel Lapostol left the base, walking rapidly, and he stopped in the outer gardens, about 50 meters south of the guard post. Fifteen minutes went by, and he saw General Arellano approaching. There, they spoke again about the three prisoners, and the general "insisted that a new court-martial was necessary for those three people, alleging that the sentences were too light," recounted Colonel Lapostol.

General Arellano and Colonel Lapostol were in the middle of that conversation when Captain Vargas, who had just returned from a mission in Vallenar that Colonel Lapostol had given him, approached them. After asking General Arellano for permission, Captain Vargas reported to Colonel Lapostol about the mission. When he finished, Colonel Lapostol briefly informed him of General Arellano's mission and the new court-martial that was supposedly being carried out inside the base. "Stay with me," Colonel Lapostol ordered Vargas, perhaps needing the presence of one of his officers to alleviate the tension.

There they were, standing in the gardens that spring had already painted with vibrant colors, when they heard the shots. Colonel Lapostol was startled and ordered Captain Vargas to go into the base to find out what was happening. Vargas returned in a few minutes.

"Report," ordered Lapostol.

"There are 15 people dead on the pistol range."

At that moment, more shots were heard.

"General, what is going on?" Colonel Lapostol asked.

"It must be the result of the court-martial," General Arellano answered acerbically.

There is nothing in the case record indicating what they said or what they felt for the next few minutes. It was established that a short time later Commander Arredondo entered the gardens. Lapostol stated, "He approached General Arellano to report something secret."

In his statement to the judge, General Arellano reported what Arredondo had said to him in the gardens, "He told me that the sentence had been carried out," reaffirming that he thought it was the three death sentences that had to be carried out by order of the Military Court in Santiago.

Did Arellano not hear the report given by Captain Vargas regarding the 15 people shot? "Yes, of course he heard it," Colonel Lapostol said to Judge Guzmán. Nevertheless, General Arellano said he could not have heard it because Captain Vargas "did not return" and therefore did not report what had happened.

From the murders in La Serena, according to General Arellano's account, a chaotic picture of the Chilean army arises. Three of the officers of his entourage "acted on their own," defying the powerful General Arellano Stark and all of the High Command. Arellano ordered the establishment of a court-martial and was disobeyed, finding out about the insubordination 13 years later. Moreover, a captain disobeyed the order given by his commander in front of a general and did not return with the required information.

The 15 victims of La Serena were buried secretly and thus joined the ranks of the disappeared. In October 1998, a few days after the arrest of General Pinochet in London, the bodies of these 15 men were exhumed from a mass grave in the local cemetery and, after the bodies were identified, their families had the right to give their loved ones proper funerals and graves with headstones. The great music maestro, Jorge Peña Hen, who was among those killed in La Serena, received an honor from the entire city — his body was finally laid to rest in a dignified manner in a public park.

Copiapó

In Copiapó, the murder of 13 prisoners occurred on October 17, 1973, in the early hours of the morning, and three more people were shot in the afternoon of the same day. General Arellano kept his version of these events unchanged: "When the 13 prisoners of Copiapó were shot, I was not in the city," he affirmed, explaining that he still had not arrived. And regarding the other three executed men (García, Castillo, and Tapia), he blamed the local Commander, Colonel Oscar Haag, and his jurisdictional superior, General Joaquín Lagos. They were the ones, he said, who decreed the death sentences, and he only had to verify that the sentences were carried out during his stay in Copiapó.

Indeed, General Arellano continued to insist on his version of the first 13 people shot, who died without sentences from a court-martial: "No matter what the date, I'm convinced that there was no participation by the members of my military group." As explained when this case was discussed earlier (see Chapter 6), Sergio Arellano Iturriaga, General Arellano's son, said that his father was not informed by local officers of the mass shooting that had occurred a few hours before his father's arrival in Copiapó: "He only found out when he returned to Santiago, while listening to Radio Moscow."

General Arellano told Judge Guzmán that he found out about the shooting through Commander Haag in Copiapó, who purportedly described it to him "as an event that occurred before my arrival."

What did the members of General Arellano's entourage say when they testified before Judge Guzmán? Brigadier Pedro Espinoza said he knew nothing about what happened in Copiapó. Colonel Arredondo said he knew nothing at the time. It was later, he said, that "I found out that there had been shootings, possibly during or after our passing through Copiapó." Colonel Moren Brito said that at the moment they left Copiapó to go to Antofagasta, "before leaving, Colonel Arredondo told us about some shootings that had been carried out in the city." Later, Colonel Moren Brito corrected his statement: "In Copiapó and La Serena, I witnessed part" of the executions.

Of all the officers in this group who testified before Judge Guzmán, Officer Juan Chiminelli, aide to General Arellano, appeared to be the person who had the best memory. He even contradicted his superior, saying, "I recall that there was heavy shooting, since the people shot were not in very good condition." He added, however, defending the innocence of his group, that they were all in the hotel "when we found out that there was a shooting as a result of an escape attempt by the prisoners. This means that none of the members of the entourage participated in those events. The ones who participated were members of the Copiapó Regiment." Moreover, in defense of his superior, Chiminelli stated, "These events occurred during the night we were in Copiapó. I recall that General Arellano insisted that Commander Haag should clarify the situation, to make it clear that there was no participation by General Arellano's entourage."

What really happened in Copiapó? Where did the two mass executions take place on October 17, 1973? Could these events have become confused in the witnesses' memories? Let's first look at the testimony of Lieutenant Enrique Vidal Aller, who was Colonel Oscar Haag's aide. He told Judge Guzmán that as soon as the group arrived, he met with General Arellano in the commander's office along with Colonel Haag and the Military Prosecutor, Captain Brito. Then, he stated, "General Arellano asked for all the folders of the people under arrest, both on the base and in the Copiapó jail. After meeting for two or three hours, Captain Brito went down with the folders that General Arellano had studied, of which 13 were put aside, belonging to the people who were later killed."

Lieutenant Vidal added, "Once the meeting was over, an order was given to transfer 13 people to La Serena, an order given by General Arellano himself to Commander Haag. This mission had to be carried out by Captain Patricio Díaz Araneda, who asked me to accompany him. I responded that I was an aide to the commander and that I could not take orders from him. Later, Captain Díaz named three second lieutenants who had just graduated from the military school." What happened next? Captain Díaz reported that when they stopped at Cardone Hill, "the prisoners fled the truck and were machine gunned so that they would not escape." Later, the bodies were buried secretly in a mass grave in the cemetery.

During his first interrogation, Officer Patricio Díaz Araneda said that he remembered nothing about what had happened in Copiapó. He said that those years, 1973 and 1974, were the "most difficult years of my life" and that was why he had "mental gaps" when he tried to remember those days. However, those gaps were apparently filled in after he spent six months under arrest, and, in late January 2000, he confessed to what had happened:

At approximately 11:00 p.m. on October 16, Díaz Araneda said, "I was called to headquarters, where Commander Haag was, along with his Deputy Commander, Major Carlos Enriotti, and I was told to execute 13 prisoners and that this mission must be carried out only by officers.

"The commander [Haag] was very upset because he is a very nervous person. He was very emotional. He told me he had to carry out the order to execute 13 people mentioned on a list he had. He was very scared.

"I appointed Captain Ricardo Yañez Mora and Second Lieutenants Waldo Ojeda Torrent and Marcelo Marambio Molina. I must add that the only person I told about the mission at that time was Captain Yañez, who asked me if there was any way of not going through with this order. I responded that there was no way to evade the order."

Díaz Araneda said that he drove the truck himself to carry out the mission. First, they loaded four prisoners who were on the base, and then they went to get the other nine from the jail. (The Court of Copiapó verified, from the guards' logbook in the jail, that the prisoners were handed over at half past midnight on October 17, 1973.) At approximately 1:00 a.m., with the 13 prisoners on the truck, he took the Pan-American Highway heading south. After about 20 kilometers, he recalled, "I drove west into the pampa for approximately 200 meters, and I stopped the truck.

"The prisoners had their hands tied behind their backs. We took them from the trucks in groups to execute them: first three, then three, then three, and finally four. Seconds before killing them, the soldiers would cover the prisoners' heads with sacks used to hold sleeping bags."

In his January 2000 testimony, Captain Díaz Araneda accepted all military responsibility for the. mission he was ordered to carry out: "I participated in the shooting of the four groups, and we used SIG 7.6 mm assault rifles with a military load. The shootings were carried out with the prisoners standing up, facing the firing squad at a distance of approximately 8 meters. They died instantly with the first shots; it wasn't necessary to give them a coup de grâce." He added, "Because I was nervous, I didn't realize that my weapon was set on automatic, and I shot two of them like that."

The above description revealed what happened to the first 13 prisoners from Copiapó. However, how did the order come about to murder them? The Commander of the Regiment, Colonel Oscar Haag, gave a detailed account in several testimonies to Judge Guzmán. To begin with, Colonel Haag identified the officers who participated in the meeting held in headquarters that evening of October 16, 1973: General Arellano, Brigadier Espinoza, Military Prosecutor Captain Brito, Military Attorney Daniel Rojas Hidalgo, and the local uniformed and civil police chiefs, among others. Colonel Haag was present and very uncomfortable because, he said, "At the moment when the document was shown in which General Pinochet named General Arellano as Officer Delegate, I was relieved of command, and he thereby became my superior officer."

According to Colonel Haag, Captain Brito brought the files of the prisoners to General Arellano and "showed him the file that corresponded with each prisoner, and General Arellano sometimes made notes on the sides." At the end of the meeting, Colonel Haag added, General Arellano presented the list "on which he had marked the names of 13 people, ordering that they should be executed as soon as possible. These people were executed with their indictments pending because the general's order had to be carried out, given his high rank."

In that way, the fate of 13 prisoners was sealed. However, how was it decided that the other three prisoners should also die? Commander Haag stated that General Arellano examined the files of García, Castillo, and Tapia. The court-martial had already decreed capital punishment for these men, but Colonel Haag, as military judge, still had not confirmed the sentences. After Arellano examined the papers, Haag said, "He told military attorney Rojas Hidalgo to close the case, that he would give him a document to sign in a meeting the following morning with the official confirmation of the death sentence."

What happened next? In the confrontation between Colonel Haag and Captain Díaz Araneda, in January 2000, the following came to light. Haag said that he took the list with the names of the selected victims and gave it to his executive officer, Major Carlos Enriotti, "telling him that General Arellano had ordered the executions." Captain Díaz Araneda was called to carry out the macabre mission, and he subsequently reported to Colonel Haag and Major Enriotti. Díaz Araneda heard the order that Haag gave him — that only officers could participate and that the execution should be outside the base — and Díaz Araneda asked whether the action could be avoided. "I told him it was a superior order and that, given General Arellano's high rank, it was impossible not to follow the order," Haag told the judge.

According to Colonel Haag, Captain Díaz Araneda selected the people who would make up the firing squad for the illegal execution, and the high-ranking officers ended their mission a little before midnight. "I invited General Arellano, Colonel Arredondo, and attorney Rojas to a light supper to recover from the long day of work," Haag said. And after supper, the group of officers left together to drop off General Arellano at the Turismo Hotel, located in front of the main square of Copiapó. Then Commander Haag's account became chilling: "In my vehicle, with Arredondo and attorney Rojas Hidalgo, we drove up the highway that goes to La Serena, in search of the military truck that belonged to the base that was carrying the 13 detainees."

When they arrived at the summit of Cardone Hill, Colonel Haag, Colonel Arredondo, and Rojas Hidalgo did not see the truck (it may have been heading into the pampa). Colonel Haag recalled, "Since Arredondo was angry because we could not find the truck, he ordered that we return to Copiapó. On our return, a few kilometers from Copiapó, we found the military truck on its way to the city." The two vehicles stopped. The dead were covered with a tarp, and blood dripped onto the pavement. "Arredondo climbed into the truck, lifted the tarp that covered the bodies, and counted them to verify the 13 dead." In his statement, Colonel Haag continued, "Later, on Arredondo's order, we went to the hotel where General Arellano was staying, and he received us in his robe." In addition, Haag witnessed the moment when Colonel Arredondo said, "Orders accomplished, General; the 13 people were executed, and I personally verified it."

Meanwhile, attorney Daniel Rojas Hidalgo denied any participation in the events, but two witnesses added another charge against him. According to their testimony, he falsified the death certificates that were given to the families of the victims.

Regarding the executions of engineer Ricardo García, general manager of the El Salvador copper mine, and of labor leaders Benito Tapia and Maguindo Castillo occurred in the yard of the Copiapó base on the evening of that same day, October 17. Moreover, Commander Haag told Judge Guzmán that Lieutenant Ramón Zúñiga Ormeño led the firing squad that night. In fact, General Joaquín Lagos, who was commander in chief of the First Army Division, a zone that included Copiapó, explained the role played by General Arellano Stark in these events. General Lagos clarified that the death sentences had been decreed by the court-martial; however, "the decision of the military judge of Copiapó, Lieutenant Colonel Oscar Haag, was still pending." The case was still being heard, and "General Arellano, without further proceedings, went on to sign the death sentences." Moreover, Daniel Rojas, who had been a military attorney in 1973, told the judge, "If General Arellano was in Copiapó on that date, it must have been his decision. . . . I recall that he had brought the delegation from the government Junta to be able to confirm the sentences officially."

General Arellano, when confronted with Colonel Haag and officer Díaz Araneda, stated over and over that he had not been in the regimental headquarters on the night of October 16, saying, "I insist I was in my hotel."

The 16 victims of Copiapó were buried secretly; thus, they were considered "disappeared detainees" for two decades. Judge Juan Guzmán's investigation was able to locate the remains of the first 13 victims. As this edition goes to press, early in 2001, the search for García, Tapia, and Castillo continues.

Antofagasta

Fourteen prisoners were slaughtered on the night of October 18, 1973, while General Arellano Stark and his entourage were in the city. In Antofagasta, the highest military authority was General Joaquín Lagos Osorio, commander in chief of the First Army Division, who, due to the military coup, also had the position of governor, the highest political authority in this zone under a state of siege.

When he appeared before Judge Guzmán, General Arellano stated throughout his testimony, "I did not learn about what happened that night until the following night in Calama, where I was informed by Major Pedro Espinoza." In addition, he insisted that General Lagos should be charged "for the crimes of obstruction of justice and concealment." In January 2000, General Arellano was confronted with Colonel Arredondo and stated that perhaps in Copiapó and Antofagasta "incompetent commanders permitted personnel under their command to act in the executions, taking advantage of our presence in those places." That is, General Arellano denied giving the order and testified that the officers from Antofagasta "unduly used people under my command" in the extrajudicial executions.

What did the members of the entourage testify? Colonel Sergio Arredondo told Judge Guzmán, in the presence of General Arellano, "The executions in Antofagasta happened during the night, before we left for Calama. I told General Arellano that 14 people had been shot." And when the judge asked him why he was present at the execution, Arredondo answered, "Because it was clear that that was one of the orders that had to be carried out."

Brigadier Pedro Espinoza told the judge that he knew nothing about what had happened, but in the proceedings, a sworn statement was added that he made in 1990 to Eduardo Avello, a notary public. In that statement, Brigadier Espinoza said that the entourage was having dinner in the hotel — with the exception of Arredondo — when there appeared "a superior officer, a subordinate of General Lagos, and without any explanation, he said that the members of the military group must accompany him. Lieutenant Chiminelli and I did not follow that order."

Lieutenant Chiminelli, General Arellano's aide, stated the following: "I recall that persons of the Antofagasta staff went to get members of the entourage, that is, Moren, Arredondo, and Fernández Larios, without giving them any explanation. Later the following day, I found out that they had gone to the south sector of Antofagasta, where there had been some executions."

Meanwhile, Colonel Marcelo Moren Brito testified to Judge Guzmán — in the presence of General Arellano — that he had witnessed the executions in Antofagasta because "Colonel Arredondo gave us an order to witness the executions. I even recall that we were eating, and we were ordered to 'get up to do an errand.'" In another statement, Moren Brito said that he had not actively participated in the executions of the 14 prisoners in Antofagasta for the following reasons: "The members of the Commission did not normally participate. We were like authenticating judges. The people from the base would be in charge of burying them, and we would know where they did so."

"Were *corvos* used in the executions?" the judge asked.

"I didn't see the use of *corvos* in Antofagasta or in Calama," replied Colonel Moren Brito.

The Commander in Chief of the First Army Division, General Joaquín Lagos Osorio, testified several times before Judge Guzmán, and he always held firm to the version he had given since 1986 (see Chapter 7), that he knew nothing about what had happened until the morning of October 19, when General Arellano had already left for Calama. He added some details to contradict Arellano regarding the "hatred" that had existed between them. The first evidence was the fact that General Arellano stayed at General Lagos' house, a fact that is parallel with the courses of their lives up to that time: They had been neighbors when they were in military school, their sons had been friends since childhood, Lagos had helped Arellano enter the War Academy, and then, in the United States, Lagos made arrangements to get him a house when Arellano took a course at Fort Leavenworth.

October 19, 1973, was a day imprinted with fire in the memory and conscience of General Lagos, when he ordered doctors to "reassemble" the slaughtered bodies of the victims to return them to their families and gathered his division officers to try to understand what had happened. His aide, Officer Juan Emilio Zanzani Tapia, testified to the judge that he had rushed to the governor's office and found General Lagos "smoking like a chimney and very upset," as Lagos gave Zanzani the account of the shootings carried out by General Arellano's entourage.

The next day, on the morning of October 20, General Lagos received a call from General Arellano, who had returned to Antofagasta. Each general maintained his version regarding the meeting they had later.

Arellano said, "I came back to clarify what had happened in Calama and Antofagasta.

Lagos said, "He [Arellano] called to thank me for the kindness he had received, and I ordered him to come to explain what had happened."

The fact is that they met behind closed doors, which was confirmed by the aide Juan Emilio Zanzani: "I saw General Arellano come in, and I asked him to step into General Lagos' office. They spent almost an hour talking behind closed doors, and I didn't hear what they said. But, in any case, the voices were a bit louder than normal."

General Arellano stated that the enraged General Lagos did not allow Arredondo to enter the explanatory meeting and that Lagos did not accept an investigation of the events.

General Lagos confirmed this point and explained his reasons: "I did not permit Arredondo to enter because the commander of that group was General Arellano, and he was the one responsible for the actions of his people."

The military attorney of the First Division at that time, Lieutenant Colonel Marcos Herrera Aracena, characterized what happened in Antofagasta as "an aberration because the executions occurred at a time when they were unnecessary, since Antofagasta was under control and quiet." The 14 victims of Antofagasta were not buried secretly, as had been done in the other cities. "General Lagos personally took charge of giving the bodies to their relatives after General Arellano's entourage passed through," stated Herrera.

Calama

In Calama, the 26 victims were slaughtered during the afternoon of October 19, 1973. General Arellano Stark held firm to his version of the events: He said that in the morning he met with the Military Prosecutor, Commander Oscar Figueroa, and they agreed that a court-martial would meet in the afternoon. Then, after lunch, he went to visit the Chuquicamata mine with the Regimental Commander, Colonel Eugenio Rivera Desgroux. On his return, he found out about the executions in which Colonel Sergio Arredondo, his chief of staff, had participated. Arredondo reported that the prisoners had mutinied during their transfer and that he [and the other officers] had had to kill them. General Arellano ordered Colonel Arredondo to report in writing what had happened, and this written statement was later added to the indictments of the 26 victims. General Arellano then found out from Espinoza about the slaughter in Antofagasta the night before and decided to return there to clarify everything with the Division Commander, General Joaquín Lagos.

What did the other members of the entourage say about these same events? Brigadier Pedro Espinoza had two versions for the judge. First, he said that while he was in the yard of the base on the afternoon of October 19, he saw the movement of vehicles and decided to follow the column in a Jeep. Then he changed his version of the story: He said that he returned to the base and found out that "Commander Arredondo had been looking for me, and at that moment he was going to the Topater sector." The fact is that Espinoza went by Jeep to Topater and saw that the truck had stopped, that the prisoners were led out of the truck, and that Colonel Arredondo and other officers from Calama were there. Espinoza said that he turned around and returned to the base, that he didn't know what happened in Topater sector.

Colonel Sergio Arredondo testified, "The general [Arellano] was always informed about the executions and their number." He added, "When the general returned from Chuquicamata, we were already in the barracks of the Calama Regiment. And during the first moment we had alone, I reported the number of people executed." Colonel Moren Brito admitted to only witnessing the executions, "by order of Colonel Arredondo." Lieutenant Chiminelli, General Arellano's aide, narrated his superior's reaction when he found out: "I recall that General Arellano was shouting and jumping around and rebuked Commander Rivera, since he had not ordered any executions."

General Arellano told Judge Guzmán, "In Calama and La Serena, officers Arredondo, Moren Brito, and Fernández Larios acted on their own. That's my impression."

The Second in Command of the Calama Regiment, Colonel Oscar Figueroa Márquez, who was the military prosecutor for the regiment, told Judge Guzmán what happened in the meeting on the morning of October 19, 1973, recorded on page 2075 of the case: "General Arellano requested the list of all people indicted, and the general personally checked a certain number of persons' names and ordered a court-martial" for them. After lunch, Colonel Arredondo "asked permission from General Arellano and Commander Rivera to interrogate the prisoners who were in the Calama jail, who turned out to be same ones that General Arellano had previously checked off from the list he had."

The checkmarks of death appeared once again.

Hernán Núñez Manríquez, who is now a brigadier general in the army, denied any participation in the slaughter of 1973 when he was a young lieutenant. Nevertheless, he verified that he had been the person who took the prisoners from the jail:

"After finishing lunch, I received an order — I don't recall who gave it to me — to go to the Calama jail with a list of some 20 names. It's not clear to me who gave me the order; I have the impression that it was from someone from the entourage" of General Arellano Stark. Núñez Manríquez followed the order, accompanied by a noncommissioned officer named Von Schakman. He put the 26 prisoners in a military truck and ordered the vehicle to go in the direction of Topater, as he had been told. Núñez did not know who would receive the prisoners there, nor did he know that they would be executed. That is what he told Judge Juan Guzmán.

Second-Lieutenant Patricio Lapostol Amo, son of the commander of the La Serena Regiment, had a traumatic experience that day in Calama. In the morning, just after the entourage had arrived, he was surprised by a personal attack from Colonel Moren Brito:

"He told me that he hoped I wasn't a coward or a fag like my father. He said this because my father had opposed the executions in La Serena." Then, that same day in the afternoon, Lieutenant Gustavo Mandiola took Lapostol to the Topater sector "because we had to set up a guard where the shootings took place." Patricio Lapostol told the judge that he could never forget what he saw:

"The bodies were in a pile, and I was struck by how mutilated they were. Some of the bodies had large wounds. It was sufficient to have killed these people with one shot but not 10."

In the meantime, on the base, there was a meeting of the court-martial ordered by General Arellano. The legal adviser of the court-martial, attorney Claudio Messina Schultz, told Judge Guzmán that they were analyzing the cases when the shooting was announced; therefore, "the meeting was adjourned."

The Commander of the Calama Regiment, Colonel Eugenio Rivera Desgroux, has maintained the same version of the events since 1986 (see Chapter 8). That is, he found out what happened only when General Arellano's helicopter departed that night toward Antofagasta. Everything that he witnessed before that time seemed "normal," given the rank of Officer Delegate that General Pinochet had given to General Arellano: That is, for Arellano to review the cases in the morning; to order the formation of a court-martial; to authorize the Chief of his General Staff, Arredondo, to interrogate the prisoners; and, finally, to sign the documents that the military prosecutor showed him before dinner. Since the objective of General Arellano's mission was "to review and expedite the cases," it seemed normal that the military prosecutor would give Arellano papers that corresponded with the sentences of the court-martial.

General Arellano insisted that he never signed death sentences or any other documents in Calama. He said that after finding out about the incidents, he ordered Colonel Arredondo to write a document giving an account of the prisoners' mutiny and their execution. On the other hand, Colonel Arredondo told the judge that this never happened. "I wasn't ordered to sign any document," he stated.

Thus, the 26 victims of Calama were buried in the desert on the night of October 19, 1973, and became categorized as among those who had "disappeared." Commander Rivera stated that it was Colonel Arredondo who gave the order to "scatter the bodies in the pampa," an order that was followed by Captain Carlos Minoletti. A short time after the transition government of President Patricio Aylwin was elected in 1990, the judiciary located the bodies, and the remains of 13 victims were found and returned to their families.

The Entourage

The identity and number of the members of General Arellano's entourage still has not been determined with absolute certainty. For example, it is said that the group consisted of between 10 and 14 members. However, there is absolutely no doubt that General Sergio Arellano Stark, as General Pinochet's Officer Delegate, commanded the entourage. There is also no doubt regarding the presence of Arellano's aide, Lieutenant Juan Chiminelli. As to who was chief of Arellano's General Staff during the mission, several pieces of evidence indicate that Colonel Sergio Arredondo had that mission only for the trip to the north of Chile. Regarding who was chief of the General Staff for the trip south, the name of Major Carlos López Tapia crops up in at least two confessions of other members of the group (Espinoza and Chiminelli). It is also a fact that Brigadier Pedro Espinoza, Colonel Marcelo Moren Brito, and Major Armando Fernández Larios went to the south as well as the north. Based on the testimony of Lieutenant Enrique Vidal from Copiapó, Second-Lieutenant Hugo Julio was also a part of the Caravan of Death. According to the testimony of officer Juan Chiminelli, Arellano's aide, two army corporals who still have not been identified must be added to the list. In addition, three officers piloted the Puma helicopter. For the trip south, it is known that Antonio Palomo was the pilot and that Emilio de la Mahotier was the copilot. For the trip north, de la Mahotier was the pilot, and Luis Felipe Polanco was the copilot.

General Arellano's son, attorney Sergio Arellano Iturriaga, told Judge Guzmán that the entourage was made up of 14 soldiers, 10 of which "were directly under his command." When asked about the four officers who were not under General Arellano's command, Arellano Iturriaga stated, "One was an intelligence officer whose participation was requested by General Lutz, and the other three officers were outside his command. . . . Of the entire group, only three men directly participated in the executions. They were Arredondo, Moren Brito, and Fernández Larios, all of whom showed their extreme psychopathic character. I must underscore that no officer under his [General Arellano's] command participated in the events."

The above statements given by his attorney have provided the core of General Arellano's defense since the case became public in the mid-1980s. In short, as General Arellano himself declared, officers Arredondo, Moren Brito, and Fernández Larios "were assigned to me" and were "all people outside my General Staff." However, let's examine what happened in the investigation with the first two men, since Fernández Larios could not be confronted with General Arellano's testimony because he was in the United States.

Were those three officers really from outside his group, that is, from the Santiago Center Combat Group (Agrupación de Combate Santiago Centro)?[1] Who assigned them to become a part of the Caravan of Death? The answers to these crucial questions were revealed at the end of January 2000, during the hearings that Judge Guzmán conducted in the Army Telecommunications Command (Comando de Telecomunicaciones del Ejército).

"There are documents where my direct subordination to General Arellano is verified, dated September 10, 1973, demonstrating that the members of the Commission were not imposed on General Arellano," Colonel Sergio Arredondo told the judge in January 2000.

"Does that indicate dependence upon or subordination to General Arellano during his trip to the north of the country?" Judge Guzmán asked.

"Yes, what I just stated indicates my direct dependence upon and subordination to General Arellano. In addition, as the general's chief of his General Staff, I became the second in command after General Arellano. If I had not been his chief of General Staff, I would not have gone on the Commission to the north. In those same documents, the dependence of Colonel Marcelo Moren Brito upon General Arellano is also established," Colonel Arredondo said.

Judge Guzmán then asked General Arellano to clarify this same key point in his testimony.

General Arellano said, "Colonel Arredondo and Major Marcelo Moren Brito were assigned to me by the Santiago Center Combat Group. Major Moren Brito belonged to the La Serena Regiment. Lieutenant Armando Fernández Larios belonged to the Infantry School that was part of the Group. Lieutenant Colonel Arredondo and Major Marcelo Moren Brito were named by me to be a part of the Commission to the north of the country. This was not the case with Second-Lieutenant Fernández Larios; I don't recall how he joined the group that traveled to the south and north."

The judge asked General Arellano to be more specific.

"I acknowledge that Colonel Arredondo was under my command in that operation. I named him as my chief of General Staff on September 10, 1973, which demonstrates that Colonel Arredondo was under my command," General Arellano asserted.

The same document, dated the day before the military coup, forced General Arellano to admit before the judge that he had personally named Colonel Moren Brito to the entourage. Moreover, Colonel Moren Brito told the judge that there was another document signed by General Arellano himself and his chief of the General Staff, Colonel Arredondo, in which he was ordered to join the entourage to the north and south. "I was under the command of General Arellano at that time, and I could not have been appointed by another person who was not General Arellano as a member of the group," Colonel Moren Brito explained.

"I agree with what Colonel Moren Brito said. There is no problem in that regard," General Arellano finally acknowledged.

Legally, therefore, it has been clarified that General Arellano himself named Colonels Arredondo and Moren Brito to be a part of his group. And, even though he said that he did not recall what the situation was with respect to Lieutenant Fernández Larios, everything seems to indicate that the same thing happened with him, since the lieutenant was a young officer in Arellano's Santiago Center Combat Group.

Let us now look at the issue of the "psychopathic character" of these three officers, as General Arellano's son described them. In fact, General Arellano himself explained the criminal acts of the officers saying, ". . . it was violent frames of mind that provoked the lack of control of these officers." He underscored the case of Lieutenant Fernández Larios, "whom I do not hesitate in characterizing as a psychopath."

In November 1999, Colonel Moren Brito asked the judge to confront General Arellano, having in his possession another statement given by

General Arellano's defense to the Rettig Commission, different from the one that had been publicly disseminated ("... he accomplished that mission accompanied by a General Staff that 'was almost completely appointed by other army authorities.'" See first section of this Epilogue). In the complete statement to the Rettig Commission, Arellano said, verbatim: "These three people, Arredondo, Moren Brito, and Fernández Larios, were imposed on me as members of my General Staff on the trip to the north, and the three of them had in their military records evidence of showing signs of brutality and cruelty since before September 1973."

Thus, when on January 26, 2000, General Arellano was confronted with this evidence, he had to retract himself, stating, "I could not have pointed out that Major Moren Brito had shown brutal conduct in his career before September 11, 1973, since I did not have any link to him at the professional level." He added, "I do not recall having made that statement to the Truth and Reconciliation Commission, and, therefore, it is not the truth."

On the following day of testimony, January 27, 2000, General Arellano also had to retract his earlier statement in reference to Colonel Arredondo. He stated, "The expression 'extreme cruelty and brutality' in his behavior must be understood as referring to Second-Lieutenant Armando Fernández Larios and not regarding Colonel Arredondo or Colonel Moren Brito." In addition, General Arellano insisted that he did not remember having said that phrase to the Rettig Commission. He stated, "That phrase must be eliminated because I never said it. Therefore, I hereby state that what was expressed in that phrase is not true."

Two days later, on January 29, 2000, General Arellano evidently had cleared up his forgetfulness as he complained to the judge, "Moren Brito read the statement of one of my lawyers that was given to the Rettig Commission. By law, the documents of that Commission are secret, and I think that it is a crime to use them publicly."

The alleged military record of "cruelty and brutality" of these officers was what had backed up General Arellano's statement that the three officers had acted "on their own" — or on the orders of DINA — in this macabre mission. Even General Arellano's defense attorney, Jorge Ovalle, stated in a document, "What happened was only possible given the abnormal circumstances of the times, which created propitious conditions to duplicate the chain of command, just as in Nazi Germany, the Soviet orbit countries, and other dictatorships."

Does the above statement imply, then, that in Chile, right after the military coup, the chain of command had been duplicated? General Joaquín Lagos Osorio, commander in chief of the First Army Division in 1973, explained to Judge Guzmán what the components of a "military mission" were and the four conditions it must have:

1. That a commander be named (as officer in charge) to carry out the mission;

2. That means be assigned to him (personnel and matériel) to carry out the mission;

3. That the specific objectives and the time frame in which they must be accomplished for the mission be defined;

4. That the region in which the mission is to be executed be set.

General Lagos added:

The commander completely assumes the responsibility of the means that are given to him for the implementation of the mission. . . . What Arellano and his lawyers state, that in the Caravan there were officers who were not subordinate to him, is completely unacceptable. That is simply not possible. No one who knows the least bit about the army could believe such effrontery. . . . The responsibility of command is unavoidable and, in time of war, a subordinate must strictly follow the orders of his superior. If he does not, he is liable to be severely punished, even sentenced to death. It is not honorable, in the armed forces, to exonerate oneself of responsibilities and to attribute them to a subordinate. The commander is responsible for what his unit does or does not do.

Did the three officers of the Caravan act on their own? Colonel Sergio Arredondo said, in his testimony for this case, "As chief of the General Staff of General Arellano, my obligation was to report to him all the actions that were carried out without lying. In the army's doctrine, it is held that the link between the commander and the chief of the General Staff must be kept perfect. Not to do so means the violation of the most elemental, ethical principle of a General Staff officer and a lack of loyalty to the commander."

Colonel Moren Brito was emphatic in rejecting the possibility that the three officers had acted on their own in the crimes: "That is unlikely. It is even more unlikely that it would happen in the army due to the concept of chain of command or hierarchical rank."

The fact is that if Colonel Arredondo acted on his own, forcing other officers under his orders to commit criminal acts, as General Arellano asserts, the logical consequences of such independent acts did not occur. The army did not punish Arredondo — on the contrary, he was immediately promoted to colonel and named director of the Army Cavalry School. Moreover, General Arellano also was not punished for having been purportedly disobeyed by his subordinates. He acquired greater powers, as he was promoted to division general and named commander in chief of the Second Army Division, the most important one in the country. Indeed, General Arellano did not demand an investigation into the events, punishment for himself, or for his designated chief of staff.

Finally, logic indicates that an honorable general would have broken any relationship with Colonel Arredondo, who, according to General Arellano, transformed his mission into a bloody trail of criminal acts — as General Arellano's defense had led everyone to believe for 15 years. But that version collapsed on January 27, 2000, when, after five hours of confrontation, Colonel Arrendondo gave Judge Guzmán a letter that General Arellano had sent him four years after the Caravan of Death. In that handwritten letter, dated November 11, 1977, General Arellano addressed his "very dear friend," Colonel Arredondo, and lamented Arredondo's forced retirement from the army "because you were denied the rank of general as a culmination of your brilliant career." At the end of the letter, Arellano repeated, "I wish to express my sorrow because an excellent general has been lost."

Judge Guzmán read the letter and gave it to General Arellano. He read it and had no other recourse but to recognize its authenticity, saying, "It is a letter sent by me to Colonel Arredondo."

The Mission

General Arellano stated before Judge Guzmán that he had lost the document that named him "Officer Delegate of the President of the Government Junta and Commander in Chief of the Army," which specified the mission he had to accomplish. No copies of that document existed in any of the files of military facilities that he visited throughout Chile in September and October 1973 (from Arica in the north to Puerto Montt in the south).

General Arellano stated that when General Pinochet gave him the mission, officer Sergio Nuño Bawden was present. However, General Sergio Nuño Bawden asserted, "I was not present when orders were given by General Augusto Pinochet Ugarte to General Sergio Arellano Stark regarding missions to be carried out in different parts of the country during the months of September and October 1973."

For his part, General Pinochet did not clarify what mission he had given General Arellano. When Judge Guzmán sent a questionnaire to

General Pinochet in London, the general responded in October 1999 through deposition letters, saying that because he was deprived of his liberty he would not be able to give "an appropriate response to the questions." He added that although his "principal objective was clarifying the facts and my non-participation in them," he could not "analyze the legality of the procedure or give, in your case, and appropriate response to the questions."

General Arellano asserted to the judge, in August 1998, that the mission "was that all the people charged would have an appropriate defense and that bar associations would be used in those cities where they existed to take over that responsibility." He added, "In all the cities I visited, I told all unit commanders and personnel not to abuse the power we had at that time, so that a good image of the armed forces would be left with the civilian population." In fact, the general was even more explicit: "I must emphatically state that I did not give any orders for executions, and I would never have done so since my mission was quite the opposite."

In January 2000, General Arellano stated before the judge that his mission did not indicate "that I would assume command of the unit or that I would have functions as a military judge." However, there were many high-ranking officers who, when they read the document that named General Arellano as the Officer Delegate of General Pinochet, assumed that they had before them the alter ego of the president of the government Junta and commander in chief of the Army. To them, therefore, he had every power.

General Washington Carrasco, commander in chief of the Third Army Division in 1973, testified that General Arellano called him on the telephone before entering his jurisdictional zone and told him "that he came as the delegate of the government Junta to control the situation." What situation?: to fire the commander of the Talca Regiment because he was "soft" or too lenient. General Carrasco said that he explained to General Arellano that he had already investigated the matter and that he had the situation under control. Nevertheless, General Arellano, "notwithstanding the aforementioned, relieved Commander Jaña of his military duties and position as governor of Talca" on September 30, 1973.

Commander Jaña's dismissal was ample evidence of the power vested in General Arellano. With regard to his function as supreme military judge, another general contributed the evidence. The Commander in Chief of the Fourth Army Division in 1973, General Héctor Bravo Muñoz, testified to the judge that General Arellano "added his signature to mine" on the sentence that condemned 12 people to death in Valdivia.

Let us examine what the legal proceedings were able to determine regarding the "mission" in the five cities that were the focus of the investigation of this book.

- In Cauquenes, Commander Castillo Whyte testified, "General Arellano told me that I should review the cases." And that is precisely what he did, checking the names of the people who were later murdered.

- In La Serena, Commander Ariosto Lapostol said that the document "that was shown to me by General Arellano also stated that criteria would be harmonized in the entire country, especially regarding the punishment that was going to be applied." General Arellano also reviewed the cases, checked the names of the 15 who were later murdered, and ordered the constitution of a court-martial.

- In Copiapó, Commander Haag testified that, after the review of the cases ended, he received from General Arellano the list "in which he had marked the names of 13 people, ordering that they should be put before a firing squad as soon as possible. These persons were executed while formal charges were pending against them, because the general's order had to be obeyed because of his high standing."

- When he arrived in Antofagasta, General Arellano did not show the document or speak about his rank as Officer Delegate to General Lagos — maybe because Lagos was a division general with more seniority (Arellano was a brigadier-general) or maybe because they were old friends. That was not cleared up in the investigation. General Lagos testified that General Arellano explained to him that he was going to "harmonize criteria on the administration of justice" and that is why he ordered the military attorney to show him the proceedings, listing those who had been sentenced and those who were still awaiting a decision. When the Caravan left Antofagasta, the result was 14 murders.

- In Calama, Commander Eugenio Rivera said that General Arellano told him, after showing him the document, that "he came to review and expedite cases." That is why General Arellano met with the military prosecutor, Colonel Oscar Figueroa Márquez, who testified, "General Arellano requested the list of all the people indicted, and the general himself checked off a certain number of people and ordered the formation of a court-martial" for those prisoners. All of the men whose names were checked were slaughtered a few hours later.

The key to understanding the mission of the entourage sent by General Pinochet is contained in the official military phrase explaining the purpose of the mission, cited several times in this volume: "To harmonize criteria and expedite cases." Insofar as expediting the cases, there is proof of the mission's actual criminal results. Regarding the part, "to harmonize criteria," the question that arises is, with respect to what? In its thousands of pages, the legal case was able to determine that every time the Caravan's Puma helicopter landed in one of the five cities, a group of officers appeared in combat gear, heavily armed. This image is in strong contrast with that of the local troops, dressed in normal grayish-green uniforms.

General Arellano's chief of General Staff, Colonel Arredondo, testified that in all the cities the entourage told local officers "that in Santiago there was a climate of war, that there were frequent confrontations in the streets, and that snipers shot at soldiers." Colonel Arredondo recalled that in Antofagasta, "General Arellano ordered a meeting of officers to talk about these issues, explaining the quality of the enemy we were facing, the proliferation of weapons in the country, and the political climate that, in short, had provoked the revolution."

For now, let us recall what the Rettig Commission on Truth and Reconciliation said in its 1991 report about General Sergio Arellano Stark's mission: "With its official and extraordinary character, with its high authority, emanating from the Commander in Chief that presided over it, with its sequel of shocking executions without trial, and with its ostentatious impunity, it could only give officers of the Armed Forces and Police one message: that there was only one command and it had to be exercised harshly."

Thus, this mission began the "hardening of October" — as the Rettig Commission called it — changing the Chilean army forever.

General Pinochet's Responsibility

In military circles, General Pinochet's responsibility does not merit discussion. He was the person who named General Arellano as his Officer Delegate. In the General Staff's doctrine, according to General Joaquín Lagos, "The bearer of the document carries the representation of the commander that issues it and acts on his behalf. An officer delegate is sent when a subordinate commander is not acting with strict fidelity, according to the ideas, spirit, and wishes of the commander in chief."

However, the objective of the legal process that began in 1998 was not to determine military responsibilities but, instead, criminal responsibilities. Logic, both civil and military, would indicate that if General Pinochet ordered the mission and this mission violated his orders, then the members of the entourage should have been indicted, punished, and expelled from the army. The facts show that precisely the opposite happened: All the men in the entourage were promoted and rewarded by the Commander in Chief of the Army and President of the Military Junta. Those promotions were based directly upon decisions made by General Pinochet — not by an Officers' Qualifying Board — because a decree-law was used that gave him that function.

As noted, General Pinochet was informed about the Caravan's actions in Antofagasta by General Joaquín Lagos, while the general's plane had a layover for technical reasons en route to Santiago. A few days later, General Lagos received an order to go to Santiago with a list of all the prisoners executed in his jurisdictional zone. Thus, on November 1, 1973, he entered General Pinochet's office and gave him the secret memorandum with the list, clearly separating the persons executed by decision of a court-martial and those killed by order of the Delegate of the Commander in Chief of the Army, Brigadier General Sergio Arellano Stark.

Moreover, that same night, General Pinochet's aide, Colonel Enrique Morel, came to the house where General Lagos was staying (his daughter's) and told Lagos that he had to rewrite the memorandum, that is, rewrite the list of the executed without specifying what had been done by General Arellano. Those were General Pinochet's orders.

Regarding Colonel Morel's instructions, General Lagos testified, "Immediately, he returned the document of people executed and told me that the lines and handwritten words that were on it had been made by the Commander in Chief. The next day I followed the order." And then, General Lagos handed Judge Guzmán a copy of the original memorandum that he had kept for more than 25 years — containing General Pinochet's handwriting.

In fact, General Arellano's defense also aimed at Pinochet when it said that, in the army after the coup, conditions were created "to duplicate the chain of command, just as it happened in Nazi Germany, in Soviet orbit countries, and other dictatorships." Pinochet was the supreme commander and, therefore, it must been he who decided to "duplicate" the chain of command. That alleged duplication alludes to DINA.

According to his defense attorney, General Arellano, in his role as the victim of an internal plot, suffered a "brutal isolation from the army, an institution to which he dedicated his life." That "brutal isolation," Arellano's attorney Jorge Ovalle asserts, was clearly accepted by General Pinochet. Thus, General Arellano's son, attorney Arellano Iturriaga, in testimony to the judge on November 1998, aimed directly at Pinochet: "What does surprise me is the support that the army invariably gave Colonel Arredondo." Arellano Iturriaga also listed the positions that Colonel Arredondo held after his participation in the entourage, including his promotion to the rank of colonel and appointment as director of the Cavalry School. In addition, "He was then named by Pinochet as military attaché in Brazil where, according to what Pedro Espinoza told me," Arellano Iturriaga added, "he was the superior of all DINA officers accredited in the country. Later, when he was due to retire, the then Minister of Justice, Monica Madariaga, was asked to give him a high position in her ministry 'for distinguished service.' This information was given to me directly by the former minister herself," Arellano Iturriaga concluded.

The fact is that, on October 1999, when Pinochet had been under house arrest for approximately one year in London, Judge Juan Guzmán decided the time had come to interrogate him. The Spanish magistrate prepared 75 questions that the Supreme Court of Chile accepted to be sent to Great Britain as deposition letters. Judge Guzmán gave Pinochet one month to answer the questions, given "the length of the questionnaire." A few days later, General Pinochet replied that he would not answer the deposition letters. He said, as quoted previously, that although his "principal objective was clarifying the facts and my non-participation in them," he could not answer the questionnaire because "I am not able to analyze the legality of the procedure or give, in your case, an appropriate response to the questions."

His "non-participation" in the events, however, was contradicted by the legal investigation, since it had established that General Pinochet delegated the power of his office to General Arellano for this mission. And Pinochet's position as author of this mass crime was revealed — according to the accusers — precisely in the three roles he played to make possible the commission of the crimes. He delegated his power for the mission, as the president of the Junta, and as the commander in chief of the army.

A Final Statement

In the days before the Supreme Court of Chile would render its decision on stripping General Pinochet's parliamentary immunity as senator for life, on August 8, 2000, I met for the second time with General Joaquín Lagos Osorio. I had not seen him since 1989, when I was about to finish the journalistic investigation for the first edition of this book (see Chapter 7). Eleven years later, he seemed younger and in better spirits. General Lagos told me that he felt his conscience was at peace, and he was happy about his crucial role in clearing up this case, which had produced so much pain for the families of the victims and a "painful confusion," as he said, in the army. During our recent interview, he talked again about the values inculcated into officers:

"Honor, dignity, loyalty to the army and the country, respect for law, the impeccable example that you must give your subordinates, and the responsibility of command: all of these things are in play in this case, so that we don't repeat this tragedy," General Lagos told me, as he looked into my eyes and held his head high.

General Lagos, 27 years after his retirement from the army, continued being a soldier. A disciplined soldier even in narrating events, he also answered questions precisely, saying only what he needs to say, no more. That is why I was surprised at his answer when I asked him what had happened during his second meeting with General Pinochet on November 2, 1973.

General Lagos recalled, "I gave him the redrafted document, and I said to him, 'So, with this I'm left as the only person responsible for what your delegate did in my zone.'"

"How did he react?" I asked, referring to Pinochet.

"He said, 'Don't worry, I'll straighten this out.'"

"And?"

"I told him: 'Straighten what out? They're all dead! Look, remember what I'm telling you, some day all of us are going to be judged for these crimes. And especially you because you are commander in chief.'"

"What did General Pinochet say?"

"He remained silent, and I continued talking. I insisted that I should be relieved of my position as commander in chief of the First Division and governor of Antofagasta. What had happened was so serious that I wanted to leave the army immediately."

"And he didn't agree?"

"He ordered me to return to Antofagasta. And my resignation didn't come through for another eight months."

"General, almost three decades have passed since the Caravan of Death. What has happened to your family?"

"I could speak a lot about the suffering of my wife and two sons, but it's obviously nothing compared with what the families of the victims suffered and continue to suffer. In any case, I now have a wonderful family — with six grandchildren — who love me, respect me, and are proud of what I've done."

"And almost three decades later, do you have an explanation for what happened?"

"Only one explanation — power, the struggle for power, the urgency of acquiring all power," he concluded.

As he saw me to the elevator at the end of this interview after so many years, General Lagos Osorio mentioned his meeting with General Oscar Bonilla, then Minister of the Interior, early in November 1973:

"He was my friend, and obviously I went to see him to tell him what had happened. He was very angry, and he paced his office from one corner to another. He could not believe it was true."

In November 1974, General Augusto Lutz, who was director of the Military Intelligence Service at the time of the coup, died suddenly and unexpectedly. His family asserts that, a short time before his death, he confronted General Pinochet about the repressive actions of DINA, and the family believes that Lutz could actually have been murdered for speaking out. Similarly, a few months later, General Bonilla — who came next after Pinochet in the army's chain of command — had to leave the Ministry of the Interior and was transferred to the Ministry of Defense. The reason: his conflict with Pinochet about the repression against dissidents. In March 1975, General Bonilla and his entire crew died when their Puma helicopter had a strange accident.

At the end of 1975, Division General Sergio Arellano Stark, after serving for more than one year as commander in chief of the Second Army Division and then going on to join the Chief of Staff, retired from the army. Meanwhile, General Pinochet was able to consolidate his power. After the initial announcement in September 1973 that the presidency of the military Junta would rotate, so that all the commanders in chief of the Chilean Armed Forces would have a turn, approximately nine months later, in June 1974, General Pinochet passed a decree-law whereby he appointed himself the

"Supreme Commander of the Nation." However, apparently that was not enough, and six months later, in December 1974, he became "President of the Republic of Chile."

All this provides further evidence of the conflict for power. This same conflict for power explains the scenario in which the tragic history of the Caravan of Death developed — a power that required the invention of an internal state of war to justify many years of dictatorship, as many years as necessary to rebuild the very foundations on which Chile had been built throughout its history. And it was a power that required the presence of the armed forces aligned behind the hard line of a "Supreme Commander" — a power that used maximum terror to frighten the Chilean population and crush any civilian opposition.

In fact, as illustrated in this volume, 27 years later, the dark history of the 1973 Caravan of Death began to appear in the courts. I went to the hearings held in the Supreme Court of Chile, and I could not help noticing attorney Carmen Hertz, seated a few feet in front of me in the courtroom. Carmen Hertz symbolizes the long struggle of all the families of the victims to obtain justice. Carmen, though physically frail, had endured the pain of losing her husband; her spiritual strength enabled her to overcome every obstacle throughout this long process.

Carmen Hertz was working as legal director of the Ministry of Foreign Affairs when Pinochet was arrested in London. She resigned from her high position to file a lawsuit against the former dictator for the disappearance of her husband, Carlos Berger. As narrated in Chapter 8 of this volume, Berger was the attorney and journalist from Calama who was among the 19 victims of the Caravan who continue to be categorized as "disappeared" and are, therefore, legally considered "kidnapped." Ironically, Berger is also one of the 19 victims whose "kidnapped" status stripped from General Pinochet the parliamentary immunity that had, until then, protected him and placed him in the defendant's seat when the Supreme Court lifted his immunity on August 8, 2000.

Carmen Berger and I shared a glass of wine and a few thoughts on that historic August night: "Everything seems to indicate that the foundational act of the dictatorship is the one that will eventually bring Pinochet down," I said.

"The circles are finally closing," Carmen said.

"It is also very impressive that the culminating act of terror, the attempt to make the bodies disappear, is turning against him like a boomerang, overthrowing his own amnesty law, as the disappearances are officially classified as kidnapping."

"Yes, he believed that by eliminating the bodies he could bring about the perfect extermination. Even Senator Sergio Diez, when he was Pinochet's ambassador to the UN, stated that the disappeared had no legal existence in Chile, that they were persons we had invented. In the end, the extreme perversity of the method opened a loophole through which the victims could continue to demand justice."

"Carmen, now that Pinochet's immunity has been lifted and the members of the entourage have been arrested, what has the legal process meant to you?"

"It has allowed us legally to determine the truth about what happened, because the truth that was established by your book [*Los Zarpazos del Puma*, in Spanish][2] was undoubtedly extraordinary and invigorating. However, the truth as determined in a court of law heals not only to the victims and their families, but also society as a whole — because the crucial dilemma of Chile, a crucial point in our national agenda, continues to be the issue of justice versus impunity. So, which road are we going to follow now? Depending on the road we follow, the society we choose for our children will emerge, and I'm talking about our children and those of the criminals."

*****

On January 29, 2001, Judge Juan Guzmán indicted General Pinochet for planning and covering up the massacres committed by the "Caravan of Death." Furthermore, Judge Guzmán admitted the journalistic work contained in this volume as key evidence in the judicial process against Pinochet.

Notes

1. The Agrupación de Combate Santiago Centro was created ad hoc in order to carry out the military coup and take control of the capital militarily. General Arellano Stark was in control of this organization at its inception.

2. In Chile, the title of this volume by Patricia Verdugo was *Caso Arellano: Los Zarpazos del Puma*, when it was first published in 1989. The current English edition, published in 2001, *Chile, Pinochet, and the Caravan of Death*, is an updated and expanded version of the original book.

Production Notes

This book was printed on 50 lb. Joy White Offset, 512 ppi, smooth finish text stock.

The text was set in 11/13 Times, with 18 point Bookman headlines, at the North-South Center Press's Publications Department, using Adobe PageMaker 6.0, on a Power Macintosh G3 computer.

The paperback cover was created by Publications Director Mary M. Mapes, using Adobe Photoshop 5.5 for the image and Quark XPress 4.0 for the composition. The cloth for the hardcover version is Kivar 7, kidskin finish.

The book was edited by Senior Editor for Spanish and English Publications José Grave de Peralta and Editorial Director Kathleen A. Hamman of the North-South Center Press at the University of Miami.

The book was printed by Thomson-Shore, Inc., of Dexter, Michigan.